The Mathematics Laboratory:

A New Teaching Approach

The Mathematics Laboratory:
A New Teaching Approach

by Ralph S. Vrana

PARKER PUBLISHING COMPANY, INC.
WEST NYACK, NEW YORK

© 1975, *by*

PARKER PUBLISHING COMPANY, INC.
West Nyack, N.Y.

Library of Congress Cataloging in Publication Data

Vrana, Ralph S
  The mathematics laboratory: a new teaching approach.

  Includes bibliographies.
  1. Mathematics laboratories. I. Title.
QA16.V72   510'.7   74-17174
ISBN 0-13-563171-8

Printed in the United States of America

Also by the Author

Junior High School Science Activities

*This book is dedicated to all those who
teach mathematics as if it were an
experimental science.*

The Classroom Mathematics Laboratory: A Practical Teaching Approach

This book will help provide a unique, more interesting, and more meaningful mathematics program. Unusual, thought-provoking experiments are emphasized in every chapter. As an additional aid to the math teacher, a specific listing of math concepts and relationships to be covered is provided at the beginning of each chapter and section. This will simplify quick reference when the material is used to supplement a particular facet of the math program.

Special assignments and activities have been included at the ends of the chapters to provide projects—all related to the laboratory approach—which might be given directly to students. It will be helpful to review and actually complete a project before introducing it in the classroom. Some of the problems are also good material as starters for mathematics workshops. The activities and problems have been selected because they have aroused student interest. They have been *proven* effective in the classroom.

Many of the projects start simply but conclude with rather complex examples. Remember that this book is a condensation of much trial-and-error work. Your students will need more time to dig through an activity than you will in the reading. For example, in many cases, such as in the "Neuron Game" (Chapter 6), only by practice can the ideas begin to make sense. Since this book emphasizes the math laboratory, it often refers to activities which no amount of words can describe. They must be worked through—the author believes it will be fun for all involved to do so.

The following principles have guided me in writing this book:

1. Science and mathematics can best be learned as laboratory work involving three-dimensional objects where possible, and in which natural forces can be observed. Mathematics is more than this, of course, but this approach represents an excellent start. Any science program with or without emphasis on quantitative work tends to be interesting and to "take hold" with students when they *see for themselves*, as distinguished

from being told by others. Likewise, a study of quantity is made significant to young people by clothing it with real objects, and supplementing
it with science-related materials. Even harmless experiments on our own
bodies have been included whenever possible so that students may consider their own presence as worthy of consideration, and discover that
their senses are not always accurate.

2. A classroom can be organized around the students actually doing
experiments and activities. Not only do the students see for themselves,
but they are also the controllers and are able to repeat at will an activity
which captures their interest. Classrooms can be modified to make this
aspect a more natural one. Accessibility is important. Easily replaceable,
inexpensive, and free materials are emphasized so that the teacher can
obtain them in sufficient quantity for each student.

3. Puzzles intrigue students (as well as teachers) although the puzzles may at first appear to be devoid of math content. The math process
used in solving them is very like scientific research. The student practices
by doing puzzles. He provides himself with "drill." Many puzzles and
games which have a mathematics content and which interest students
have been sought for inclusion.

4. New uses for old materials have been emphasized. Equipment is
fabricated, for the most part, much of it by students themselves. The
guiding rules for such construction are that it must be simple, student
operated, sturdy, and insight-producing. You should use the equipment
to take observable measurements whenever possible.

5. Many areas of mathematics are complex. These have not been
avoided if analogies are simple. For instance, the vibration of a
drumhead can be described mathematically with rather complex equations. But the vibrations can be heard, felt, and seen so we experiment a
bit and move on. Much good school work can be described as forays.
There is danger in a compulsion to be complete, to tie everything up
with ribbons. This work is a probing, exploratory . . . and practical
foray . . . aimed directly toward increasing student interest *and involve-
ment.*

Ralph S. Vrana

"The primary value of mathematics is that it is man's chief tool to help him understand his world and to master that world in his behalf. Mathematics is a partner with physics, chemistry, and the other sciences, including more recently the social sciences. Mathematics has a purpose, and that purpose lies outside of mathematics. If we do not present that purpose, we are failing to utilize the strongest motivation for studying mathematics."

Morris Kline in New York University
Education Quarterly, Summer 1973

Contents

The Mathematics Laboratory:

A New Teaching Approach

1

Discovering Patterns and Cycles
in the Math Laboratory

Mathematical concepts include: volume,
parallels, infinity, perspective, regular
polygons, pyramids, quadrilaterals,
trapezoids, cubes, tetrahedrons, octahe-
drons, parallelograms, pentagons, prisms,
geodesic figures, equilateral triangles,
right angles, angular measure, planes,
vertex-face-edge relation, vernier principle, tangents, intersections, rate, sine
curves, minimum area problems

Three Dimensional Geometric Models

The world around us is in three dimensions, yet we often think in
terms of two. The following puzzle illustrates this: How can you arrange
six toothpicks (with ends meeting) so that they form four triangles? The
problem can be solved only by resorting to three dimensions, yet we tend
to lay the toothpicks out on a flat surface, trying to form a two dimensional figure. This is unfortunate, for experience with three dimensional
geometric figures aids in visualizing one's environment more ade-
quately. Those who use their hands gain this experience. Indeed, any
active person continually experiences this 3D aspect.

One of the unfortunate consequences of a classroom with everyone
in his seat working with pencil and paper is that this essential 3D aspect is

muted. It is refreshing now and then to put paper and pencil aside and work with materials in three dimensions. When we consider the design of such materials, how they fill space, their shapes and sizes, we become involved with mathematics. The following activities are designed to introduce ways of bringing out the 3D nature of our world and thereby understand it better and interpret it more completely.

Stereo Viewing–Three Dimensions from Two

Related Math: parallax, angles, parallels, infinity, perspective

We can easily make two drawings of the same object spring up into a three dimensional image. It is a pleasant mystery to be able to give this solidity to pictures and photographs, and we begin to understand the meaning of having two eyes and the attendant concepts of parallax and perspective (see figure 1-1).

Following are two sketches of a pyramid viewed from the top, but at slightly different angles.

Figure 1-1. A pyramid in three dimensions will rise between these diagrams if the left eye looks at the left one and the right eye looks at the right one.

If you look at the left pyramid with the left eye and the right one with the right eye, the images will merge in your brain and you will see a single pyramid rise out of the paper toward you. The difficulty is to get the eyes to look separately. Some people require practice. If you look over these sketches at a distant object the eyes will separate properly. Then look down quickly at the sketches or push them up into your line of vision. If your eyes remain focused separately you will see one pyramid between the original two. This middle pyramid is the one which comes up from the paper.

Another method of seeing the 3D image is to use a low power hand magnifier in front of each eye and look at the sketches from a distance which will keep them in focus. Also good is a hand stereo viewer such as is used with aerial photographs. These viewers have a lens for each eye.

DISCOVERING PATTERNS AND CYCLES IN THE MATH LABORATORY 21

A plastic viewer can be obtained from a science supply house and is handy in studying aerial photographs of the local area, or even two ordinary photographs taken a short distance apart and made into stereo as in the pair of photos in figure 1-2. The camera was moved one foot sideways between shots, exaggerating amount of depth since no one has eyes this far apart. (See problem 1 at the end of Chapter 2 for a simple way to "spread the eyes apart.")

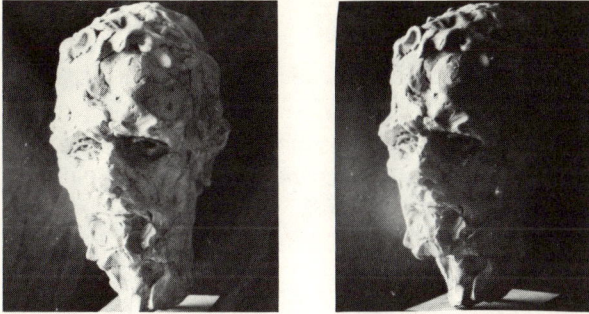

Sculpture by Howell Pinkston

Figure 1-2. Photos of the same object were taken with the camera moved one foot between shots. The result can be viewed in three dimensions.

Figure 1-3 is another example of a design which has distinct 3D illusion when viewed as previously described.

Figure 1-3. When these designs are viewed stereoscopically (with left eye on left, right eye on right) a pronounced 3-dimensional effect will result.

Many other designs are possible, but if they are complicated it is difficult to picture how they each would look when viewed from slightly different angles. Any repeating design can be viewed with each eye on corresponding parts to give an illusion of depth. The design of figure 1-4 can be made with a typewriter and can easily be seen in 3D. (The diagonal lines have been inked in.) Note that the central part of the design is slightly further to the right in each subsequent unit. It appears to be below the surface of the paper when viewed stereoscopically.

Figure 1-4. This design was made on a typewriter (diagonal lines were added) and when viewed stereoscopically seems to go into the paper.

Still another method of obtaining two different views of a subject is by means of a camera lucida. This is a device which artists sometimes use to get a tracing of a scene. A very simple one can be made by slanting a single sheet of clear glass on a table top downward toward the object to be viewed. As you look down into the glass a portion of the light from the object will be reflected up to you, but you will also be able to see through the glass and thereby make a tracing on paper underneath it of the object viewed. A more permanent arrangement than this is necessary for practical work. Simple devices of this sort can be obtained from art stores or science supply houses. For stereo, two tracings are made, a short distance apart.

Models from Sugar Cubes, Styrofoam, Toothpicks

Related Math: polyhedra, parallelograms, cubes, squares, symmetry, prisms, volume, minimum area, geodesic figures, equilateral triangles, angular measure, ratio, Euler's formula

The orderly arrangement of atoms in many compounds results in crystals of evenly sculptured geometric figures observable in many rocks. Sometimes a complete form will be preserved such as a cube or pyramid. More frequently, just a glittering surface indicates part of a crystal in the rock. There are several kinds of shapes possible in minerals and the shape of an unknown mineral is a guide to its identity. Our study here will involve methods of constructing geometric figures, many of them similar to the real crystals which might be part of the classroom equipment. Mineral crystals can frequently be obtained from rock found near the school. More perfect crystals can be obtained from science supply houses.

One common crystal system is that which forms cubes. The cubes are a result of atoms positioned as though they were at the corners of a square box, with box piled on box. If a house were made with square bricks, one directly over another, many varieties of architecture would still be possible. Similarly, many varieties of crystals are possible by piling cubes. One common form is a pyramid, and such a pyramid is easily made with sugar cubes (and white glue if a permanent arrangement is needed). Two photos of such a pyramid, as in figure 1-5, can be viewed in stereo.

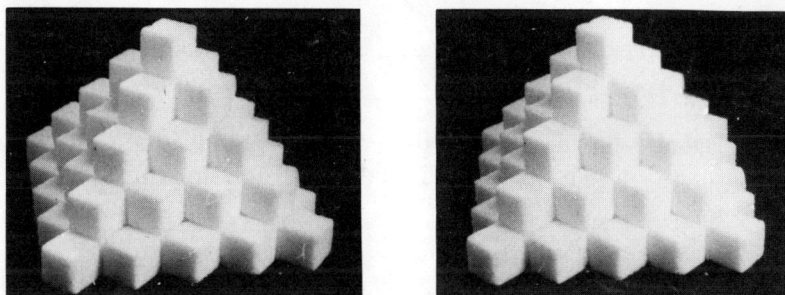

Figure 1-5. A sugar cube pyramid fastened with white glue and viewed from two places to give a stereo impression.

Another shape common in minerals of this cubic (or isometric) system is an octahedron, a double pyramid with eight identical sides. This can be obtained by gluing two sugar cube pyramids back to back. With a little care an octahedron can be cut out of a potato or molded from clay.

Toothpicks and bits of styrofoam can be used to construct crystal models. The styrofoam represents the atoms, and the toothpicks hold the atoms in their proper positions with respect to one another. The bits can be cut from a large block of styrofoam or can be obtained as small balls from a gift shop. The styrofoam is very light and rigid, and one piece will hold up some 20 or 30 units easily as shown in figure 1-6.

Toothpicks should be used to first fasten one unit to a large styrofoam block and then build other units on the well-anchored first unit. (Flat toothpicks are safer than the pointed kind which, when mounted, become a large pin cushion.) Constructing these crystal models will help students grasp the concepts later studied in solid geometry.

Relations Between Crystals and Models

Merely by changing one dimension, a whole new class of models can be constructed. The work with these toothpicks and styrofoam bits paral-

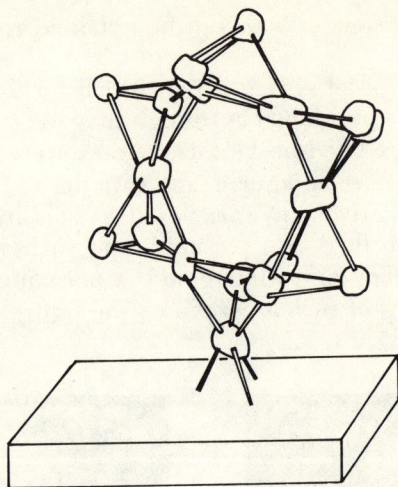

Figure 1-6. The units of this model are tetrahedra each made of four toothpicks (flat kind) and four bits of styrofoam. It is quite rigid.

lels the work of nature—on a scale that can be easily handled and studied. In the construction of cubes with toothpicks we used the same length toothpicks. If we have two different lengths of toothpicks we can start with rectangular boxes as the units. Even boxes with parallelogram sides are possible. The length of the toothpick represents the distance between atoms, and variations in this length produce whole classes of geometric shapes, examples of which can be found in mineral crystals. Instead of toothpicks, nature uses electricity to fasten atom to atom.

Other Methods of Making Models

1. *Styrofoam balls* can be packed together to produce much the same figures as with sugar cubes. Different colors and sizes of styrofoam balls afford the opportunity to experiment. White glue holds them together quite well.

2. *Envelopes* can be cut and shaped to make various figures. A tetrahedron can be made from a sealed envelope. Standard small size envelopes (6½ inch x 3¹¹/₁₆ inch or 16.5 centimeters x 9.4 centimeters) can be cut across the middle from top to bottom. Each side will make a tetrahedron. Marks are placed at the middle of each side of the cut edge and a line drawn from the marks to each of the opposite corners. Folding outward on these lines produces the tetrahedron. Many tetrahedra, all the same size, can be produced this way and pasted together to form a larger design.

3. *Spaghetti tetraheda* With a few strands of uncooked spaghetti, white glue, and care, reasonably accurate tetrahedra can be made. One long strand of spaghetti can extend out from one edge of the figure for a handle (see figure 1-7). The figure can be dipped into a soapy solution or into "dippity glas" (a liquid plastic which solidifies rapidly on exposure to air). The dippity glas leaves a translucent coating on the tetrahedron frame which hardens into a permanent film as a record of the rather interesting internal structure formed. If two opposite legs of the tetrahedron are removed and the framework dipped, a saddle-like surface of minimum area will form. Finding this surface mathematically is quite difficult.

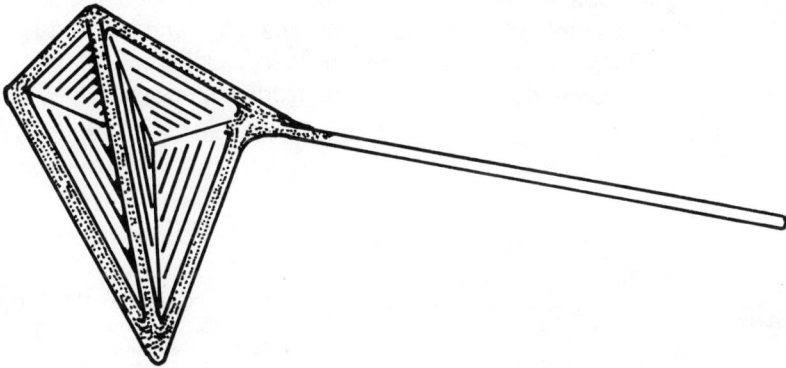

Figure 1-7. A tetrahedron of spaghetti fastened with glue and dipped in liquid plastic.

4. *Cardboard models* can be made from a number of circular platters such as those used under cakes and pies, or the smaller ones used under cocktail glasses. As many platters are needed as finished sides in the model. An equilateral triangle is a good basic unit with which to start. It is inscribed in one platter and then transferred to the others. To inscribe it, a compass is set at a length equal to the radius of the platter and then used to mark off the circumference. Six marks will be made and, by connecting every other one, an equilateral triangle will form with flaps along each edge. The flaps serve to attach the triangle to its neighbors with staples or paper clips. The flaps are easiest to leave on the outside, but with a little care can be put on the inside for a more finished appearance as in figure 1-8. Squares with flaps are also easily made by drawing two diameters on the circle at right angles. The ends of these diameters are connected to form the square, and folding the flaps makes it possible to connect the square to others to form a cube. Other models can be constructed by adding triangles and other figures of the proper size.

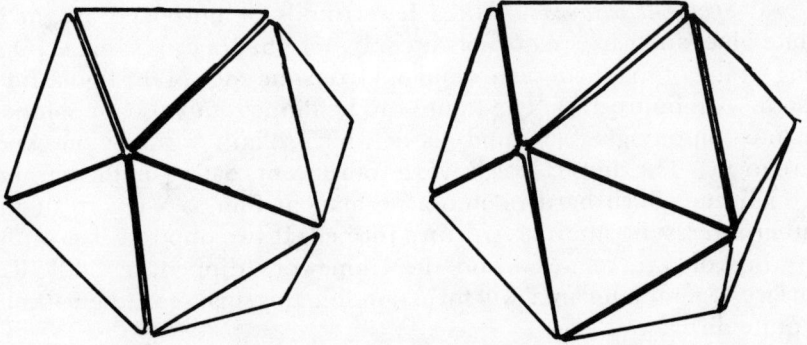

Figure 1-8a. An icosahedron can be made from pie platters. They are folded into equilateral triangles and stapled. Twenty platters are required for this model whose flaps have been folded inward and are nearly concealed.

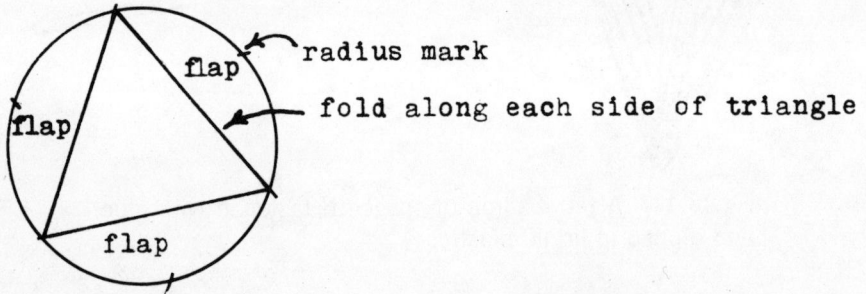

Figure 1-8b. A disk is the basic building unit and can be any size. When it is made from large pasteboard boxes, the interior will serve as a classroom planetarium. Fifteen units are required for the dome and the flaps should be folded outward for a smooth interior.

5. *Velcro material* can be used as a border on triangles or squares so that they can be rapidly assembled and disassembled. The material is really two types of cloth. When these are brought together they stick, but can be pulled apart easily. The two edges which are to be fastened must each have a different type of cloth since the cloth will not stick to its own type. A small strip of the cloth fastened with staples to each edge at the corner will provide enough sticking power to make models, illustrated in figure 1-9. Plywood works well with the velcro cloth, but it is a tedius job to cut the squares and triangles just the right size. Heavy cardboard or plastic is a good compromise.

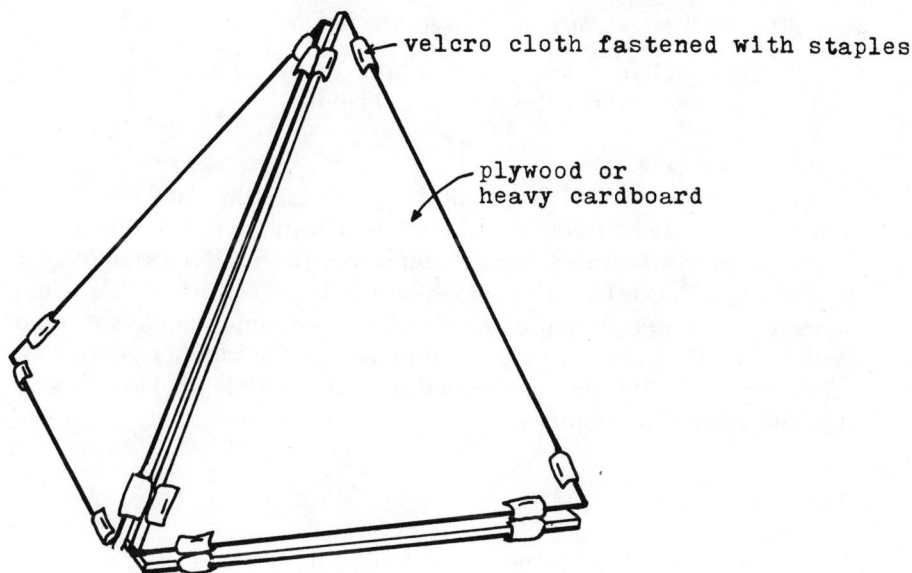

Figure 1-9. A quickly assembled tetrahedron of plywood fastened by velcro cloth.

A Little Model Math

How many models can be made using only squares? As soon as more than six sides are involved it becomes necessary to use other than right angles, and since we have only right angle corners to work with, only the cube can be made. Remember, the restrictions are severe: No two adjacent squares can lie on the same plane, and no indentations in the model are allowed.

How many models can be made using only equilateral triangles? Note first that the sum of angles around a point on a plane is 360 degrees. At most, six equilateral triangles will fit together around one point and since the sum of their angles at this common point add up to 360 degrees, they will all lie in the same plane. Thus six won't work, but five triangles coming together will form an angle less than 360 degrees, so this is a possibility (see figure 1-8a). Four triangles create a pyramid and two of these back to back make a model using only triangles. Three triangles produce the tetrahedron. With enough building units students can build these figures and experiment with them. Pentagons, hexagons, octagons, and rectangles should be available in quantity with sides of unit length (or multiple as in the case of the rectangle). Four squares (or four rectangles) and eight equilateral triangles will produce a pyramidal prism.

How the Vertex, Face, and Edge Are Related

Every model we make, no matter how complicated (as long as it has no holes through it), has the following relation:

$$V + F = E + 2$$

In the above equation V is the number of vertices, F the number of faces, and E the number of edges in the model constructed. If we take this equation literally we can assume that it is true for models with irregular length edges, since length is not mentioned, only number. We could squeeze the model, stretch it, even smear it out on a plane if we could remove one face, and, as long as we preserved the number of vertices, faces, and edges, the aforementioned relation would hold. This is topology, the subject of another chapter.

Moiré Patterns

Related Math: parallels, trigonometric functions, angles, curves

A really intriguing experience with the interplay of designs can be obtained by using moiré patterns. Moiré patterns are nothing more than ruled lines on two pieces of transparent plastic (obtainable commercially), or, in fact, any overlap of simple designs which produce a third design. Two picket fences, one behind the other, can produce such a pattern, especially if viewed while driving by them in a car. Moiré patterns have been used to enlarge and to represent certain concepts mathematically. Such uses require accurate patterns and training in their use. However, our purpose is only to generate shapes and designs which change as the patterned units are rotated. The student becomes familiar with this interesting effect which he later may find useful.

The following methods have been found satisfactory for manufacturing the patterns at home or in the classroom:

1. *Homemade*—A series of parallel straight lines can be drawn on a sheet of transparent paper with the aid of a felt pen and T-square. (The paper should be tacked to a sheet of poster board or a drawing board.) Two such papers, one over the other, will produce a moiré pattern when the lines on one sheet are nearly parallel to those on the other. Two sheets, each consisting of a series of concentric circles, will also provide interesting patterns when one is laid over the other. These patterns (and the commercial variety) can be projected on an overhead projector for the whole class to view.

2. *Corduroy material* may be printed on to paper. The corduroy material may be dusted with graphite or lampblack and pressed onto the paper. It may be inked with printer's ink using a roller such as those used

in making linoleum cuts. Or perhaps simplest of all is that the corduroy may be pressed onto a stamp pad and then onto paper. When one impression is laid over another at a slight angle the result is a third series of lines running crosswise.

3. *Khaki material* prints very nicely. The khaki can be pressed onto a stamp pad with the thumb and then pressed onto a piece of paper with the thumb still in position. The cloth is then lifted from the paper, rotated slightly, and pressed down in the same spot. The pattern produced is like hexagonal tiling.

4. *Wire screen* can be used to produce moiré patterns just by holding one piece over another. Rotation then produces varying designs. Intriguing prints can be made with a stamp pad. The screen wire is pressed onto the pad and then onto paper. Carbon paper also works well as a transferring material. Just place paper on a desktop with carbon paper over it and the screen over the carbon paper. Rub the screen with a spoon, and a pattern of short line segments will appear on the paper below. When the screen is rotated slightly and rubbed again, the moiré pattern will appear on the paper. The design is subtle and continually appears and disappears. It is most clearly seen with peripheral vision.

5. *Clear plastic* is a good, permanent medium for the creating of moiré patterns. The pattern of a wire screen can be pressed onto a piece of plastic with a hot iron. The plastic to be printed is placed on a piece of metal. Over it the wire screen is laid, and then the iron is held over the wire screen. Experiment will determine how long to keep the iron in contact. The piece of plastic should be small enough to be covered by the iron and screen. It should be thick enough not to wrinkle easily. Arnelite plastic for tables and shelves was found to be a good material. The iron should not be moved during the pressing as this may shift the wire and distort the result. After the screen has been imprinted on the plastic and removed, some dark chalk can be rubbed into the design to make it stand out. Two such pieces of plastic can be held together at one corner with a thumb tack fastened over a white board. The lower one can be fastened with another tack so that it won't move while the upper one is rotated at various angles to study the effect. (See figure 1-10.) The same piece of plastic can be stamped twice with the screen wire impression, leaving on it a permanent record of the moiré pattern.

6. *Halftone photos*—Newspaper offices often have plastic halftone photos which they discard. These have a very fine dot pattern which, in the lighter portions of the halftone, can be used to produce moiré patterns. Two such halftones are placed together and held up to the light to produce the effect. Since the dots are very precisely placed, the pattern is quite pronounced. The halftones must be cleaned and their backing removed, a rather tedious and messy job, but well worth the effort. The dot pattern is most pronounced in the light background

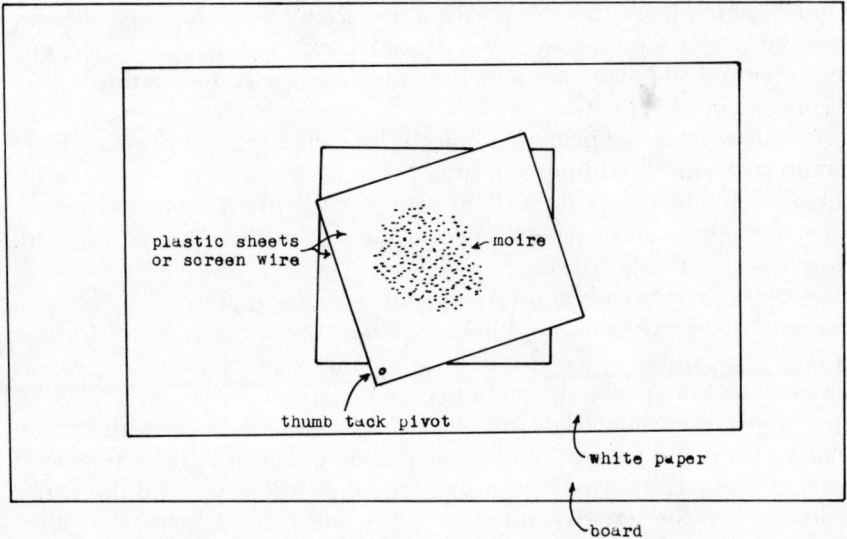

Figure 1-10. A method of studying moiré effects.

parts of the halftone. If the halftone is inked, it can be printed onto any available paper, then reprinted at a slight angle to the first printing. Very pronounced moiré patterns will result, which are actually enlargements of the dot patterns. Printing can easily be done with carbon paper. First, place a sheet of paper on the desktop, then carbon paper, then the halftone. A spoon is rubbed on the halftone and the dot pattern will appear on the paper. If the halftone is rotated and another print made over the first the moiré pattern will appear. In this process the embossed side of the halftone must face down toward the carbon paper for it to pick up the dot pattern.

7. Some *bathroom window glass* has an embossed pattern on one side. Two pieces of such glass (small squares 2 or 3 inches on a side will do) when placed one over the other will give a moiré pattern. These pieces of glass are easily projected and the change in appearance as one piece is slightly rotated will cover a large area of the darkened room. One such piece of glass when held over a newspaper illustration will form a moiré pattern with the dots in the illustration. The embossed side of the glass must face *upward* to achieve the effect.

8. *Typewriter ribbon* has an extremely fine weave and already is inked. A strip of it can be pressed onto a piece of paper with a finger and it will leave a very fine grid. Another grid slightly offset from this first one will leave a pattern so delicate that to see it properly you will need a magnifying glass.

Moiré Patterns and Science

The moiré effect has been used to clarify certain observations in the physical world. Wave fronts, electric fields, and heat flow are examples. The moiré patterns lay out problems in these areas by analogy. Other applications are being discovered. As for the mathematics of the patterns themselves, we can "nibble" at them in various ways:

1. Crossed lines—Whenever two lines cross (at a small angle), at their junction there is a thickening both as they come together and as they separate. You can check this easily with two lines made with a felt pen. Thus we have a sequence of thick-thin-thick for just two lines. If we start with two parallel lines extending outward from our location and then bring their farther ends together at some small angle, say one degree, this crossing will be remote from us. If the lines are 1 centimeter apart, they will begin to intersect (their thickest point) 57 centimeters away. If the angle is increased to two degrees the distance to the intersection is much closer, 30 centimeters. As the angle increases the lines cross closer and closer to us but the change in angle has less and less effect on the movement. This characteristic is observed when two sets of lines are slightly crossed. A whole series of thick-thin-thick lines appear as each line in one set crosses each line in the other. The moire ´ pattern moves more rapidly when the two sets of lines are nearly parallel than when they are crossed at a large angle. What we are seeing is the tangent function in action.

2. Dot patterns work much the same as lines. For simplicity we can consider a series of dots in a line. Another line of dots set at a slight angle to the first will give a thick-thin-thick sequence, or possibly a single thickening depending on the spacing of the dots. If a hair is laid over a halftone newspaper photo so that it makes a slight angle with the dots in the photo, a series of dark streaks will appear along the hair. This is due to the periodic thickening effect of dots close to the hair. If the dots are close to the hair we tend to see both hair and dots. When they are separated we see neither. Why do we see the intricate tiling effect with the khaki print and the halftone? Because the dot grids, unlike a series of lines, run in two directions. One dot grid, such as a halftone photo, laid on another creates patterns in at least two directions.

Tiling Patterns

Related Math: area, angles, polygons, angular measure, central angles, the plane, congruence, symmetry

One rather simple and restful way to learn about designs is to use various geometric figures as tiles that are laid alongside one another to form a design. A large number of flat, wooden shapes are needed. We might set the problem of filling a plane such as a tabletop. There are many ways to achieve this but if only regular polygons are to be used (all sides are the same length and all angles between sides are of the same value) we find that triangles, squares, and hexagons are the only figures which will do. Octagons leave spaces and pentagons don't seem to do well at all. If squares and octagons are combined, the plane can be filled, but the sides of the octagon and the squares must be of the same size (or the octagon can be a multiple of the square).

If the polygons can have sides of different length, then, besides the figures discussed, rectangles, any triangle, trapezoids, and parallelograms will tile the plane. Will quadrilaterals work? If they are the same size and shape the chances seem good since the sum of the angles of a quadrilateral is 360 degrees. A number of the quadrilaterals can be made for the experiment. More simply, one shape can be made and its outline traced onto a large piece of paper. Then another outline is traced alongside it and if done properly the paper can be filled without blank spaces by the addition of sufficient forms. An example of this pattern is seen in figure 1-11.

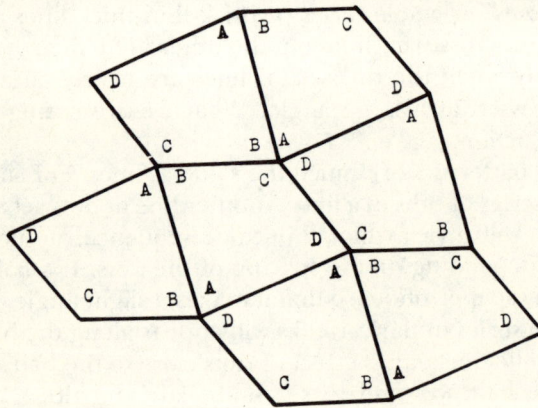

Figure 1-11. Tiling a plane with a quadrilateral form.

Sound Vibrations

Related Math: sine waves, graphing, multiplication, counting, measuring, maxima and minima, rate, averaging, angular measure, coordinates

Sound is so fundamental that it is rooted in us. We have evolved into hearing creatures and it is therefore important and interesting to show the many aspects of sound. Vibrations of all sorts can be created and observed by each student. The equipment for the most part is simple and involves interesting mathematics.

Vibration is a repetition of a cyclic sort with a certain number of these repeated movements each second. These vibrations can send out a wave which vibrates the air. The speed (velocity) of this wave is related to the number of cycles per second (frequency) and the distance between waves (wavelength):

$$\text{Velocity} = \text{wavelength} \times \text{frequency}$$

Thus, even when we talk we are illustrating number. A deep voice has a lower number (of vibrations) than a high voice. And we might ask, "Why the trouble of having vibrating organs to deliver and receive this sound?" One answer to this is simply that sound is a continuous excitement of a material, and intelligent delivery requires that this use of energy be continuous. Clicks won't work nearly as well. We need continual, attention-getting tone which can be modified in many different ways to obtain language. Simple mathematical formulations lie at the root of sound, and therefore language sounds as well.

Bicycle Fork Vibrations and Determining Pitch

Bicycle forks (after removal from the front wheel of the bicycle) vibrate loudly and for long periods of time when struck. The large forks work best, but a variety of types are good to have in order to compare pitches. A styrofoam cup tied by a rubber band to one of the prongs of the fork (see figure 1-12) will make the sound come out more clearly. In order to record the vibrations, a pencil or ball point pen cartridge can be tied to an end of one of the prongs with a rubber band. The bike fork is set in vibration and drawn lightly across a piece of paper. A wavy pattern on the paper will result which gradually decreases in amplitude but remains constant in frequency. A string tied to one of the prongs and held taut at the free end while the fork is vibrated will make a wave pattern in the air. It will be a "standing wave" with "nodes" where the vibration is least, in between each of which are other places where there is a great deal of motion. If the string is replaced by rubber bands tied together to lengthen them, they will vibrate wildly at a certain tension, indicating the interesting and useful phenomenon of resonance.

One of the important things to accomplish with the bike fork is to determine its natural frequency or pitch. It is easy enough to get a pretty record of the wave pattern, but how to find out how many cycles of the wave pattern are recorded each second? If we can find this we can use the device to measure other speeds. Our problem is that the vibration record essentially stops within one second and we must have start and stop marked quite accurately on the paper. The following methods have their weaknesses but do give some approximation:

a. Learn how long a second feels by watching a sweep second hand clock and noting the time between seconds. Then run the bike fork with

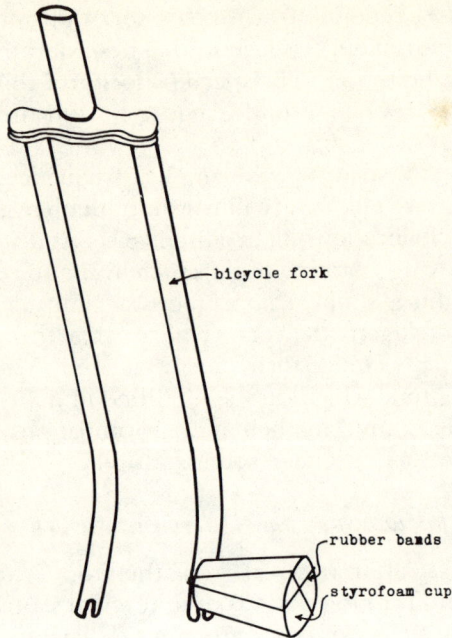

Figure 1-12. A method of obtaining quite audible vibrations from a bicycle fork.

pen attached across a paper for the same length of time. Do this several times and then count the number of cycles in each pattern and average them.

b. Compare the tone with one on the piano. If you can find one which matches the tone on the bike fork you can look up the frequency of the note on the piano. Middle C on the piano is 262 cycles per second, and while each note below it does not diminish in frequency exactly evenly, each C below middle C is half the frequency of the one above. From this the frequency of notes in between can be deduced.

c. Compare the record of the bike fork pattern with the record of a regular tuning fork whose frequency is known. Both forks must be in contact with the paper for the same length of time. Here again averages from a series of records can be made.

d. An interesting method of finding the frequency is to vibrate the fork over a closed tube. However, low pitched forks require a very long tube of about ten feet. Two close-fitting cardboard tubes held telescope fashion with the open end close to the vibrating bike fork can then be lengthened or shortened until the tone becomes louder, indicating resonance. Once the increase in sound is detected the length of the cardboard tube is measured and the frequency of the vibrations can be found by using the formula:

$$\text{Frequency} = \frac{1087 \text{ (in feet)}}{4 \text{ x length of the tube}}$$

If the metric system is used, replace 1087 by 331 (in meters).

Other Vibration Sources

There are many other sources of sound vibrations, and every effort should be made to record them. You can experiment with the human voice, a drum, a loudspeaker, band iron, stretched rubber bands, or reeds (from a soda straw). Only by recording these vibrations can we see the differences in their patterns as well as their similarities. The emphasis should be on devices which will permit a student to work by himself rather than those which require so much equipment that only a classroom demonstration is feasible. As a teacher you will still have much to do in gathering material and altering some of it to suit the purpose at hand.

Sound Patterns from Loudspeakers

A loudspeaker can be rigged so that it will record sound vibrations. Figure 1-13 shows just one method of doing this. The styrofoam cup sits on the paper cone of the speaker and is held in place with four rubber bands fastened to the speaker mounting holes. Coat hanger wire is pushed through the cup and this wire vibrates when the speaker is in

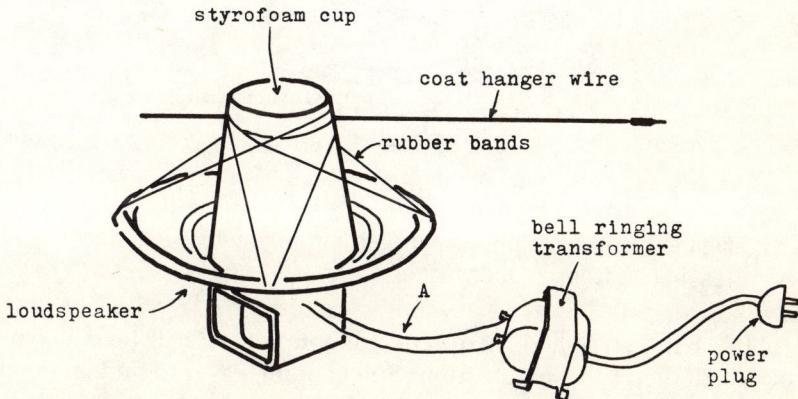

Figure 1-13. A method of recording vibrations from a loudspeaker. In this case the recording is of powerline vibrations of 60 hertz.

operation. At the end of the wire the felt tip from a worn out pen is fastened with a short rubber band and dipped into *washable* ink. In order to get recordable vibrations the speaker should be connected to a bell-ringing transformer (available at a hardware store) as shown. The speaker is connected to the side of the transformer which ordinarily is connected to the doorbell. The other side is connected to an electric power outlet. All connections should be taped on the powerline side to avoid shock. A very loud sound will issue from the speaker and a switch placed at A in figure 1-13 will make it easier to turn the speaker on and off. Some other transformers will work. In fact, if the speaker is obtained from an old radio or television it may already be connected to an "output" transformer. Two wire leads from this transformer will already be connected to the speaker. The other two leads on the other side of the transformer can then be connected to a power cord. The speaker will not vibrate as loudly in this case. If a "filament" transformer is available (used to light the tubes in a radio) it can be used in the same way to obtain a loud tone.

The speakers used in these experiments preferably should be expendable since they are easily damaged. The paper cone is easily punctured. One way to protect the cone is to stretch a large rubber balloon across it, holding it stretched with paper clamps as shown in figure 1-14.

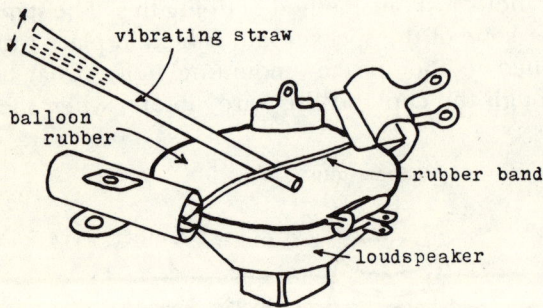

Figure 1-14. A simple way of getting large vibrations and resonance from a loudspeaker.

A rubber band stretched across the balloon rubber will hold down a straw which then will vibrate visibly. Still another way is to find an empty tin can which has the same size opening as the speaker (a size 2½ can fits a 4 inch (10 centimeter) speaker). Remove the bottom from the can and stretch a rubber balloon over one end, holding it in place with one or two rubber bands. When the open end is placed over the speaker the balloon will vibrate like a drumhead. Cinnamon sprinkled onto the rubber will whirl around, and centers of vibration will be detectable. A straw or light felt pen may be attached and a recording made as before. The speaker cone vibrates the rubber balloon, but is itself far enough removed to be fairly well protected from injury. Of course there are other variations of this, and experimentation will no doubt produce good records. For instance, it is worth experimenting with the length of the straw. Place your finger under the straw and move your finger along as the straw vibrates. At certain critical positions of your finger the vibrations will increase violently. A piece of spaghetti can be used in place of the straw and even more violent vibrations will result.

Other methods of obtaining wave pattern records may be tried as many students enjoy doing this work. A length of coat hanger wire with a felt tip from a pen tied to the end with a rubber band can be held with the other end pressed to a table. When the felt end is pulled down slightly and released the wire will vibrate, and this can be recorded on paper held lightly against the felt tip. It is a highly damped vibration (stops soon) so you will have to be quick with the paper. (It is good to use two people for this.) Band iron used in tying lumber will also vibrate, or a hacksaw blade will do.

Vibrations and Sine Waves

As the various vibrations are recorded and compared a similarity among them will be seen. The shape of the wave is distinctive. It is a *sine wave*.

We can construct a pattern which will vary like these records using simple geometric tools—a compass, protractor, ruler, and lined paper. Draw a one-inch-radius circle at one end of the lined paper and extend a line through the middle of the circle to the other end of the paper, at right angles to the lines as in figure 1-15. With the protractor draw a 30 degree, a 60 degree, and a 90 degree angle as shown. Label the lines and lay out AB on the 30 degree lines, CD on the 60 degree lines, and OE on the 90 degree lines. The 120 degree line has the same length to the axis as the 60 degree line and the 150 degree line has the same length to the axis as the 30 degree line, and so on all the way around the circle to 360 degrees. By connecting all the points a sine wave will be formed. Here rotating motion produces a sine wave when the proper coordinates are chosen. If the circular motion takes place between two walls, then the velocity of a particle travelling on the rim of the circle with respect to either of these walls will vary as do the numbers in a table of sines, and as does this wave that we have constructed. If the two walls are magnetic with one a north pole and the other a south pole, and if the particle is a copper wire, an electric current will be created in the wire as it is rotated. This electric current will vary in strength as do the numbers in a table of sines vary.

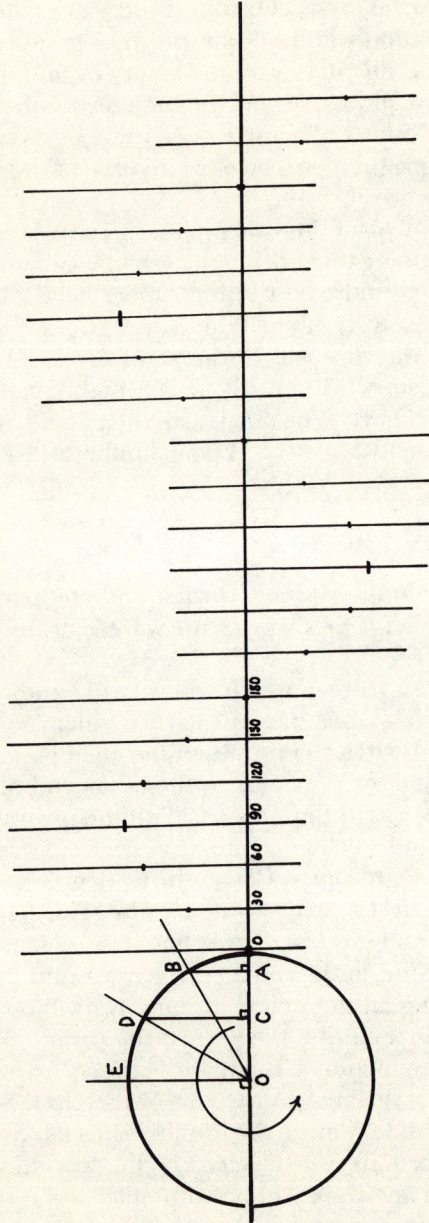

Figure 1-15. The relationship between rotating motion and the sine wave can be demonstrated.

Puzzles and Problems

1. Hold a ruler or strip of cardboard as shown in figure 1-16 so that its end A is in contact with the line Y-Y, while point B, a few inches from the end, is in contact with X-X. Mark the location of the end of the ruler, or some convenient point on the ruler if the paper is too small (point C). Move the ruler slightly, keeping A and B in contact with the axes as before, and mark the new location of C. Do this until you have made about 20 dots all the way around the axes. What figure do you have when you connect the dots?

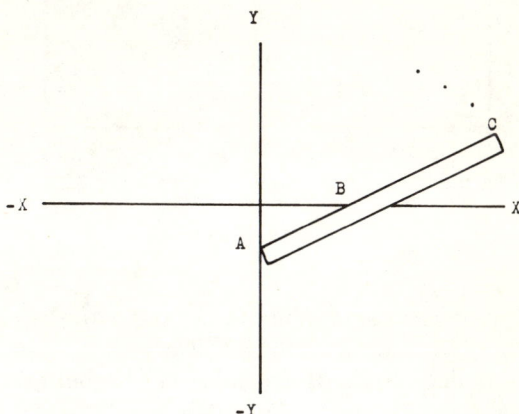

Figure 1-16

2. Try the same as in #1 but have the X and Y lines cross at less than a right angle. Do you get the same kind of a figure? Try this with an L-shaped cardboard or plastic triangle so that A, B, and C are not in a line. Does the shape produced by connecting dots change?

3. Divide the square (figure 1-17) into four equally shaped parts with the same area. You must draw the shapes between dots. One easy way is shown by dotted lines. How many different ways can you divide the squares? Try a square with five dots on a side. How many ways can it be divided into four equally shaped parts? Try other squares with three dots on a side, six dots, etc.

4. Using the shape in figure 1-18, fill in the rectangle. How many shapes do you need? How many ways can you tile it? If the rectangle is twice as wide, how many of the shapes will you need to tile it? How many ways can you tile this larger rectangle?

Figure 1-17

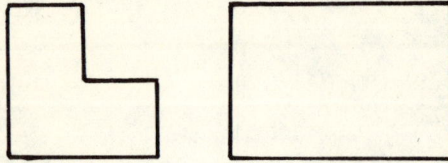

shape   rectangle

Figure 1-18

5. Obtain some potassium alum (from the drugstore) and dissolve as much as you can in about a half cup of hot tap water. If you can use boiling water the results will be better. Pour off the dissolved portion into another glass and let it stand after hanging a string or thread in the liquid as shown in figure 1-19. Crystals will form on the string in an hour or so if the solution is concentrated enough. While these crystals will not be perfect you may be able to figure out what shape they tend to form by

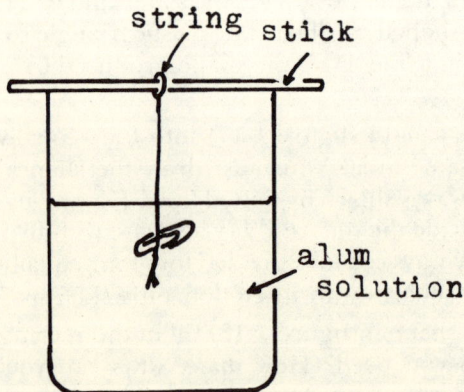

string stick

alum
solution

Figure 1-19

careful observation with a 10 power magnifier or 20 power microscope. If you can let the contents of the glass stand indefinitely the crystals will grow larger on the string as the water evaporates. Some common household chemicals will show crystalization if they are first dissolved in water and then the water allowed to evaporate in a shallow glass dish. Salt crystals quite a bit larger than the ones in table salt can be grown this way.

6. View the design of figure 1-20 stereoscopically and you will see

$$\ni A_\wedge \mid A^\vee$$

Figure 1-20

of what the world is always in need. The A's must be superimposed. Almost any word can be taken apart and brought back whole by viewing it stereoscopically. At least one letter of the word should be complete so that the eyes can look at this letter and see the rest of the word with peripheral vision.

BIBLIOGRAPHY

Association of Teachers of Mathematics. *Notes on Mathematics in Primary Schools*, London: Cambridge at the University Press, 1967. (Three dimensions, pp. 122; tiling is described on pp. 131-160.)

Carson, George S. "Soma Cubes," *The Mathematics Teacher*, Nov. 1973, p. 583.

Courant, R. and H. Robbins. *What Is Mathematics?*, New York: Oxford University Press, 1956. (Soap bubble mathematics, pp. 385-397.)

Elliott, H. A. *Numbers, Shapes and Patterns*. Toronto, Canada: Holt, Rinehart and Winston, 1967.

Inexpensive Science Teaching Equipment Project. *Guidebook, Vol. II.* Science Teaching Center, University of Maryland, College Park, MD, 1972. (Crystal models, pp. 193-222.)

Stong, C. L. "The Amateur Scientist," *Scientific American*, Feb. 1973. (Molecular models, p. 110.)

2

Understanding Math Principles in Size and Shape

Mathematical concepts include: angles,
trigonometry, ratio, measurement of distances, loci, cones, proportions, scale,
fractions, solid geometry, parallels, symmetry, volume, area formulae, Pythagorean theorem, equations, pedals, sampling,
envelopes

The words "size" and "shape" are both mathematical terms, each
derived from certain qualities seen in the forms around us. The words
lie at the basis of various geometries. Their study gives us the power to
transcend their conventional meaning so that we see them without
blinders, without the human temptation to make ourselves the measure
of what is large or small, and we begin to understand relativity.

Making a Pegboard Rangefinder

Related Math: parallax, angles, triangles, estimating distance, loci, inscribed circles, bisectors

A rangefinder is designed to measure a distance by optical means.
We can stand in one place, sight the object to which we wish to find the
distance, and read the distance directly on the rangefinder.

A rangefinder similar to those found on cameras can be constructed
from dowels, mirrors, rubber bands, and pegboard, as shown in figure

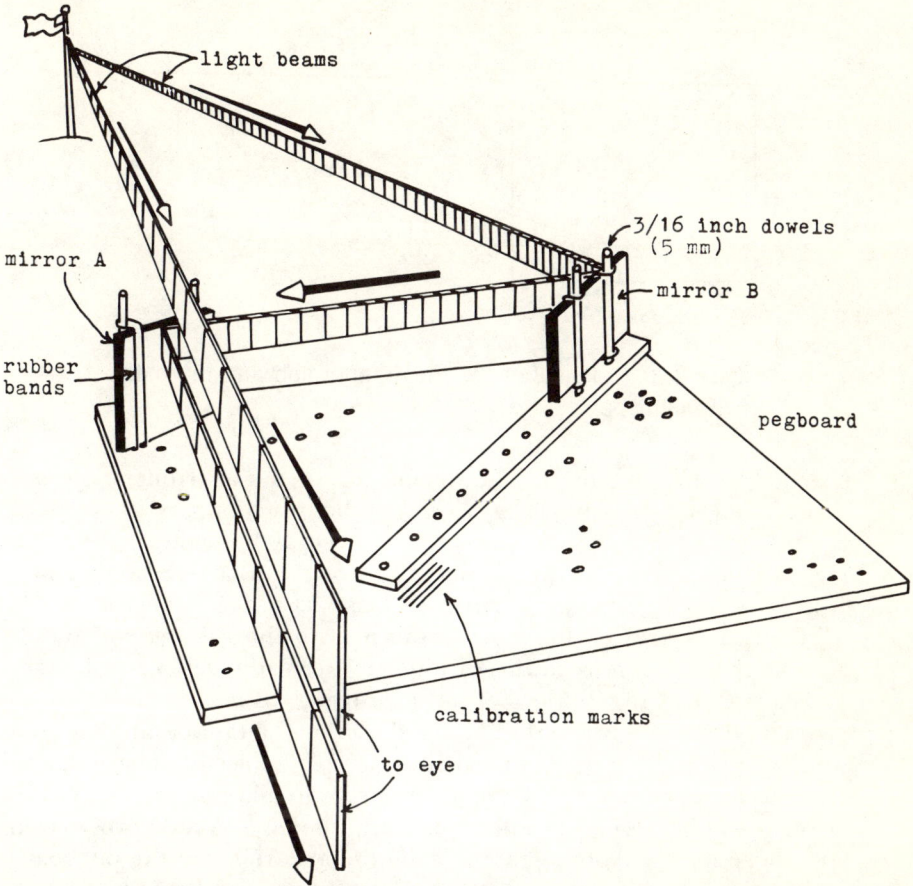

Figure 2-1. One beam of light from the distant flagpole is sent through the rangefinder and one arrives directly. The viewer arranges one beam over the other to determine distance.

2-1. This is a demonstration instrument which works quite well for measuring distances in the classroom.

In order to operate the rangefinder, sight over the mirror A to the object whose distance is to be measured. At the same time adjust mirror B so that it reflects the same object into mirror A and then into your eye. Mirror B is adjusted by moving the arm until the object is seen directly over its image in the mirror at A. If the rangefinder has been calibrated you can read the distance which is marked on the baseboard under the arm. The arm holds mirror B and is adjustable by pivoting on a dowel

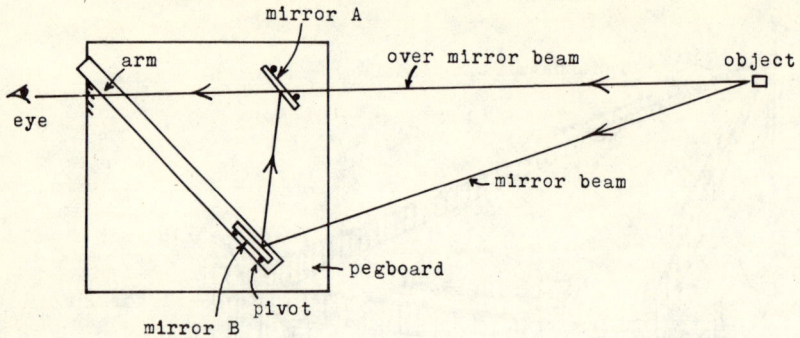

Figure 2-2. Top view of the rangefinder showing the paths of the light beams.

fastened to the baseboard. The dimensions of the instrument are not critical, especially if only distances within the classroom are to be measured. However, for objects between 1000 feet (300 + meters) and 2000 feet (600 + meters) mirror B will turn through an angle of only about 1/30 of a degree, assuming 2 feet (2/3 meter) between mirror A and mirror B. It is not easy to construct this instrument with these materials accurately enough to read this difference. No mathematics is necessary to calibrate the rangefinder beyond measuring distances.

The first job is to build the rangefinder and get it operating so that students can see that they can actually line up an object in mirror A and also have it appear above the mirror. In order to calibrate the rangefinder, sight an object of known distance, and, when it is located properly in and above mirror A, draw a line along the arm right on the pegboard and label it with the known distance. Do this for several other objects at various known distances. The difficulty of measuring distances beyond 100 feet (30+ meters) will become apparent.

Activities with the Rangefinder

a. Estimate the distance to a tree, wall, or pole on or near the schoolground. Then use the rangefinder to determine the distance. Measure the distance to see how accurate each method is. Measuring off may be done quickly with a click wheel (see page 190).

b. Find those locations which are equally distant from two corners of the school building. To do this, sight the rangefinder on one corner of the building and then without changing the position of the arm sight it on the other corner. If no change in position of the arm needs to be made then the two corners are the same distance from the location of the rangefinder. This spot should be marked on the ground and another one chosen and tested. If enough tests are made a locus of points equidistant from the two corners will be found. How close can the range-finder come to giving the exact point midway between the two corners of the building? A level table on which to rest the rangefinder while using it will increase its accuracy. Any tipping of the rangefinder will change the reading slightly.

c. Line up a flagpole or tree in the rangefinder from about 25 feet (7.5 meters). Keeping the rangefinder at that setting, walk toward the object from another direction until the rangefinder again reports that the same distance is obtained. Do this several times, marking each spot where the distance is the same. A circle of spots will be created with the object at the corner.

d. Set up three poles in the schoolyard and ask the students to find the location which is the same distance from each pole. Some sort of reward or prize could be buried at that spot to create a game.

Principle of the Rangefinder

Why does the rangefinder work? The two mirrors and the distant object form the vertices of a triangle two of whose angles (A and B) and the side between them (side AB) are known, as shown in figure 2-3a. The mirrors, shown in figure 2-3b, merely construct the triangle with light

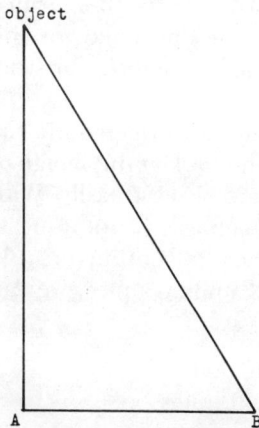

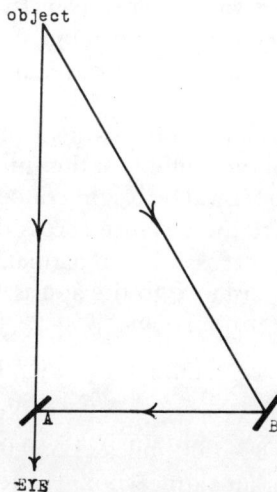

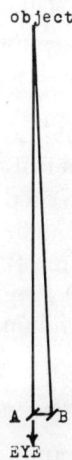

Figure 2-3a. The basic triangle with the object at one vertex and the rangefinder "see-ing" it from the other two vertices.

Figure 2-3b. The straight beam from object to eye is made to pass directly over the reflected beam out of mirror A.

Figure 2-3c. A more real view of the rela-tive distances, show-ing why this method eventually fails.

rays. The mirror at B must be rotated slightly for every change in object distance if the eye is to see the object over the mirror at A and also in the mirror. This rotation of the mirror at B is therefore an indicator of the distance to the object. It is amplified slightly by the arm and can be determined directly when marks have been placed under the arm of the pegboard. Figure 2-3c shows a more realistic view of the shape of the triangle. If A and B were one foot apart, then the object in figure 2-3c would be 19 feet distant. The angle shown at the object is 3 degrees so that any measurements taken from 19 feet to infinity will be crowded between this three degrees and zero degrees. If the base (distance between mirror A and mirror B) is lengthened greater distances can be measured.

Pinhole Camera Rangefinder

Related Math: pencil of lines, cones, similar triangles, ratio and proportion, right angles, diameter, transformations

An oatmeal box (the larger the better) can be made almost instantly into a pinhole camera by punching a small nailhole in the base and spreading an unwrinkled sheet of wax paper over the open end, held there by a rubber band wrapped around the side of the box. Inverted images will appear on the wax paper screen. In order to see them, since they are not usually very bright, the room must be darkened, or the person viewing must have a dark cloth over his head to block out stray light.

One quick measurement with this instrument is to determine the diameter of the sun. Aim the nailhole at the sun and look at the image of the sun on the wax paper. It will be bright enough to observe easily. With a millimeter rule measure the distance across the image. (I got a measurement of 3 millimeters across with an oatmeal box 24 centimeters (9½ inches) long.) Since the distance to the sun is 93 million miles, we can find its diameter by the proportion:

$$3 \text{ centimeter}/24 \text{ centimeter} = x/93{,}000{,}000 \text{ miles}$$
$$x = 1{,}160{,}000 \text{ miles}$$

The actual diameter is 864,000 miles (1,350,000 kilometers)—our answer is fairly accurate for an oatmeal box. However, any box will do. Just measure its length and the diameter of the image on the back. As shown in figure 2-4, similar triangles are used to get the proportion.

Since we already know the diameter of the sun, and our figure with the pinhole oatmeal box camera was off about 25 percent, we might try to find a more accurate way to determine the diameter. Why not try a longer tube? A mailing tube, or the long tubes on which rugs are sometimes rolled, make good cameras. A larger image of the sun will be

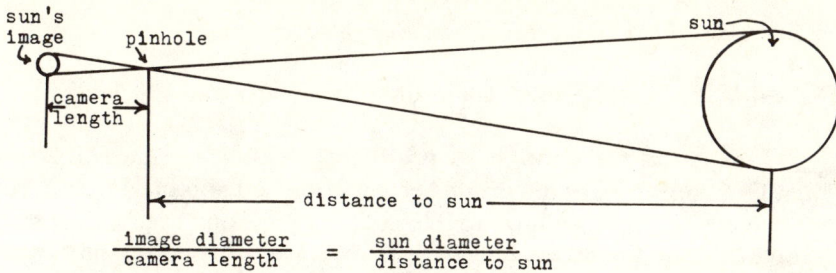

$$\frac{\text{image diameter}}{\text{camera length}} = \frac{\text{sun diameter}}{\text{distance to sun}}$$

Figure 2-4. If the distance to an object is known, its diameter or height can be determined by this method. Likewise, if its height is known, its distance can be found.

formed on the wax paper back. If care is taken (small pinhole, dark room for viewing) even occasional sunspots can be detected. At any rate, by using a mailing tube 91.1 centimeters long an image of the sun on the wax paper was obtained which was .8 centimeters in diameter. This comes out to be about 820,000 miles for the sun's diameter—a bit more · accurate than the oatmeal box. The worst source of error is in measuring the diameter of the sun's image on the screen. With a long tube which careens around while aiming, the image constantly moves on the wax paper, making it difficult to hold a millimeter rule up to it to read it. Two people are required to get a good reading. With a tube 149.5 centimeters long an image of 1.4 centimeters was obtained. This gives a sun diameter of 871,000 miles—not distant from the 864,000 mile figure. If the classroom can be darkened and the sun is shining, an even more accurate method of calculating the sun's diameter can be used. A mirror outside the building is held by someone who reflects the sunlight on to a dark blind in which there is a nail hole. On the opposite wall of the darkened room will appear the image of the sun, about 2½ inches (6.35 centimeters) in diameter. The whole class can view and measure it. If the image is not perfectly round the shortest distance across should be used for the measurement. No one can hold the mirror outside the room steadily enough to keep the image from dancing. Some sort of prop for the mirror should be used and the prop should be the same height from the ground as is the small hole in the blind.

In this case, we need to know the distance to the sun to find its diameter. We could reverse the procedure and find the distance to an object if we could know its size. If a 10 foot pole (about 3 meters) is used, distances to various objects on the schoolground can be determined in the aforementioned manner. Have someone stand with the 10 foot pole near the object and measure the size of the image of the pole on the back of the pinhole camera. It would be sufficient to use the height of the person and not use a pole at all if less accuracy is needed.

Stereoscopic Vision, a Built-In Rangefinder

Related Math: parallax, triangulation, similar triangles

One pinhole is enough to produce one image. If we put two pinholes in our camera the image becomes doubled and hard to see. Yet our two eyes do not produce double images unless one eyelid is pressed gently with one finger. As long as both eyes are focussed on one object we see only one. Nature seems to have gone to some trouble to give us two eyes and then to eliminate the duplication they produce—but nature is not in the habit of being redundant without cause. The eyes, of course, are our built-in rangefinders with instant triangulation. They serve well for those distances that our arms can reach or even at which we can poke a long stick. When we wish to find longer distances we must look at the object from one location and then move to another, which is nothing more than what we have been doing with the rangefinder and what the two eyes do at the same time. We even use this method to find the distance to nearby stars, sighting them once and then six months later when the earth has moved 186,000,000 miles (300,000,000 kilometers) from its first position. This is about as far apart as we can separate our eyes.

Peripheral Vision

Related Math: graphing, estimating angles, coordinates

While both eyes see nearly the same things there are a few items on the margin of our vision which one eye loses sight of before the other. If you wiggle a finger at the side of your head and move the finger farther and farther back it will eventually "disappear." The eye farthest from the finger loses sight of it first. Peripheral vision above and below the eyes is not so extensive (due to eyebrows and cheekbones). Evidently we have more need to see what is at our side than above or below.

Peripheral vision can be measured by having a person stand on a line marked on the floor and look at a distant object in front of that line. The experimenter wiggles a finger, starting behind the margin of peripheral vision of the subject. When the subject first sees the finger in the margin of his sight he advises the experimenter. If the line on the floor is represented as a line on a sheet of paper and a dot or x placed on it for the subject's head, a rough chart can be drawn to show approximately where the wiggling finger appears in peripheral vision. The paper shows only two dimensions, so two such charts are needed, one looking down from the top of the subject's head, and another of his profile. If one of the subject's eyes are kept closed, the chart will show more variation.

Maps and Math

Related Math: coordinate systems, maxima and minima, transformations, increments, rates, ratio, parallels, perpendiculars, intersecting lines, diagonals

Maps are symbols much as numbers are. The idea of producing a shape on a different scale from its original one is quite in keeping with the basic processes of mathematics. A great deal of abstraction must be acceptable to produce even a detailed map. We concentrate on certain aspects of land, such as its topography, ground cover, or rock type, to the exclusion of its other properties.

Topographic Maps

When the student steps out of the classroom he sees topography. Small hills, valleys, and streams in nearly any location are all described on available topographic maps. City streets and buildings, maybe even the students' own homes, can be found on these maps. Such maps are particularly appropriate for the mathematics program. Begin with maps of the area around the school and then obtain representative maps of other areas. The United States Geological Survey has topographic maps in good detail for 75¢ each. It can provide state index maps which show all topographic maps available. Portions of the topographic maps can easily be duplicated by Xeroxing. Pertinent areas can be magnified and enlargements made.

Exercises with Topographic Maps

1. What is the highest elevation on the road between _____ and _____? (You select the places from the local topographic map.) It is good to choose a road with a high point between the places selected. Wherever a topographic line intersects the road we know the elevation at that point, and it is only a matter of finding that topographic line which is the highest in elevation. Every fifth line is heavier, and somewhere along its length is labelled with the actual elevation in feet. This makes it easier to find the elevation of each line on the map.
2. Where is the steepest point on the map? While there might be vertical cliffs too low to be recorded, any large feature will reveal its steepness by the closeness of the topographic lines. It is not easy to measure the distance between two topographic lines when they are only 1/32 of an inch (.8 millimeters) apart, but an average of five or ten lines can be taken fairly easily. Suppose that five topographic lines at one particular point on the map are only a total of 3/16 inch (about 5 millimeters) apart. If there is no other point at which five lines are less distance apart, this is the steepest point.

3. How steep is the steepest part of the map? In the aforementioned case, if the scale of the map is 1 mile to the inch (or 1 kilometer to
2 centimeters) and the topographic lines are 100 feet (30 meters) difference in elevation, then we have the means of determining steepness. The
steepness is the ratio of the rise in elevation to the horizontal distance. In
this case 400 feet (120 meters) to 3/16 of a mile (300 meters), or 400/990
(or 120/300 in meters), a respectable steepness.

4. How can a cross section of a topographic map be made? First
draw a straight line on the map where the cross section is wanted (figure
2-5a). Then lay a piece of graph paper or lined paper over the line (as in
figure 2-5b) with the elevations labelled on the lined paper. Note the 200
foot (60 meter) topographic line and how it is transferred to the ruled
line as a dot directly over where the topographic line passes under the
lined paper. Vertical variations are so small in comparison to horizontal
ones on the earth's surface that it is necessary to exaggerate the vertical
as is done in this figure. We have a tendency to exaggerate the vertical
anyway since as we travel along the surface of the earth 3000 feet (or
about 1 kilometer) of horizontal surface blocks off much less of our view
than 3000 feet (or 1 kilometer) of vertical surface. The most striking
mountain ranges are deceptively steep looking but are actually puny in
height compared to horizontal distances.

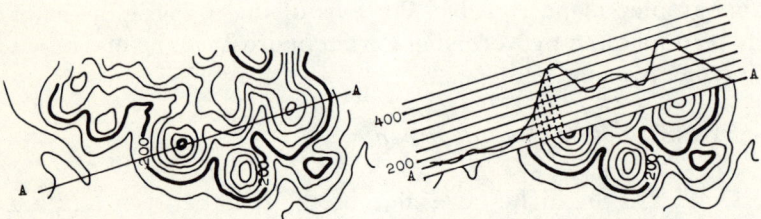

Figure 2-5a. A section of a topographic map with a line AA drawn
where the cross section is desired.

Figure 2-5b. A ruled sheet has been
laid along line AA and the cross
section completed. There is vertical exaggeration.

5. Giving a topographic map a three-dimensional appearance.
Look at the series of sketches of a topographic map (figure 2-6a) on
which ruled lines have been laid (figure 2-6b). A new pattern is developed at figure 2-6c which appears alone in figure 2-6d, giving a
three-dimensional characteristic to the map. It seems as though we have
sectioned the topography with parallel lines that run up and down the
hills. In order to obtain this pattern on a topographic map we will need
tracing paper and graph or lined paper. Trace the topographic lines of
the topographic map onto the tracing paper and lay this over the graph

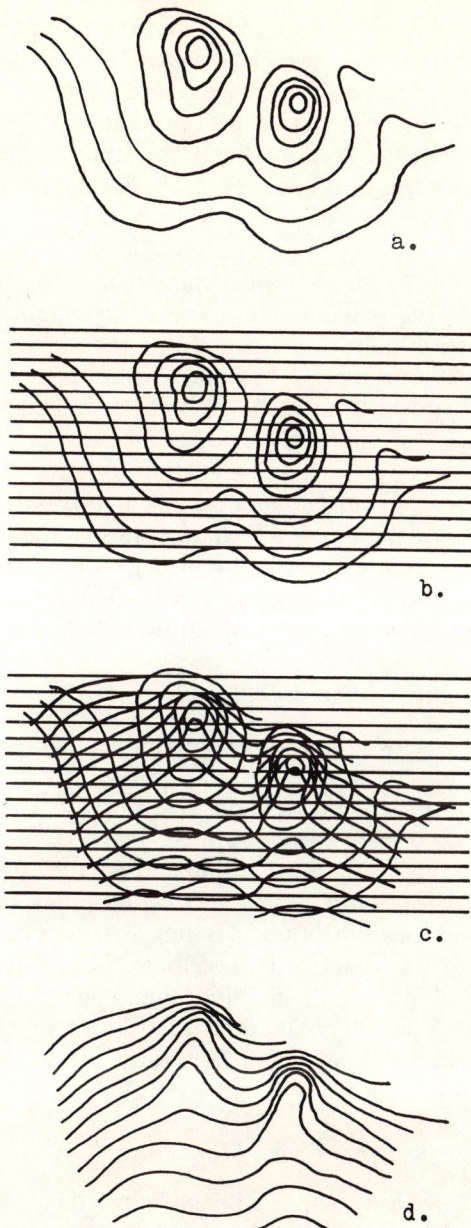

Figure 2-6. These are the steps taken in the change from the conventional topographic map at a. to the finished map at d. with a different way to express elevation.

paper. Then, wherever a horizontal line on the graph paper intersects a topographic line we start a line which we extend to the intersection of the adjacent topographic line and the adjacent line on the graph paper. (We don't need the vertical lines—in fact, they are in the way.) When we have finished we have actually sectioned our topographic map at another angle. The original contour lines were all horizontal. Now we have added some at another angle. There is much interesting mathematics here which we can discuss in the classroom. The series of parallel lines which are superimposed on the topographic map is like a smooth-faced hill which intersects the real one. By drawing one diagonal between any two pairs of lines we establish the trace of the smooth-faced hill as it cuts the actual hill. By continuing this diagonal to other pairs of lines we trace out the complete intersection of the smooth-faced hill with the actual one. The next series of diagonals requires an assumption on our part that the parallel lines now represent elevations one contour up or down as the case may be. This gives us another cut through the actual hill parallel to the first. As the actual hill changes in steepness these cuts also change and give us another view of the topography with lines running up and over the hills. These lines give a reality to the map which is frequently missing in the ordinary topographic lines.

Giving a Weather Map a 3-D Appearance

We can use the same approach with weather maps (which appear in the daily paper) and see the "highs" and "lows" a little more clearly. (See figure 2-7.) To emphasize these highs and lows, or to steepen topography, the following process can be applied. When connecting diagonals between the ruled lines, skip a ruled line and connect to the next ruled line up, as shown in figure 2-8. Topographic lines (and isobars on weather maps) wind around, and it is not always possible to connect them according to the described procedure. Start from those places which look easy and discontinue the line when you are not sure where it is to be continued. You will obtain a series of line segments in different portions of the map which, after further study, can be connected properly in many places.

A More Realistic Topographic Map

An even more realistic map can be made by altering the topographic map so that it looks as though it is viewed from an angle rather than from straight above. First, with tracing paper over the map we trace out the highest contour line onto the tracing paper. Then we raise the tracing paper a measured distance, perhaps one line on a graph paper laid under the map. At this new location of the tracing paper we trace out the contour line next to the highest, and then move the tracing paper up one more unit. We trace the third contour line from the highest at this new

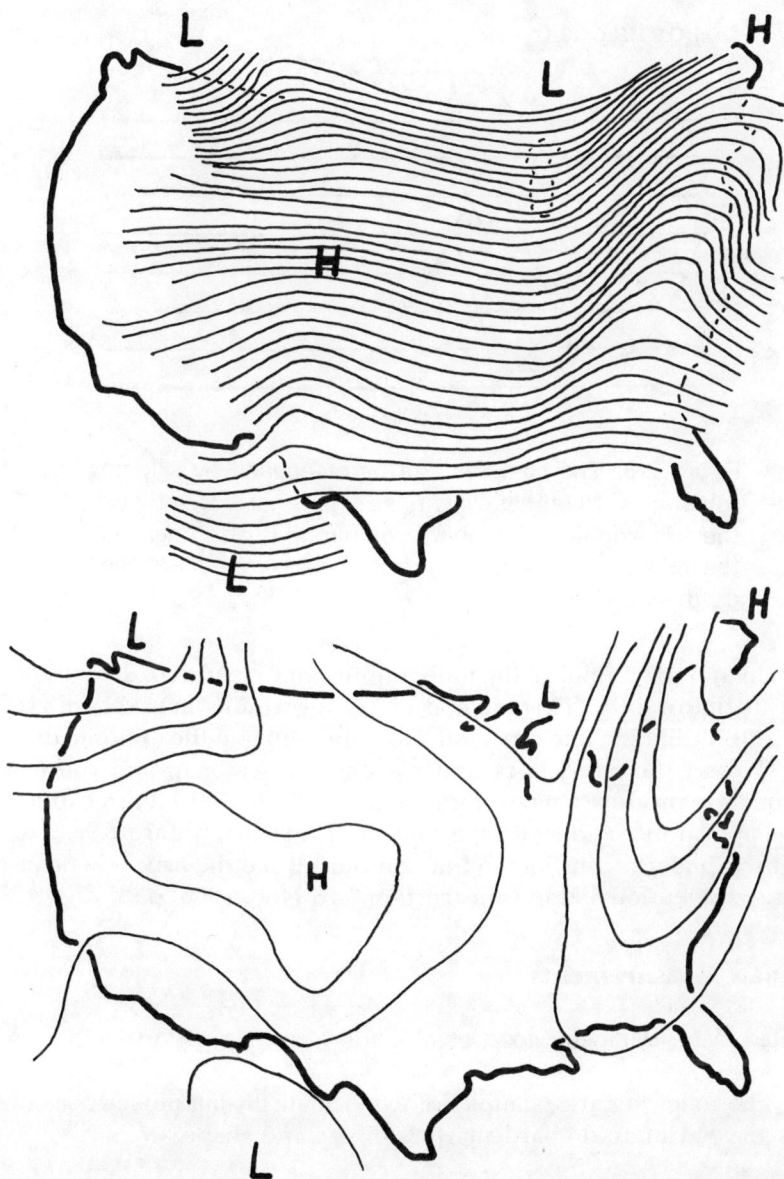

Figure 2-7. Derived weather map (top) and original. Note that high pressure areas are risings in the lines and low pressure areas are lowerings. The relationship between the two is more easily seen in the derived map. The number of lines has been increased by line skipping (see figure 2-8).

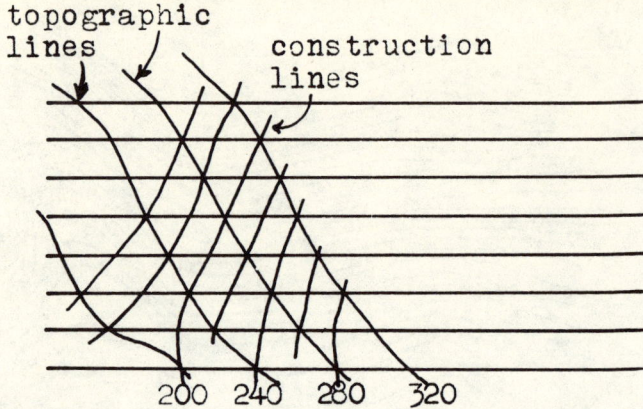

Figure 2-8. The contours can be steepened by skipping ruled lines. Note that every ruled line is used even though there is skipping. The above contouring is also finer than the original because many more ruled lines have been used.

location and so on until all the topographic lines are traced. The result is seen in figure 2-9b. This method of tracing results in a crowding of topographic lines in one direction and a spreading in the opposite direction. We set the ruled lines underneath this new map and construct diagonals to produce a map which has a more pronounced three dimensional appearance and which is a copy of the original (figure 2-9c). For a good treatment of this method of contouring see the article in *Science*, "Three-Dimensional Map Construction," 18 Nov. 1966, p. 857.

Human Measurements

Related Math: symmetry, focal point, parity

The following are examples of experiments using ourselves as subjects and having to do particularly with size and shape.

1. *Mirror writing*

Place a mirror on the table, preferably on a stand, and write your name on a sheet of paper so that it appears correctly in the mirror. A book placed so that it blocks the hand from view tends to focus attention on the mirror, but the experiment can be done without the book. Several points are worth considering after first trying this experiment with the class. Is everything reversed in the mirror or just certain lines, ie., are

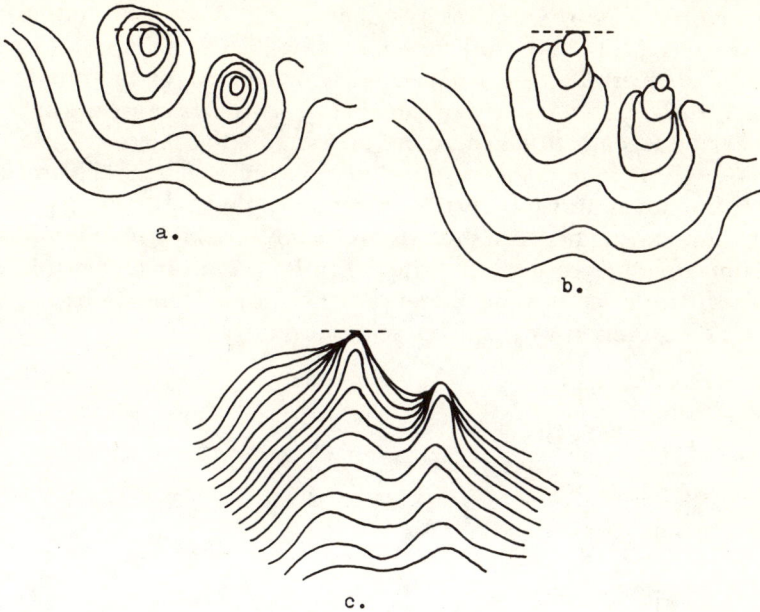

Figure 2-9. A topographic map (a.) is altered by dropping each elevation contour a measured distance (b.). Ruled lines are placed over the altered map and when diagonals are drawn, the result is the portrayal at c. The dashed lines are all of the same elevation. Line skipping has been used to improve the detail.

both up and down lines and lines drawn across reversed? Is there a quick way to write your name? Yes, there is: write your name on paper and copy its mirror image. Your own name will appear under the pencil. Will a concave mirror reverse your name the same way? We find it will not because there are two kinds of reversals possible in mirrors, one for plane and one for concave. If anything, the concave is more reversed than the plane mirror. A concave shaving mirror is not optically correct enough to use in this work, and you have to stand about 6 feet (2 meters) from the mirror before a reversed and upside down image can be seen. A better mirror can be made from an aluminum beer or soda can. The bottom of such cans are concave and they must be polished, an arduous task. First they must be sandpapered, using fine sandpaper, for the cans have irregularities which must be eliminated. Then jeweler's rouge is applied to a piece of flannel and rubbed onto the bottom of the can until gradually a polish is built up. There is some question as to whether the work involved is worth the novelty of having a mirror at the bottom of a beer can but if there are students willing, the job can be done. Even the inside of a Christmas tree ornament may be concave enough to do the trick. A small fragment of the ornament can be used because the image is smaller and it tends to take in more area than a flat mirror.

Along this same idea you can look in a mirror at a sketch of two concentric circles drawn fairly close together (figure 2-10). With a pencil, draw a line staying between the two circles while looking in the mirror at their image. More complicated tracks can be traced, but even this first one is difficult for the inexperienced. "Rightness" and "leftness" are vigorously exercised when such tracings are made.

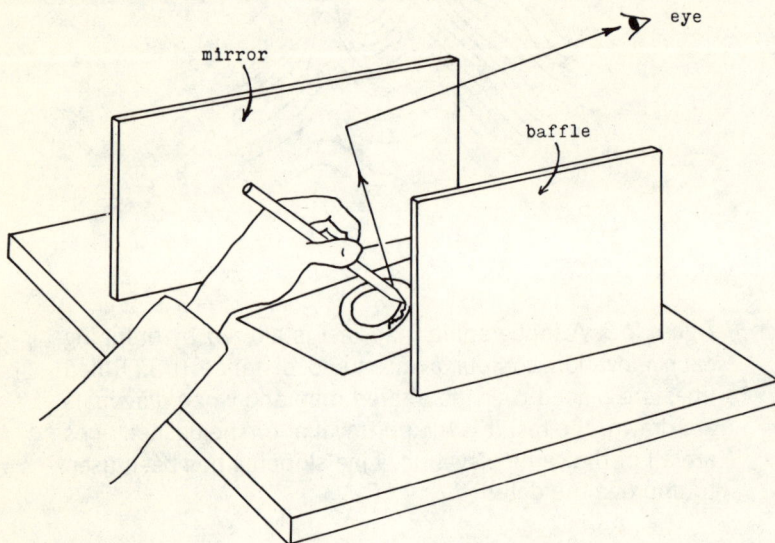

Figure 2-10. The pencil is guided so as to leave a mark in the ring while looking at its mirror image—a good exercise in opposites. It is by no means easy to do this.

2. *Finger mazes*

Related Math: closed curves, surfaces, reversals

In a few minutes a maze can be made using pegboard, dowels and rubber bands as illustrated in figure 2-11. The maze should be learned by feel alone as an experiment to determine the effectiveness of the sense of feeling in learning a new task. How does this learning compare

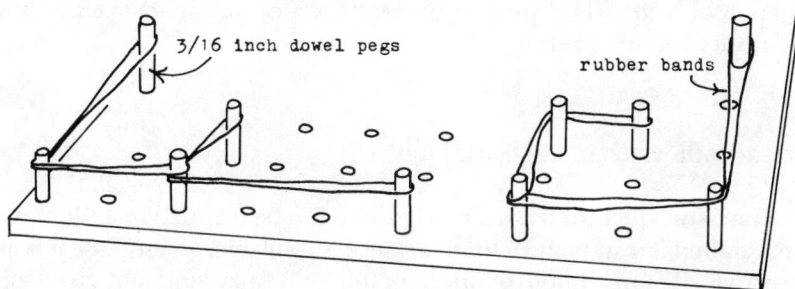

Figure 2-11: A rubber band finger maze can be built and altered rapidly from pegboard, dowel pegs and rubber bands. It should be negotiated blindfolded or while looking away since it is no challenge to the visual sense, but sufficient for the sense of touch. The above shows a beginning stage in construction.

with learning by vision alone? Which kind of learning is forgotten more quickly?

The dowels can be extended through the pegboard so that an identical maze, but reversed, can be made by stretching rubber bands across these exposed ends. Then the relationship between learning a maze and learning its reverse can be studied.

It is not easy to negotiate the maze by feel alone, and one is tempted to peek after groping about for a minute. The rubber bands provide a good wall for the pathways. One sure way of getting through the maze (without learning it) is to keep your finger on the left side (or right side) of all pathways. Inevitably this procedure will lead you to the exit.

3. *Lung Capacity*

Related Math: volume, distance measurement, fractions, arithmetic processes, averaging

Lung capacity can be roughly checked with a gallon (about 4 liters) plastic jug, a rubber hose or tube, and a wash basin. Fill the jug with water, invert it, holding a hand over the opening, and immerse the top in a water-filled wash basin. As soon as the top of the jug is in the water, the hand can be removed and a hose fished into the opening. Blow into the open end of the hose and the bottle will empty of water. Markings on the side of the bottle can be made to measure the volume of water displaced. (Much water gets on the floor.) Another way to measure lung air is to blow into a completely deflated plastic bag of at least one gallon capacity. After one full breath is blown in, the bag is sealed and immersed in a large pan of water. The amount the water raises can be marked on the pan and its volume found.

4. *Testing cigarette smoke*

Related Math: volume, fractions, ratio

The byproducts of a burning cigarette can be trapped in a filter and even weighed if a suitably delicate balance is available. In any case it is an instructive demonstration of the amount of smoke and tar given off when a cigarette is smoked. A hand vacuum pump is used to draw on the cigarette. If none is available a tire pump with leather piston reversed will work. (See page 191.) One setup for obtaining the byproducts is shown in figure 2-12.

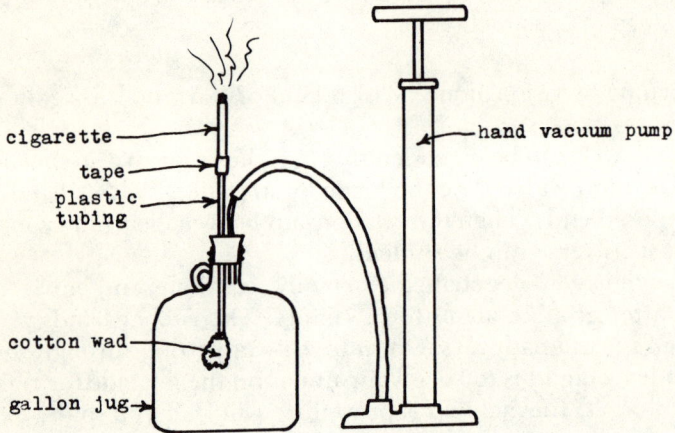

Figure 2-12. The byproducts of cigarette smoking can be measured with this device. The gallon jug quickly becomes filled with dense smoke whether the cigarette has a filter or not.

A dense smoke fills the bottle and remains there a long time. The cotton absorbs some of the smoke, and the liquids from the burning cigarette roll down the tube into the cotton. A pack of cigarettes "smoked" this way will leave the cotton quite messy, and a weight measurement of the cotton before and after smoking will be more easily made than for one cigarette. The dense smoke in the bottle can be cleared by detaching the hose from the vacuum pump and blowing it out through the hose by mouth. The number of breaths required gives some idea of how long after smoking one's lungs are cleared of noticeable smoke.

These experiments help the student visualize what happens when tobacco smoke is inhaled, a process otherwise concealed within the body. The notion that it is virile and romantic to smoke should be balanced with a little realism.

Hinged Puzzlers and Shapes That Change

Related Math: area of a triangle (and rectangle, parallelogram, square), Pythagorean theorem, right triangles, exponents, equations

The game of tangrams is played with simple, flat geometric figures which may be fit together to make many different shapes. (There are other puzzles which involve similar simple figures in which one is asked to change a square to another shape by rearranging the pieces.) The area of course remains constant. The following description of hinged puzzles requires pegboard and 3/16 inch (5 millimeter) dowels cut in lengths about 3/8 inch (10 millimeter) long. A stub is left on each piece of pegboard with a hole in it to receive a 3/16 inch dowel hinge as shown in figure 2-13.

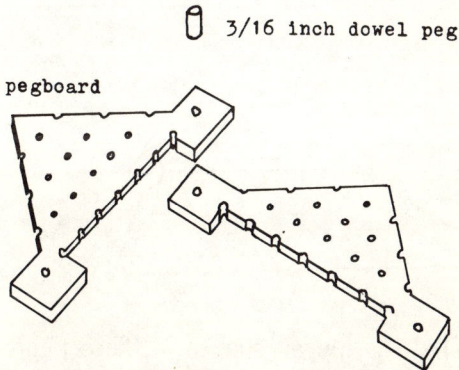

3/16 inch dowel peg

pegboard

Figure 2-13. Shapes can be cut from pegboard and hinged together to form other shapes. With care, another triangle can be cemented over the lower shape in the above figure for a flush arrangement.

1. *Triangular areas*

The area of a triangle is equal to ½ base x height. In figure 2-14a we see the triangle cut into three parts and hinged together. In figure 2-14b the same pieces have been rotated on the hinges to produce a rectangle whose area is the base x ½ the height of the original triangle. Thus if we accept that the area of a rectangle is base x height, then this device shows that the area of a triangle with the same base and height is half that of the rectangle or: the area of a triangle is equal to ½ its base x its height. If the top is hinged we can rotate the pieces to produce a parallelogram whose area is also the same as the original triangle (figure 2-14c).

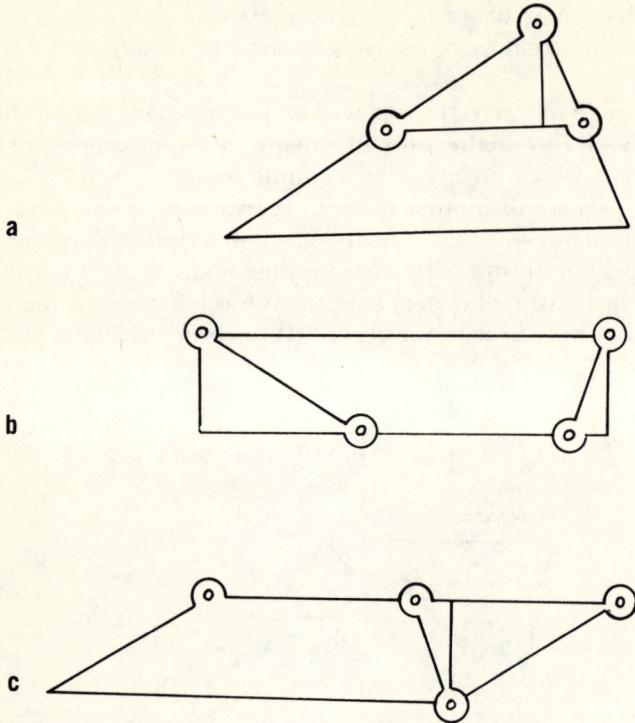

Figure 2-14. The hinged shapes in these figures can be arranged to form a triangle, a rectangle, or a parallelogram. They are helpful in developing the formula for the area of a triangle: A = ½ bh

2. *The Pythagorean theorem*

Examine figure 2-15a. Each of the four right triangles which make up the square has its hypotenuse facing outward, so the area of this square is the hypotenuse x itself, or "the square on the hypotenuse." We must show that the sum of the squares on the legs of a right triangle equals the square on the hypotenuse in order to prove the Pythagorean theorem. To do this we rotate the larger square until the four triangles

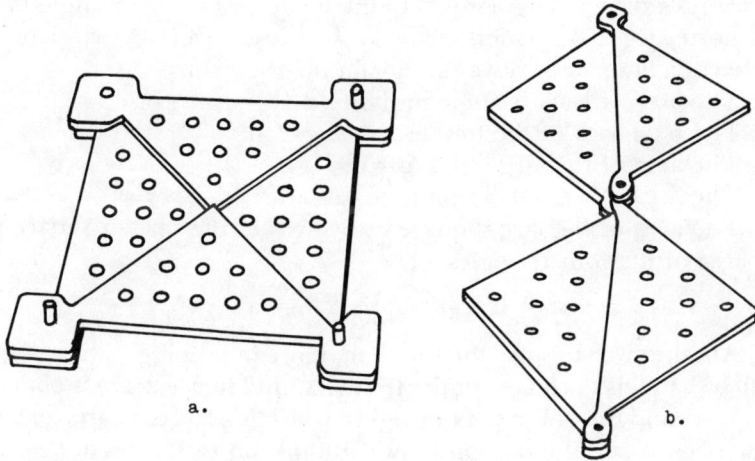

Figure 2-15. The above hinged pegboard illustrates the Pythagorean theorem for 45 degree right triangles.

make up two smaller ones (figure 2-15b). Each of these smaller squares is the square on one leg of the right triangle. Since the area of the new figure is the same as the old we know that the sum of these squares is the same as the first larger square. These were special triangles however with 45 degree angles and equal legs. The more general case is shown in figure 2-16 where a square hole exists in the center. The sides of this

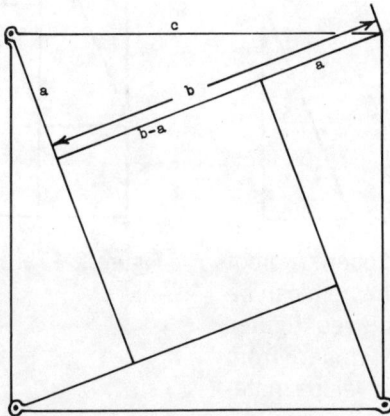

Figure 2-16. The above hinged pegboard is helpful in deriving the Pythagorean theorem for any triangle. A square hole in the center is present for all triangular shapes except the 45 degree right triangle.

square hole have a length equal to the longer leg of the triangle minus the shorter leg. No rotation seems to yield results here but if we permit ourselves a little algebra we can obtain the theorem.

The area of each triangle in figure 2-16 = ½ab.

The total area of the four triangles = 2ab.

The area of the large square = c^2

The area of the small square = $(b - a)^2 = b^2-2ab + a^2$

The area of the large square = the area of the smaller square plus the area of the four triangles, or:

$$c^2 = b^2-2ab + a^2+ 2ab = a^2 + b^2$$

Another way to solve the theorem, more in keeping with the equipment at hand, is to rotate out the triangles until figure 2-17a is obtained. Trace around the outline of this figure which is a large square, a+b on a side. Then rotate the triangles inward until two rectangles are formed. When this figure is placed over the tracing just made it can be seen that the uncovered remainder of the tracing of the large square is equal to a square "a" on a side and a larger square "b" on a side as seen in figure 2-17b. Thus the area of the large square is $a^2 + b^2 + 2ab$ (which is a roundabout way of doing algebra but illuminating). If we take 2ab away from this we obtain c^2 (discoverable in figure 2-17a), and thus $c^2 = a^2 + b^2$.

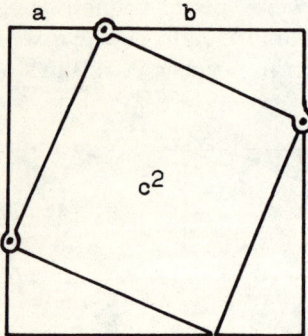

Figure 2-17a. Hinged open. A proof of the Pythagorean theorem can be obtained with the hinged figures above. They can be made from pegboard or manila envelope material.

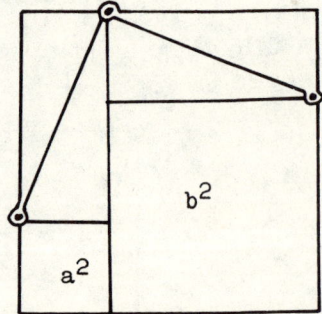

Figure 2-17b. Hinged closed.

3. *Triangles into squares*

An intriguing device is one which when hinged one way will make a triangle and when hinged the other makes a square. The hinging serves

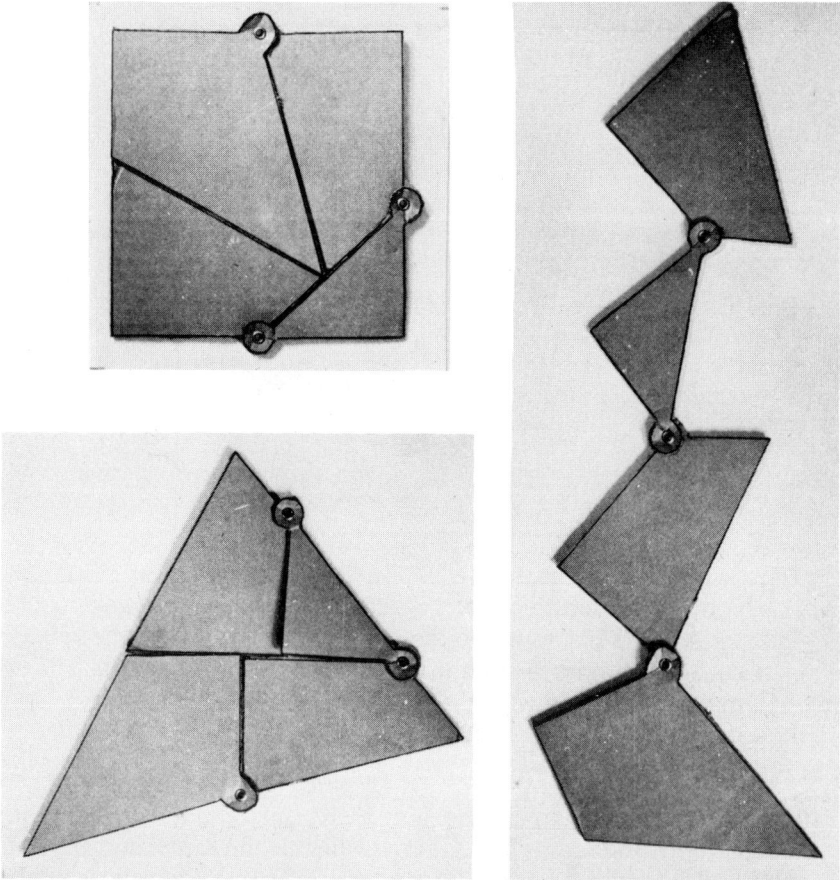

Figure 2-18. Pasteboard hinged with eyelets which have been crimped on by eyelet pliers provides a good medium for demonstrating the swinging of a square into a triangle.

to show the change quickly and is a good classroom device. Pasteboard has been used in figure 2-18. Note the eyelets which fasten the pasteboard units. Eyelet pliers can be obtained in a hardware store together with eyelets. Do not crimp the eyelets too firmly or you will not be able to rotate the pieces.

In order to make the proper cuts so that a square will rotate into a triangle, use figure 2-19. The points C and D are arbitrary, and as long as all lengths "a" are the same, and both lengths "b" are equal, you will be able to rotate this square into a triangle. I have found no easy way of designing cuts in a triangle so that it will rotate into a square. I assume this is because if we start with a square we can develop many triangles of

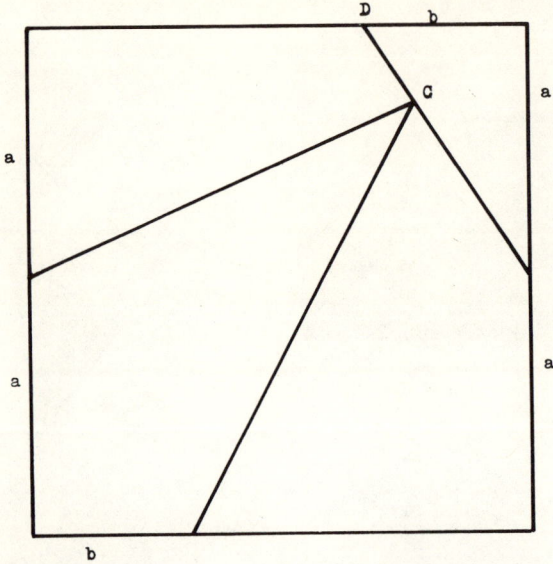

Figure 2-19. The pieces of this square can be hinged at any three of the places where the cuts meet the edge and the square will swing around into a triangle. Manila envelope material fastened with eyelets works well in constructing the device.

different shapes whose area is the same as the square, but if we start with a triangle, only one square has an area which is the same, and the cuts are therefore exactly specified. This is seen in figure 2-20 where all the cuts and sides of the square have been labelled. Note that the inside of the square becomes the outside of the triangle, and vice-versa.

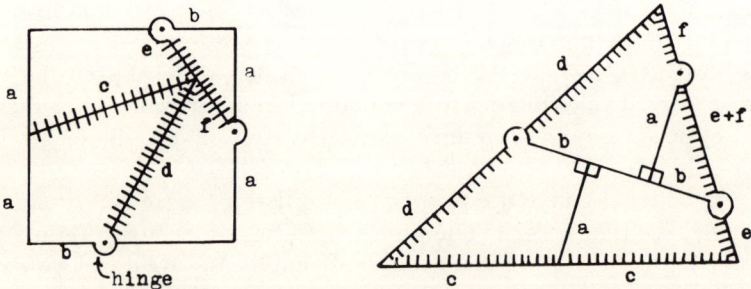

Figure 2-20. The parts of the hinged square are labeled to show where they are in the resulting triangle. Note that the internal cuts of one are the borders of the other.

Non-Bicycle Pedals

Related Math: envelopes, pedals, loci, curves, perpendiculars, tangents

Not all pedals are on bicycles. (In fact, the connection between these mathematical pedals and bicycle pedals eludes this writer.) At any rate some interesting work can be done with simple materials utilizing the principle of the "pedal."

1. In figure 2-21 we see how a corner can be slid between two pegs in a pegboard to reveal the curve of a circle. This circular curve is the pedal about the two points. While this creation of a circle with a series of right angles is an important theorem in geometry, we can go further and develop other shapes besides circles.

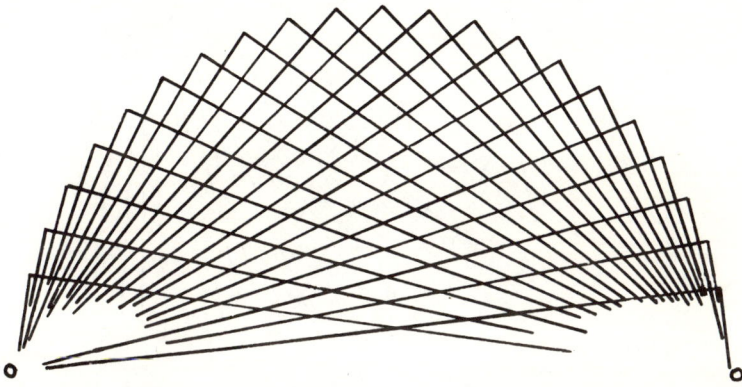

Figure 2-21. A triangle, when placed between two pegs and traced, then slid to other positions between the pegs and traced again and again, gives the circular curve shown above. A smaller angle of the triangle might be used to obtain a different curve. Note the distorted grid system created.

2. Suppose one of the pegs was replaced by a circle; what shape would we get by sliding a corner between this circle and the other peg? In figure 2-22 we see the result partly complete. The plastic triangle used in the construction is shown in position. Only lines from the circle to the corner of the triangle have been drawn. We started with a circle and obtained a looped curve. We also can start with the looped curve and obtain a circle as the figure indicates. To do so, hold one edge of the triangle on the point while the right angle of the triangle touches the looped curve. Note that this is the same position as was used to create the

looped curve. The looped curve is the pedal of the circle and the circle is the negative pedal of the looped curve. A few variations may be tried. Use a smaller angle than a right angle to create the pedal. Use a larger angle. Use an ellipse instead of a circle.

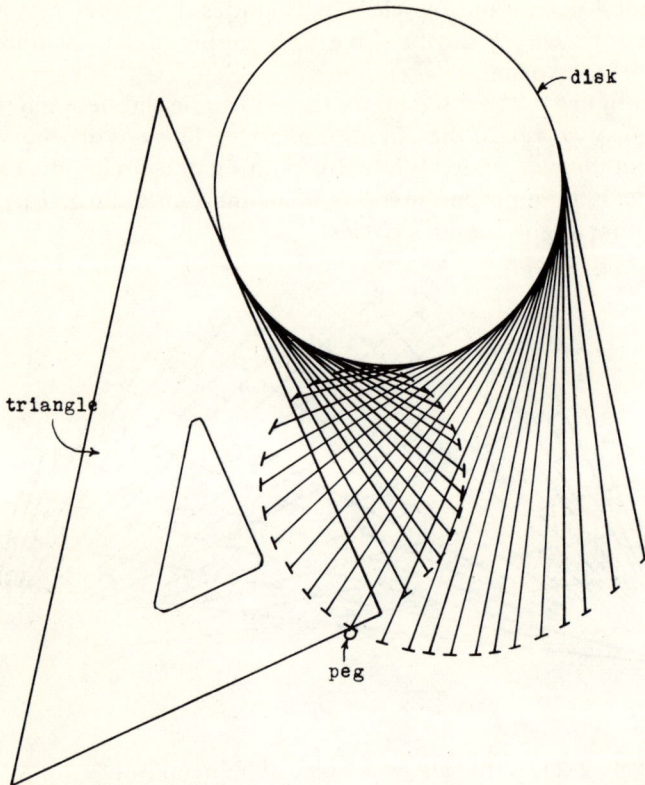

Figure 2-22. The beginning of a looped curve made by sliding a triangle between a peg and a disk. A point and a circle marked on paper will do as well if care is taken in placing the triangle.

Separating Colors

Related Math: measuring area, ratio, sampling

Some quantitative work can be done with food coloring by allowing it to soak into a porous surface such as a newspaper, paper towel, filter paper, plaster, chalk, or cornstarch. Many materials will work and you should try experimenting with them. The colors in green food coloring tend to separate out into yellow and blue. If for instance, a spot of food coloring is dropped onto a piece of filter paper which is placed over an open jar, and water or alcohol is dropped slowly on the spot, the food coloring will spread and separate into various colored rings. (See figure 2-23.) Since the color tends to bunch up at the outer edge, the material must be wide enough to contain all the spreading liquid.

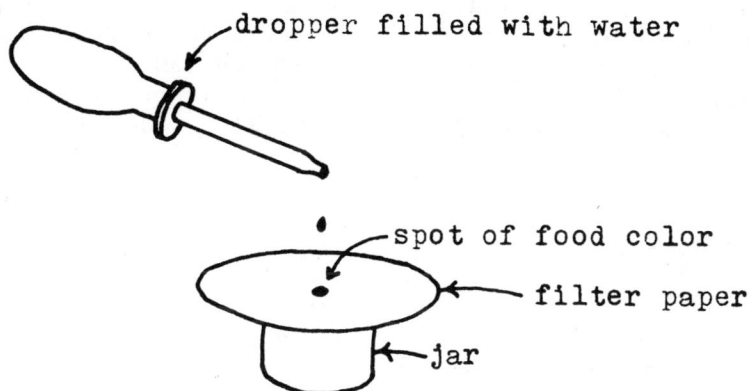

Figure 2-23. This arrangement separates the basic colors in green food coloring into yellow and blue. The resulting pattern on the filter paper can be quite vivid.

Uncooked cornstarch powder is a good medium for color separation. Add the cornstarch powder to enough water to make it milky and pour the mixture on to a sheet of glass, allowing it to cover the top. When it dries the food coloring can be added and the tests made. Color separation is quite good in this material. The yellow remains in the middle and the blue spreads out. If the same procedure is used with plaster of Paris, the blue stays in the middle and the yellow spreads out.

This work is basically the same as that of the professional who uses it to separate and identify the ingredients of a mixture. Special inexpensive paper is used which is obtainable from science supply houses. Measurement of the area of the paper covered by each color gives an idea of the relative amounts of the ingredients.

Sampling Air Pollution

Related Math: ratio, sampling, rate, areas, fractions

A window gets dirty because of particles which stick to it, and these may be removed by pressing the adhesive side of a strip of cellophane tape gently against the dirty window, removing the tape, and placing it under a microscope. At the same time another strip of the tape can be fastened to the window with gummed side out in order to trap particles. Every 24 hours another piece of tape is placed on the window beside the last piece. At the end of a week a record of the amount of material in the air hitting the window, and the rate at which it hits, will be available. A smoggy city will be most productive of particles. Pollen can be collected in this way, but an idea of its appearance should also be obtained by more direct methods such as moving the slide around inside some grass which has gone to seed. The size of the pollen can be estimated by comparing it to the width of a human hair under the microscope. (A microscope with standard optics has a field of view a little more than a millimeter across at 100 power.)

Puzzles and Problems

1. Increasing stereo vision—Hold a mirror close to your nose so that you can look into the mirror with one eye and see sideways. Then hold another mirror about 6 inches (15 centimeters) or more to the side of your face so that you can see this mirror in the other mirror close to your nose. Aim this second mirror so that you can see something ahead of you and look at the object with your free eye at the same time, as in figure 2-24.

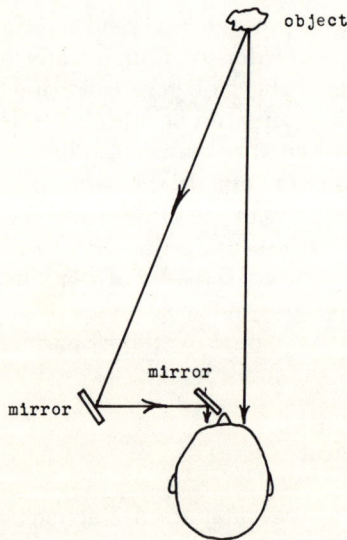

Figure 2-24. A simple method of giving more depth to real objects.

When both eyes focus on something about 10 feet (3 meters) away (a bush or tree works well) it will appear different. What is this difference and what causes it? You can use a periscope for this same problem or the pegboard rangefinder.

2. Cut out the pieces that make up the large square figure 2-25a. and rearrange the pieces to make the two smaller squares of figure 2-25b. What is the relationship between these three squares?

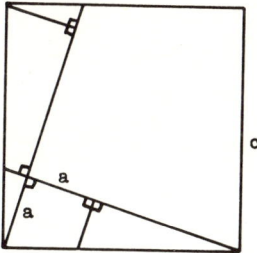

Figure 2-25a.   **Figure 2-25b.**

One square is refitted to make two squares. Does $a^2 + b^2 = c^2$?

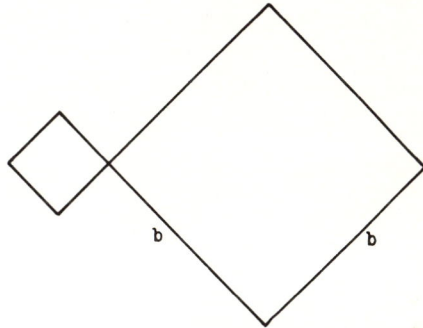

3. Place two pegs a few inches apart in pegboard. Place a plastic triangle between the pegs so that it just touches them as in figure 2-26. Draw a line along the edge of the triangle away from the pegs. Move the triangle a little and draw a line along the farther edge again. Do this until you obtain a design (or envelope). Reverse the triangle so that you can draw the curve on the other side as well. Try the same procedure with one of the smaller angles of the triangle between the pegs. Can you get a completely closed curve by using the triangle on both sides of the pegs? Variations can be obtained by changing the distance between the pegs and by placing a curved shape with a flat back between the pegs and sliding it. What curve would you obtain if you used a half-circle protractor between the pegs?

4. Use a peg and a strip of pegboard fastened to the base near the peg. With a triangle trace the edge shown in figure 2-27. Move the triangle and trace again until a pattern emerges. Use different distances between the peg and the strip. Since this curve is a parabola, a flexible mirror placed along it will focus sun-

light at a point and the concentration of the sun's rays can be observed on the paper. The reflective surface of the flexible mirror must be on the concave side of the curve and this side should face the sun.

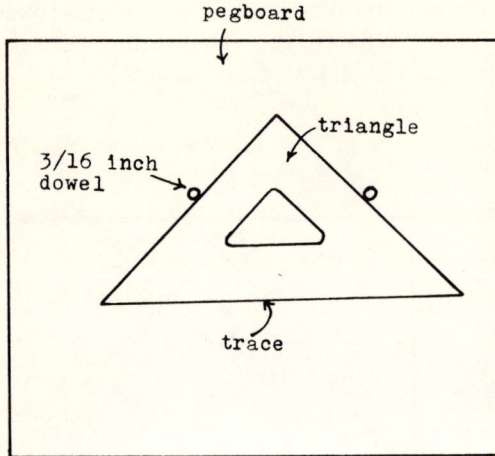

Figure 2-26. An envelope can be obtained by sliding the triangle to different positions, each time drawing a line along its longest side. The result is a curved line made from straight lines.

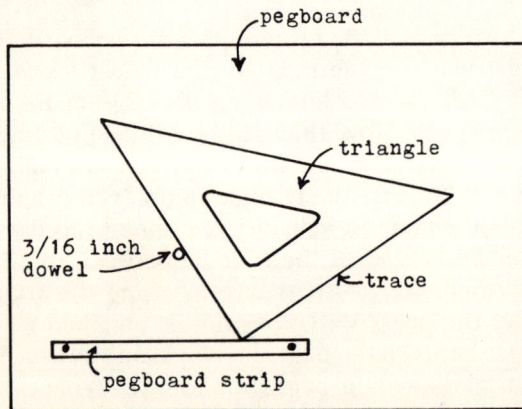

Figure 2-27. A parabola is obtained by a tracing of lines as shown. The long side of the triangle is worth tracing for its envelope also. Other tracings can be obtained by placing the smaller angle of the triangle in contact with the pegboard strip.

5. A quick ellipse—Draw a circle and mark a point not in the center of the circle. Draw several chords through the chosen point. Find the bisectors of each chord and connect them as in figure 2-28. You will obtain an ellipse. A quick way of finding the bisector is to use tracing paper on which to draw the circle. Lay a sheet of lined paper under it so that one end of one chord lies over one of the lines and the other end over a line two lines away from the first. Where the chord crosses the middle line is the midpoint of the chord (See figure 2-28).

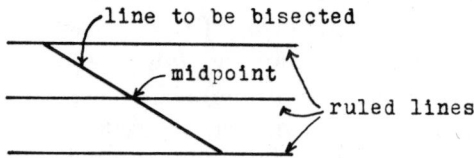

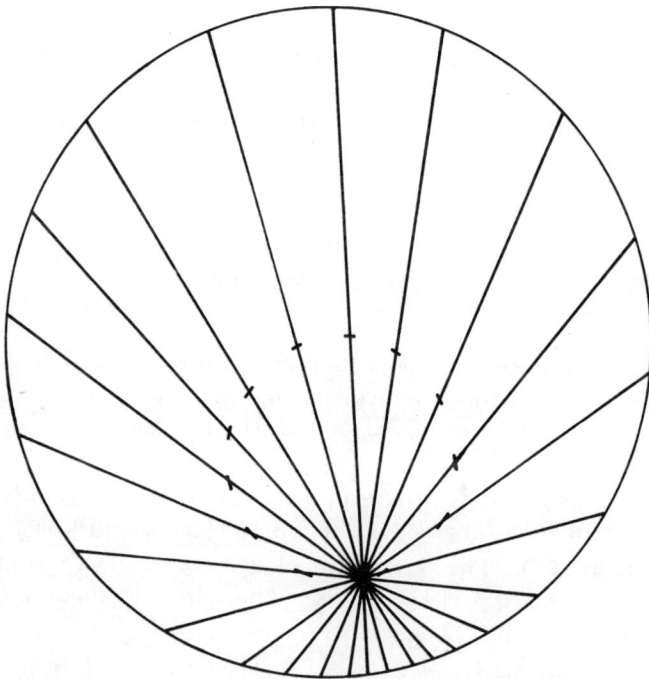

Figure 2-28. The dashes on the chords of the above circle are at the midpoints of the chords. With three ruled lines on onion skin paper the midpoints of the chords can be found quickly.

6. Do the same but use a point on the circle.

7. Do the same again but select a point outside the circle.

8. Draw a circle and with your pencil mark two points on its circumference. When you connect these two points the circle is divided into two parts. How many parts will a circle be divided into by three points connected each to the other? How many parts can a circle be divided by four such points? Five? Six? Ten? Would you get the same result by drawing points on a square and connecting them? Is there any other figure beside a circle that can be divided into as many parts by points and lines drawn on its perimeter? (Note: To get the most parts we cannot have more than two lines intersecting at the same place.)

9. Peel an onion until you obtain a very thin skin. From an ordinary slice a very thin layer can be separated with a knife or a needle. Look at this under the microscope using about 100 power. How can you obtain the actual dimensions of an average onion cell? (What happens to a plastic rule with a millimeter scale when placed under the microscope at 100 power?)

10. If you look through a tube with one eye while holding one hand with open palm against the tube in front of the other open eye, you will see a hole in your hand. To see a hole in your head replace your palm with a mirror. What license has been taken with the eyes?

BIBLIOGRAPHY

Inexpensive Science Teaching Equipment Project. *Guidebook*. Science Teaching Center, University of Maryland, College Park, MD, 1972. (Vol. I, pp. 255-256; Vol. II, chromatography apparatus, pp. 223-240.)

McBain, William and R.C. Johnson. *The Science of Ourselves, Adventures in Experimental Psychology*. New York: Harper and Row, 1962.

Pettigrew, John D. "The Neurophysiology of Binocular Vision" *Science American*, Aug. 1972, p. 84. (The why and how of binocular vision.)

Steinhaus, Hugo. *Mathematical Snapshots*. New York: Oxford Press, 1969.

3

Math Measurements of Speed and Strength

Mathematical concepts include: angles, vectors, direction, grids, graphing, angular measure, rational and irrational numbers, inverse, ratio, symmetry, equations, diagonals, triangles, hexagons, counting, sine waves, maxima and minima, formulae

The Wandering Pool Ball

Related Math: angles, vectors, grids, angular measure, symmetry, diagonals, proportions, fractions

An understanding of velocity, vectors, reflection, and numbers, both rational and irrational, can be obtained from studying the path of a moving pool ball. The pool ball represents any object which bounces off a surface. If the surface is flat, smooth, and hard and the object round and hard, the object will bounce from the surface at the same angle at which it approached the surface. Study of such bouncings strengthens the ideas inherent in the meaning of the terms direction, ratio, angle, parallel, and infinity while it also provides a diverting opportunity to do some experiments on graph paper. We don't need a pool table, but we should understand what rebound means and that the angle of approach to the cushion equals the angle of departure. We can use a diagram similar to figure 3-1 which shows the position of the pool ball at the start,

73

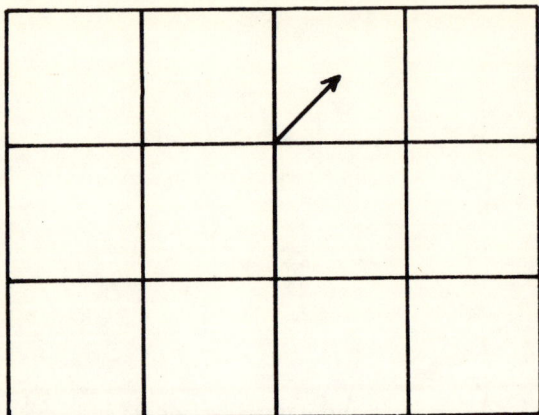

Figure 3-1. Imagine that the arrow is the direction of a pool ball and the boundary of the figure is a pool table. How will the ball rebound if there is no friction? The grid of crossed lines is added to help determine the path of the pool ball. Will the ball have a repeating path? Will it eventually go into a corner?

its direction, and a grid system laid on the table (without pockets) to demonstrate the path more clearly. We should begin with a ball aimed at an angle of 45 degrees to the side of the pool table. In the case of figure 3-1 the ball goes into the lower right corner after a few rebounds, and then retraces its path backward until it goes into the lower left corner. We assume that a ball which goes into a corner comes back on its own path. In the example the ball passes only through the vertices of the squares in the grid. Therefore, if the grid was shifted a half square sideways as in figure 3-2 and we start the ball as before, it would never go into a corner simply because the corners are no longer along the diagonals of the squares in the grid. However, the ball will have a repeating path.

We could get the same repeating path which never goes into a corner by moving the starting position of the ball in figure 3-1 half a square across, leaving the grid system as is. Now the ball in its wanderings never crosses an intersection and, since the corners are at intersections, the ball never goes into a corner.

There are many possibilities to the paths, depending on the dimensions of the table. The simplest paths are obtained with square tables. A table can be made quickly by outlining part of the grid of a sheet of large, square graph paper. While a ball can bounce at any angle from a pool table cushion, it is better to restrict our play to the 45 degree angle shots—at least in the beginning. Also, the table should be a whole

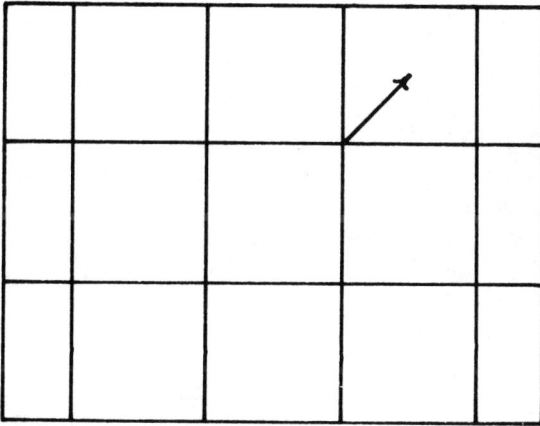

Figure 3-2. The pool table is the same as in figure 3-1, but the starting point of the pool ball has been shifted half a square to the right. Will the pool ball now eventually go into a corner?

number of units in length and width, making it easier to use the graph paper.

We define a path as the complete track of a ball on the table—until the ball repeats itself. Before venturing into the possibilities of a ball shot from anywhere on the table we start as in figure 3-1 with the ball and the corners of the table at intersections. With these restrictions we can develop many concepts about the resulting figures. For instance, a path begun at a corner continues longer without repeating than if the ball began from any other place. Thus a logical place to begin tracing a path is from a corner. Another characteristic of this motion is that the number of traverses from one side of the table to the opposite side compared to the traverses between the ends is inverse to the ratio of the length to the width of the rectangle. Thus if there is a ratio of three to five between the width and length there will be five traverses of the width to three of the length for one path before retracing occurs. Many of these concepts can be worked out by students as paths are traced on the blackboard and studied. Any conjecture can serve as the basis of a theorem. Proofs are not always easy, but a conjecture which cannot be disproven is well on its way. It is not rigorous mathematics but it exercises the imagination. Is one path in any way symmetrical to another? Under what conditions will the ball always rebound to the right? How many varieties of paths are possible on a rectangular table? On a square table? Can a path lead into only one corner? Into all four corners? Will every intersection of the squares which make up the grid trace a path? What does the total pattern of all possible paths look like?

Rational and Irrational Pool Tables

Related Math: rational numbers, irrational numbers, rectangles, grids, infinity, fractions

When a rebound takes place we can imagine a new table adjacent to the original table, but flipped over, on which the rebounding path is traced. If this process is continued at each rebound we obtain figure 3-3 with the path of the ball now a straight line. This is very helpful in analyzing this type of motion. Note the lettering which shows the position of each corner of the table.

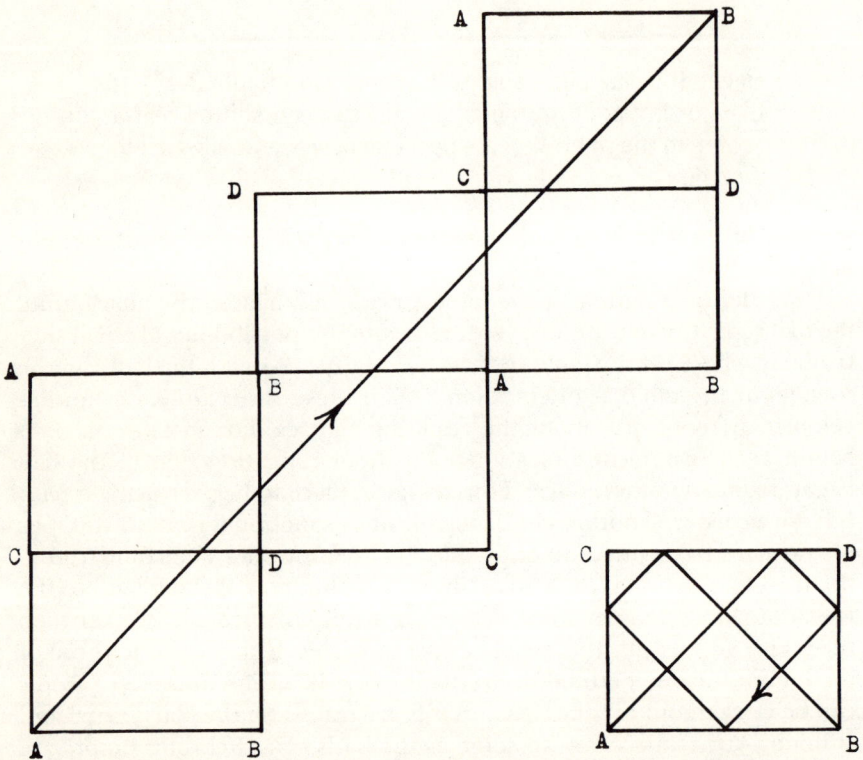

Figure 3-3a.   **Figure 3-3b.**

Figure 3-3. The path of a pool ball on a table becomes a straight line if the pool table is flopped over on one side whenever the ball hits that side. If each rectangle above was folded back onto the one at the lower left we could see the original path as shown in figure 3-3b.

If we consider a plane filled with fitted tables as in figure 3-3 then we can draw lines between any two intersections and consider that we have drawn a path on one table. If we flipped back all the tables onto the original we would see what that path looked like. We can show that no matter what the ratio of the two sides of the rectangle the ball will eventually enter a corner. To prove this we imagine a square made up of the rectangular pool tables whose sides and lengths are any given ratio, say x:y. In order to fit the rectangles into the square, the number of rectangles with side of dimension x must be y in number. Thus along one side of the large square there are y rectangles, each with side x. Along the other side with the y dimension we fit x number of rectangles. In this way each side is the same length and we have a square. The path of the pool ball will go from one corner of the square to the other (since it is shot at a 45 degree angle) and hence will finally wind up in a corner of the rectangular pool table. We have shown that the path of a pool ball starting from a corner will eventually go into a corner no matter what the dimensions of the table. We have assumed that x and y (the lengths of the two sides) *could* be expressed as a ratio and therefore we selected "rational numbers." If, however, no such ratio is possible, such as is the case with the diameter and circumference of a circle or in this case the given length and width of the rectangle, then we deal with irrational numbers. Considering an irrational pool table, will the path of a pool ball starting from one corner eventually wind up in another corner? In a very large square composed of many rectangles of the given irrational relationship, the path would tend toward the corner. However, if we want to know if it ever gets exactly into the corner we face a paradox. To construct the square we need a definite number of rectangles, but the ratio of the sides is an irrational number. How can we have this relationship? As any line can be broken into an irrational number of pieces we *can* construct the square and a diagonal which will be the path of the pool ball. Perhaps this is as far as we need go. The students who understand the dilemma might wish to carry it further and should be encouraged.

Instead of flipping over our rectangular pool tables we can construct a fine enough grid of squares within the pool table itself and achieve a similar result. If we can fit an exact number of squares into the rectangle, no matter how small they are, then the ball will inevitably go into a corner. The ball must start at a corner of the rectangle. Then the ball can only travel along the diagonals of the squares because it is shot at 45 degrees. It intersects corners of these small squares as it proceeds. If it repeats its path, ie., goes into a corner, before intersecting all the squares we have constructed in the rectangle, then we have shown that the ball does indeed go into a corner. If it does not repeat, even though it contacts all the squares we have drawn, then it will repeat after it crosses the last square since that square fits into a corner of the rectangle.

Triangular Pool Tables

Related Math: equilateral triangles, parallels, denseness, similar triangles, angles

Paths in triangular pool tables provide further study of this rather unusual geometry. In an equilateral triangle, if the path of the pool ball parallels one side the ball will rebound each time parallel to a side. It is thus rather easy to draw the path freehand as shown in figure 3-4.

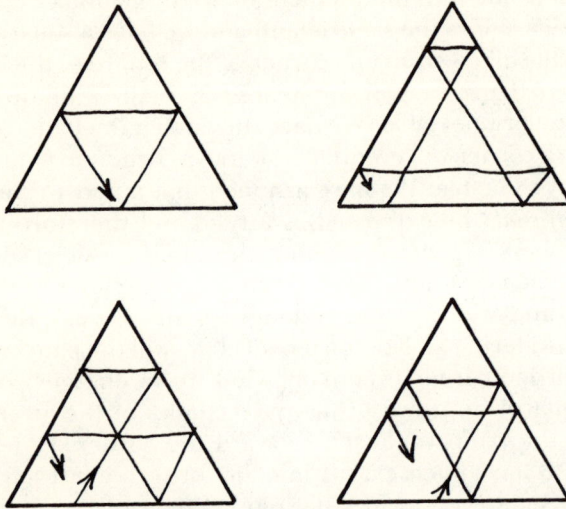

Figure 3-4. Sketches of paths on a triangular pool table when the ball is started moving parallel to one side. What path results when the ball is started perpendicular to one side?

Triangles when inverted also make the path straight as in rectangular pool tables. If the ball is started from a corner will it eventually go into another corner, no matter from what angle it is shot? We could reason that if the ball goes out from corner A as in figure 3-5 it will eventually pass through another corner, since these become more and more difficult to pass through as we add another line of triangles. But this is not true if the ball is started from A and aimed between D and E. No matter how far out D and E are from A, there is still space between them and no intersections will be passed through on the way out from A.

Although consisting of triangular shapes, figure 3-5 also serves to illustrate the path of a pool ball on a hexagonal or parallelogram-shaped table. We need only consider the hexagonal shapes or the parallelograms within the figure.

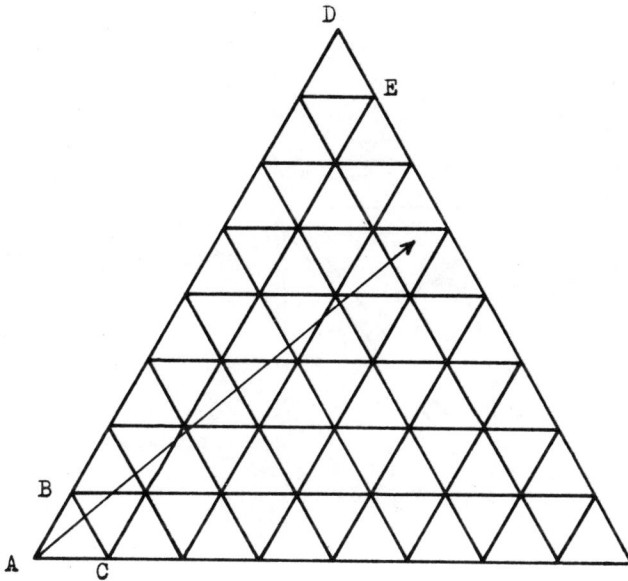

Figure 3-5. The original equilateral pool table is ABC. It has been flipped over many times to produce the whole figure. Are there angles at which the ball can be shot where the ball will not wind up in a corner of the table?

How Fast Is the Wind?

Related Math: ratio, ordinal numbers, increments, rate

There are many ways to show windspeed—spinning paper cups on a frame, or a simple weight on a string which tends to move toward the horizontal as the wind pushes it. These devices work, but some means of measuring the total number of revolutions of the spinning cups is helpful. A reasonable substitute for the factory-made device is shown in figure 3-6 in which the recording part of the instrument is an old auto speedometer salvageable from the junkyard. A portion of the cable must be saved in order that the speedometer can be activated. The device can be put together in the classroom and taken outside when readings are desired. There is a drag from the speedometer so that large cups are required to catch enough wind to turn the device. Only when the wind is rather high is there sufficient rapid turning to get a reading on the speedometer, although this can be improved by lubrication. The mileage indicator will record, no matter how slow the cups turn, and the total number of turns made by the device in about an hour can be determined, and, accordingly, the average wind speed determined. Of course,

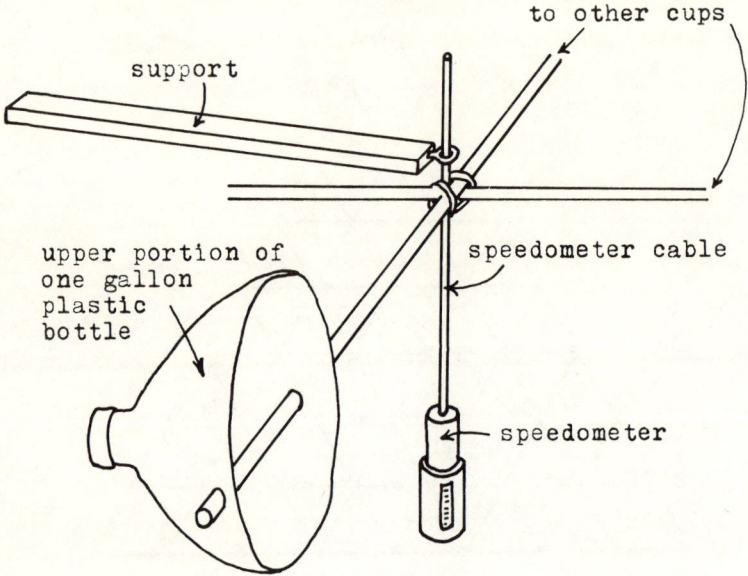

Figure 3-6. A windspeed indicator can drive an automobile speedometer. Large cups must be used for movement to take place. The above is a quickly constructed arrangement but more framework would be required to make it stand by itself. The speedometer cable is somewhat flexible and should be cut off about one foot from the speedometer end.

other means of measuring the speed of the wind must be used to calibrate the instrument. Absence of calibration should not stop its being used and estimates of windspeed can be made as students become familiar with the problem.

A Spring Pendulum As a Timer

Related Math: functions, correspondence, sine waves

A shade roller spring works well as a spring pendulum with a 2 to 5 pound (or 1 to 2 kilogram) weight hanging from it. The device will swing up and down for about 30 minutes after an initial pull. Since each swing takes the same length of time (has the same period), the device is useful as a timer. Over 1500 oscillations of the spring can be counted for one pull. If the weight could be moved horizontally while the spring moved it up and down it would describe a sine wave (see page 37). If an inking device is fastened to the weight and a large piece of paper drawn across it as the weight goes up and down, this sine wave motion can be recorded. But the weight moves slowly and the paper must be moved at least as slowly, making it a difficult task to perform by hand.

A Spring Pendulum to Make Lissajou Figures

Related Math: coordinates, curves, sine waves

Two pendulums when properly attached produce an intricate pattern which changes shape and direction. Such patterns, which can be made in many ways, are called lissajou figures. One of the simplest arrangements to produce lissajou figures is shown in figure 3-7. Two shade roller springs with weights of about 4 pounds (2 kilograms) hung from them provide the energy. The weights are pulled down a few inches and released. The weights then oscillate and the pegboard arms joined to them swing in a changing pattern which the felt pen records at their junction. The pegboard arms are held to the spring by pegs placed between the coils. Two identical arms behind the ones shown, fastened to the same pegs as they pass out the other side of the springs, make the device sturdier. The 3/16 inch (5 millimeter) holes in the pegboard will

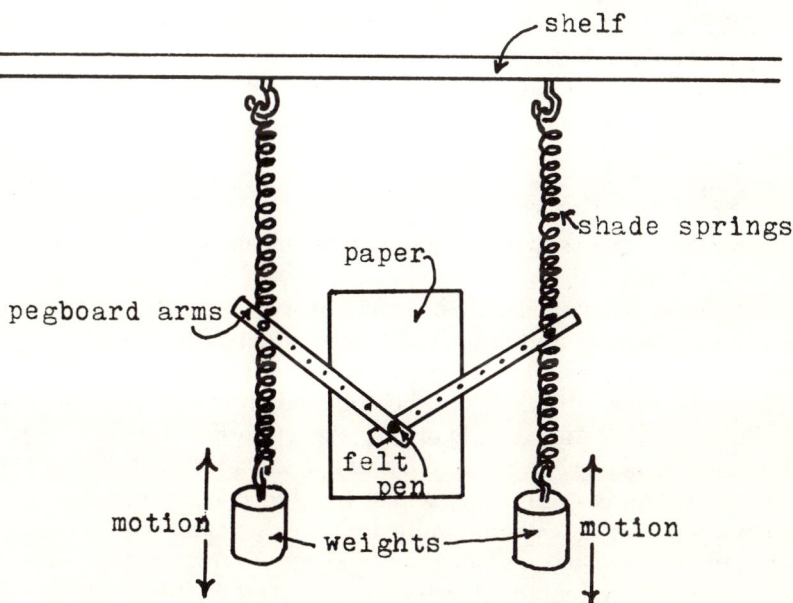

Figure 3-7a. Curved patterns called lissajou figures can be created with this device. The paper is held so that it rests gently against the felt pen.

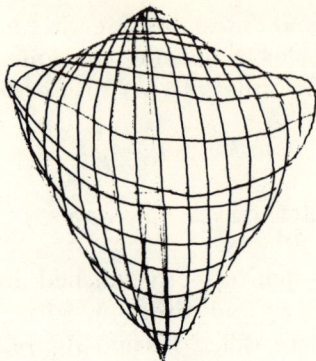

Figure 3-7b. An example of a pattern produced by the pegboard and spring device. (Irregularities are due to moving
the paper on and off the device) Different patterns can be
made by altering the weights or the length of the pegboard
strips.

have to be enlarged to accommodate the pen. Variations in the pattern
will result if the weights are varied, or if the position of the pen, length of
the spring, length of the arms, or position of the arms on the springs is
changed. A delicate touch on the recording paper is required to get a
pattern. Too much pressure slows the device radically and distorts the
curve. Heavy rubber bands can be used in place of the springs, but they
are not long-lived.

Tides and the Moon

Related Math: graphs, maxima and minima, mean, average, zero point

A somewhat similar play of forces as we observed with the weight
and spring, but on a grander scale, is the tide. Tide tables can be obtained from coastal sporting goods stores where they are handy for
fishermen. Such tables can also be obtained from the U. S. Coast and
Geodetic Survey. An example of one is given in Bowditch's, "American
Practical Navigator." For our purpose we can plot the tides on graph
paper if we have a tide table. A plot for the central California coast is
given in figure 3-8. Note that there are four fluctuations of the tide each
day and we have chosen to separate these into four curves, each showing
a maximum or minimum of water level. In plotting, the points given on
the tide chart for maximum and minimum can be transferred to the
graph paper as dots and later connected to produce the smooth curves.

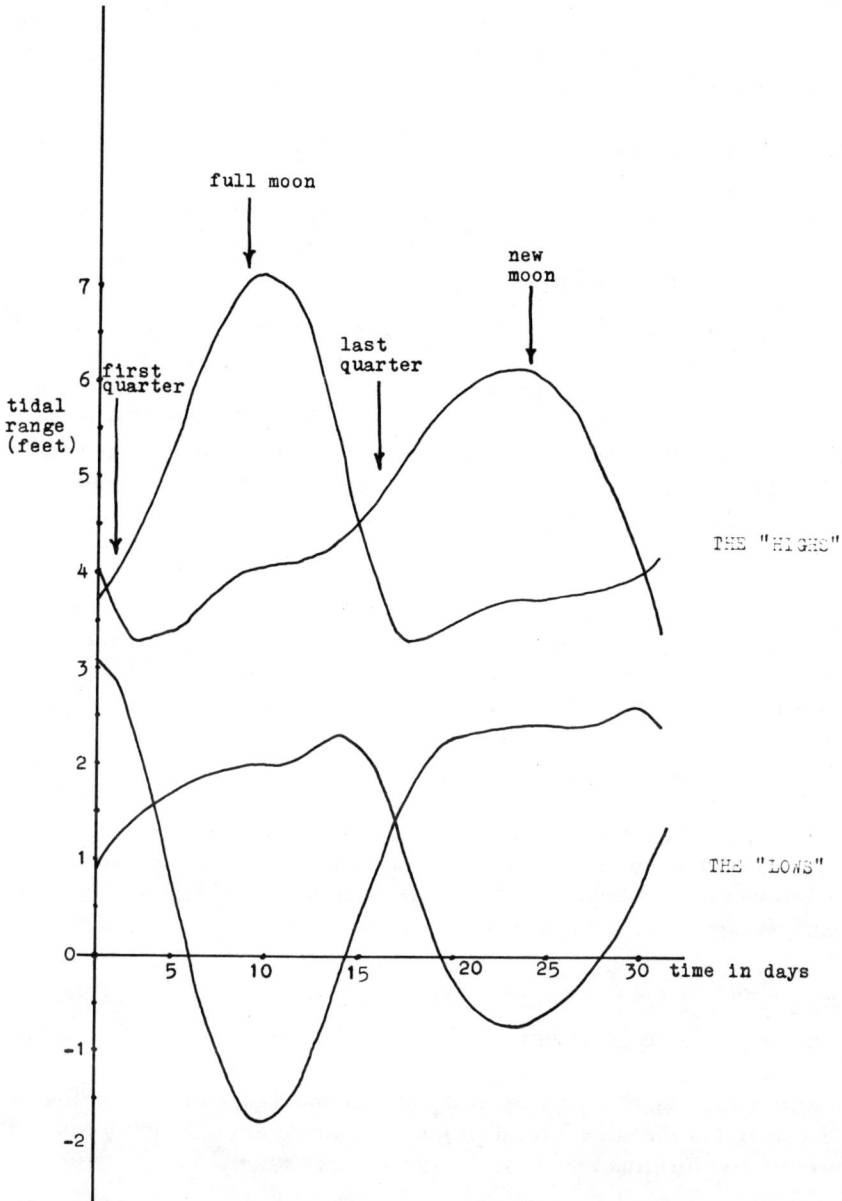

Figure 3-8. A tide range graph will show the relation between the moon and the tides. Two low tides and two high tides occur every day in the location above. The graph can easily be constructed from a tide chart.

Not all coastlines have two high and two low tides each day. If the phases of the moon are shown on the curve you will see that the tidal extremes occur during full and new moon.

Human Measurements

Related Math: acceleration, angles, rate, average, formulae

Stopping the Pendulum

A heavy washer suspended by thread can be swung from a hook over the blackboard. At the end of the pendulum is a large washer or ring. At a predetermined place along the path of the washer the subject whose reaction time is being observed stands ready with a pencil. In order to stop the washer he must run the pencil through it. A mark is placed on the blackboard opposite to where the pencil must be held. In this way the pencil must be pushed at just the right moment. While it is relatively easy to stop the washer when the pencil is held near the end of the washer's swing, it is not at all easy to do so at the middle of its swing where it is travelling fastest. Of course the thread must be very close to the blackboard so that the washer cannot twist. If the subject is allowed as much time as he wishes before making his stab he can make his job easy by waiting until the washer diminishes its swing enough that his position is at the end of the swing. But if he must make his attempt at the first pass of the washer his job is more difficult. It is an amusing game and with a washer 1¼ inches (3.2 centimeters) in diameter, with a hole 3/4 inch (about 2 centimeters) there is still difficulty in getting a pencil to enter. After a number of attempts have been made, students can be asked where they believe is the greatest acceleration. (It is at the end of each swing, *not* at the low point where the washer is moving fastest).

Reaction Time

A similar experiment involves the dropping of a vertically held ruler or meterstick by the experimenter. The subject presses his thumb against the stick to hold it against the wall and stop its fall. Reading the distance that the stick has fallen gives an indication of reaction time. If we use the formula

$$s = \tfrac{1}{2}at^2$$

where "s" is the distance, "a" the acceleration of gravity, and "t" the time, we can get the reaction time in seconds. If distance is measured in feet, "a" is 32. If distance is measured in centimeters, "a" is 980. Once this reaction time is observed for one individual we might ask: Is it the same or close to the reaction time of others? Does it vary from day to day? Is one person's reaction time the same for other circumstances, such as putting his foot on the brake of a car? Does the reaction time vary if we are responding to something we hear or feel, rather than see? There is one thing we might predict about reaction time. If we are prepared to respond, our reaction time should go down.

The Acceleration of Gravity

Related Math: acceleration, coordinates, space, points

An object thrown or fired horizontally will hit the ground at the same time as an object dropped at the same time at the firing place. We can show this with two checkers and a strip of pegboard about 10 or 12 inches (25 or 30 centimeters) long. Hold the pegboard on a desktop near the corner and place the checkers as in figure 3-9. Give the pegboard

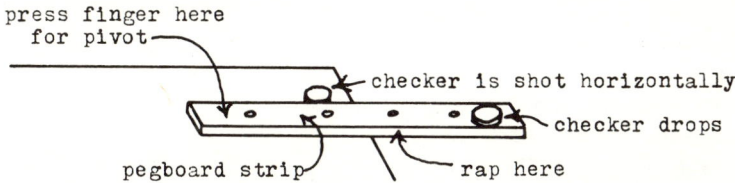

Figure 3-9. This simple device shoots one checker horizontally at the same time as the other is dropped. It can lead into a fruitful discussion of motion and relativity.

strip a hard rap and the checker sitting on it will fall to the floor while the checker in front of it will shoot out horizontally. You should hear one click as the checkers hit the floor. Many students think that the horizontally fired object will hit later. Since the floor is probably not the earth's surface we must assume that no matter how far each object falls each will always be the same distance above the ground. If the objects were viewed from the side behind the horizontally shot checker they would both seem to fall side by side. This characteristic of motion, that much depends on how one views the moving object, is present in the pool table situation, also. If we looked at the pool table from the side rather than down from the top we would see the ball moving at a steady velocity back and forth (for a ball shot at a 45 degree angle to the side). This would also be true if we viewed the table along another side. However, viewed from a corner with eye at the level of the table top we might see another sequence of motions. The ball would seem to pause for a moment, then move, then pause again, the pauses being those times the ball was actually moving directly at us or away from us. Likewise, if we looked down on the two checkers as they departed from the stick one would seem to remain still as the other moved away. Neither would seem to fall (unless we inferred this from their seeming to diminish). This device illustrates two motions present in an object and how each motion influences the object as much as if it acted alone. If any object approaches us without changing size then we cannot detect its motion. This point is a fruitful one in stimulating discussion on relativity. In a universe consisting of only two bodies which move toward one another there is no way to determine if one or the other or both moves. Further restricting the universe to only one body precludes any motion at all. The bodies being considered here must be very small and unsplittable. Motion as we know it on the earth involves three objects, two for the motion itself (one of which is most often the earth) and one for the observer. The falling checkers move with respect to the earth and we observe this relationship. Without the earth we could observe only that the two checkers moved apart at a constant speed.

Do It Yourself Thermometers

Related Math: zero point, volume, area, ratio

Unless we are used to working with other temperatures far removed from the range to which we are accustomed, we are apt to consider anything warmer than we are as hot, even though this is a subjective evaluation. We pay serious penalties when we estimate heat wrongly—we call things hot or cold which in a larger spectrum might both be called cool. Our means of measuring heat reflects this subjectivity when we call the temperature at which water freezes zero (Centigrade). What really is a degree Centigrade, or Fahrenheit? Familiarity with the temperature scale can be increased by obtaining plenty of inexpensive room thermometers. The glass tube can be removed from the scale so that the device can more easily be put into liquids and so the students can experiment with making temperature scales. Thermometers of various sorts may be manufactured in the classroom. Figure 3-10 illustrates an air thermometer. The U-tube ordinarily measures pressure in liquids by filling the bottom of the U with water. The drop is more sensitive, and, in fact, limits the range of the device since it moves more easily to the top of the tube.

How Hot Can You Get It?

Related Math: parabola, angles, focal point

If the classroom is lit by direct sunlight during any part of the day an interesting device can be rigged to show how much the sun's intensity

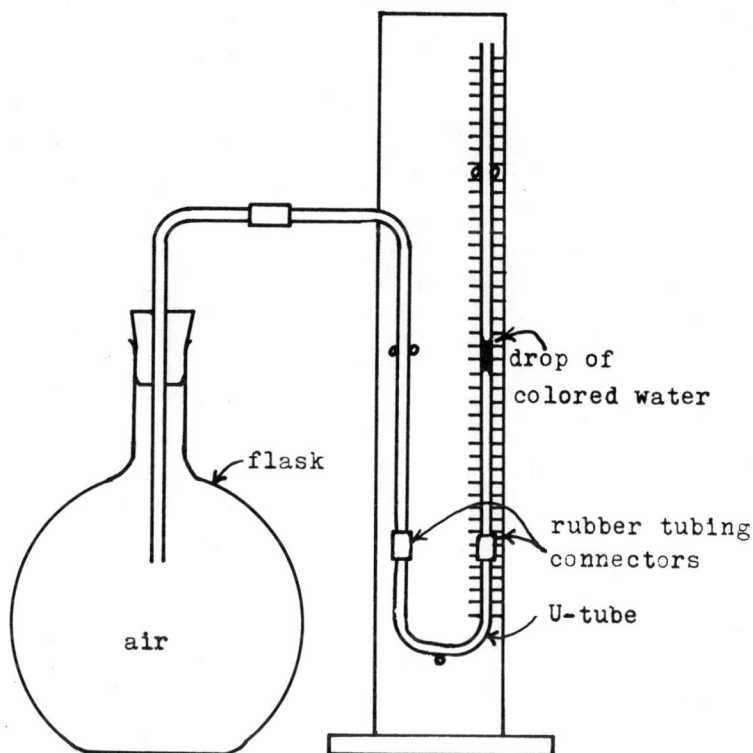

Figure 3-10. This temperature indicator is visible from a distance. A straight tube up from the mouth of the flask will also work. Atmospheric pressure changes daily and affects the reading. Plastic tubing is safer than glass. If the U-tube is filled with colored water the range will be increased.

can be increased. Several hand mirrors are needed and they are placed at one end of a board with a thermometer (such as is shown in figure 3-11) at the other end. The mirrors are placed so that the sun reflects from them and onto the flask. This experiment can be done outside with a class of students, each with a mirror. They can stand a good distance from the flask, thus providing a more pronounced demonstration of the sun's radiation. If there is snow on the ground the mirrors can be aimed at a small pile of snow which will melt if placed at the focus of the mirrors. If aluminum foil is placed in back of the thermometer or snow pile the heat will be concentrated further, but dark glasses may have to be worn by the students. Naturally, no one should be near the ther-

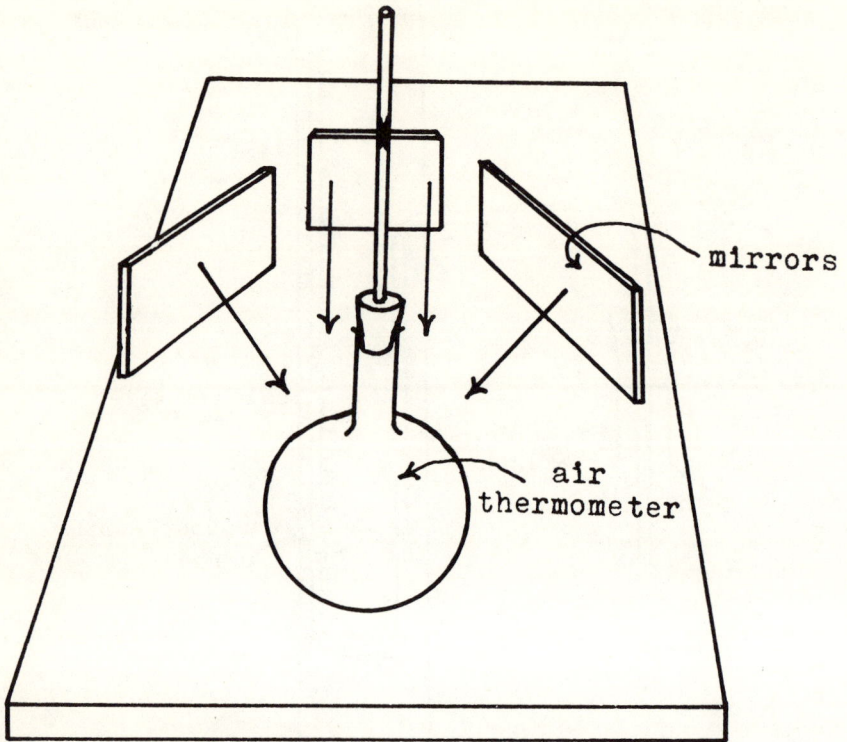

Figure 3-11. Sunlight, reflected off the mirrors, is concentrated on the flask; the air inside is heated which causes the colored water in the tube to rise.

mometer or other indicator of heat when the mirrors are at work. A wall behind the thermometer is helpful both in aiming the mirrors and in keeping stray beams from bothering bystanders.

Burning Glasses

Related Math: tables, focus, angles, perpendicular

Ordinary magnifiers of 3 or 4 inch (8 or 10 centimeter) diameter are sufficient to make various objects melt or smolder when placed at the magnifier's focus. Very dark sunglasses, smoked glass, or dark photographic film is necessary to look through while aiming the magnifier at the chosen target since the sun's light becomes so concentrated that even its reflection from the target is intolerable. An even more concentrated spot of light and heat can be obtained from a large plastic fresnel lens

obtainable at a science supply house. The appendix has a table of melting points from which an idea of the temperature range at the focus can
be obtained. It is a project to be undertaken in the schoolyard on a sunny
day.

Breaking Things for Fun and Earnest

Related Math: tables and graphs, area, increments, averages

Several items can be tested in the classroom for their ability to resist
being pulled apart (tensile strength). Rather thin samples must be used
both for convenience and safety. While the process of such testing is
simple in concept, children seem to enjoy it. The aim is to break
something—and this is near and dear to the hearts of many repressed
spirits.

Nylon fishline is a good material with which to start since its strength
is marked on the spool. Very thin nylon line of 2 pounds (or 1 kilogram)
strength should be used because even a 2 pound weight hitting the floor
can release quite a bit of energy and make a loud noise. Is it true that the
2 pound line will hold more than its rating? Will the line stretch as weight
is added? Is there any noticeable change in the length of the line just
before it breaks? To measure these factors easily some little construction
is needed. This can be done in the "Measurements Area."

Rubber bands, cellophane tape, masking tape, sewing thread,
spiderweb strands, hair, strips of paper, and very thin copper or steel
wire can be tested. The great tensile strength of steel can be determined
if there is available a wire thin enough to break with small weights. A
heavier steel wire can be filed down in one place so that it will be sufficiently weakened to break easily, but in order to compare it with other
materials, the diameter of the thin area must be known to compare it for
instance with copper wire. A strand of fresh steel wool works well. The
difference in strength between coarse and fine steel wool can be measured and the diameters estimated with a microscope.

It is important to have a large number of fairly uniform, small
weights. These need not be labelled as to actual weight in ounces or
grams, but it is nice to have them uniform because ratios between the
strengths of different materials will become apparent. Nuts and bolts,
nails, or other hardware are good counters of weight. Clothespins or
paper clamps have the advantage of being able to grip very thin materials well enough to be suspended by them, making it easier to test the
strength of such things as spiderweb strands or human hair.

A bucket made from an old coffee can or large fruit can is necessary
to hold the weights. Two holes are punched into the can near its top
through which a heavy wire is pushed as in figure 3-12. One end of the

material to be tested is then passed through the hole in the pegboard strip and a dowel passed through the hole to hold the material in place. A knot or loop in the material will help keep it from slipping through the peg.

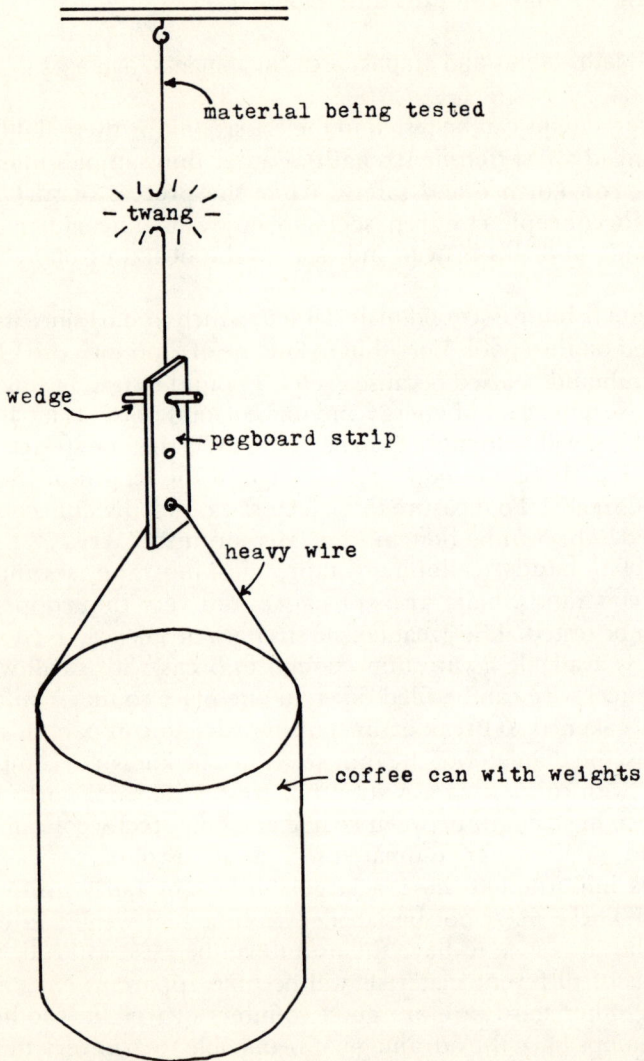

material being tested

twang

wedge

pegboard strip

heavy wire

coffee can with weights

Figure 3-12. Wire, thread, fish line, hair or rubber bands can be tested for tensile strength with this apparatus. Two or three thicknesses of pegboard strips are advisable to hold strong wire.

A Homemade Spring Scale

Related Math: ratio, formulae, zero point

Weighing devices should be abundant in the classroom. An easily made scale is illustrated in figure 3-13. A shelf or cross-rig must be available and a hole notched through it for the pegboard. Pegs in holes at the top and bottom of the pegboard strip keep it positioned and resist overstretching the rubber band. The pegboard must move freely in the slot. The lower 3/16 inch (5 millimeter) dowel peg can also serve to hang material to be stretched and broken. One end of the material can be wedged between peg and hole. Very weak material may break before the rubber band stretches. Clothespins hung from the material can give a measure of its strength in clothespin weights.

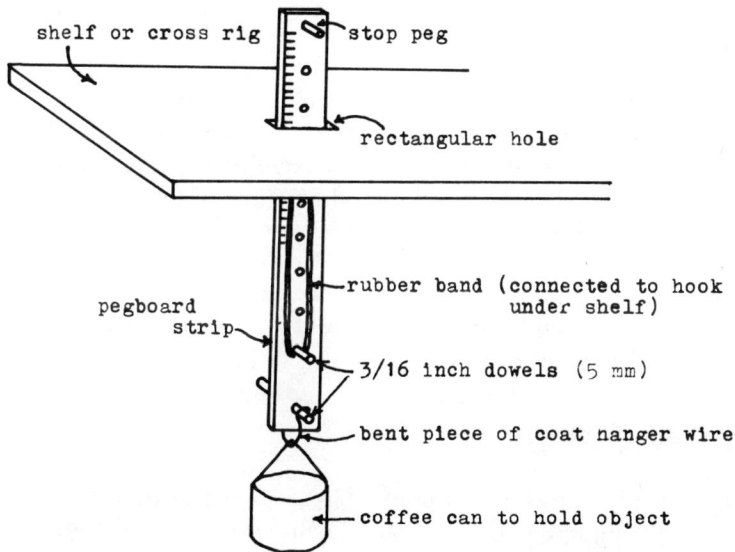

shelf or cross rig   stop peg

rectangular hole

pegboard strip

rubber band (connected to hook under shelf)

3/16 inch dowels (5 mm)

bent piece of coat hanger wire

coffee can to hold object

Figure 3-13. A versatile spring scale can be made from a rubber band and pegboard strip hung from a shelf. The capacity of the scale can quickly be changed by adding additional rubber bands.

The Strength of Paper

Related Math: averaging, acceleration, ratio, distance measurement

The strength of various kinds of paper can be found by stretching the paper over a frame and dropping a marble on the paper from various heights until the paper breaks. If the paper is laid under a Mason jar lid and the lid screwed onto the jar, a satisfactory result can be obtained, although it is important that the marble fall on the paper as it may break the glass. A golf ball works well. Grocery bags can be tested in this way, as well as writing paper and newsprint. The jar can be placed on the floor and a yardstick (or meterstick) used to calculate the height of the golf ball. A wad of cotton at the bottom of the jar will cushion the golf ball. The ball must be dropped accurately since it is not much smaller than the mouth of the mason jar. This lends a sort of game aspect to the experiment. A meterstick or two metersticks placed vertically near the golf ball before it is dropped will give a measure of the height. The ideas of force, work, and momentum underlie these experiments. The falling golf ball acquires more energy as it descends, which is turned into work when it hits the paper covering the mouth of the mason jar. If we could lay a heavy enough weight on the paper it would break through just as a small weight dropped from the proper height would break it.

The following questions suggest variations in the experiment: Does the paper break when the golf ball is dropped from the same height each time the experiment is tried? How does wetting the paper affect the height necessary to break it? Does this weakening of the paper by wetting vary from one kind of paper to another? (Paper towels in particular should be tried both wet and dry.) Does doubling the paper require the height that will break it to be doubled? Does a smaller ball with the same weight require a different height to break it? If a ball the same size but twice as heavy can be found, is the height required to break the paper now only half what it was?

Puzzles and Problems

1. Imagine a hexagonal pool table as shown in figure 3-14. Draw the complete path of the pool balls shown. Arrows indicate the direction of the pool ball at the start.

2. Imagine a pool table shaped like a parallelogram, as shown in figure 3-15. Draw the complete path of the pool balls shown in the figure.

3. How much of the path of the pool ball shown in figure 3-16a can you draw? Its path begins not quite parallel to one side. The path of a similar pool ball but parallel to one side is shown in figure 3-16b.

4. If a pool ball is aimed in a direction other than 45 degrees we can trace its path by using a grid system of rectangles rather than squares as in figure 3-17. The ball will move along diagonals of

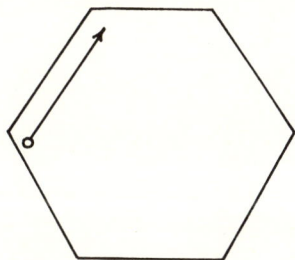

Figure 3-14a

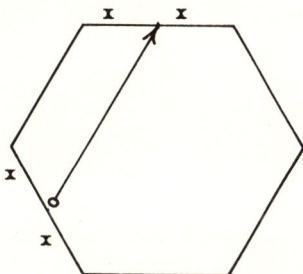

Figure 3-14b

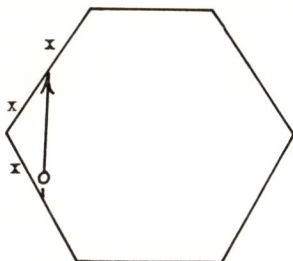

Figure 3-14c.

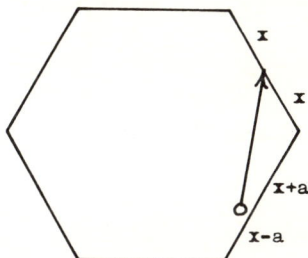

Figure 3-14d.

Pool ball paths on hexagonal pool tables.

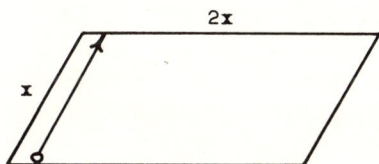

Figure 3-15a.

Figure 3-15b.

Figure 3-15c.

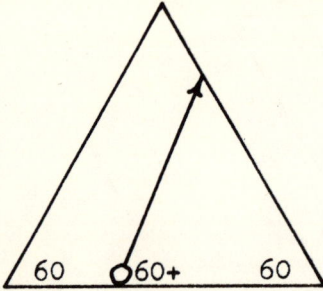

Figure 3-16a.

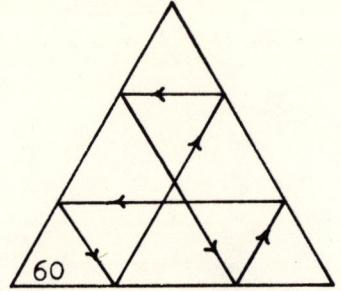

Figure 3-16b.

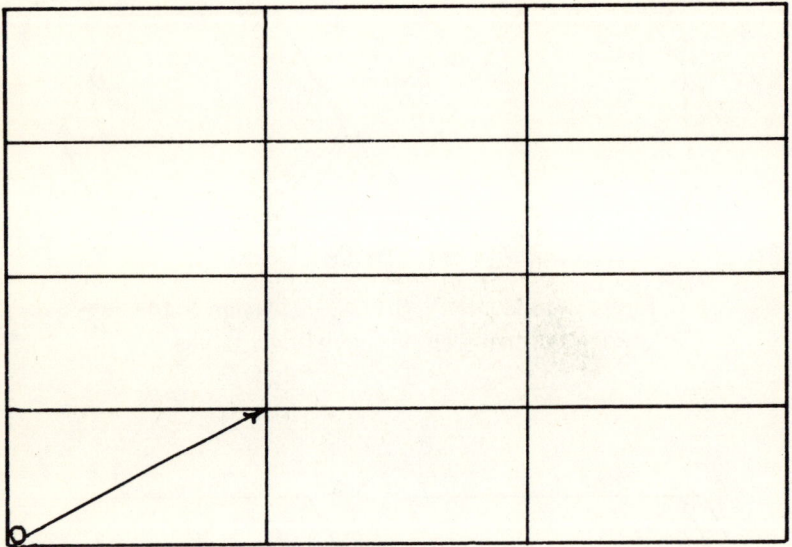

Figure 3-17

the grid system. Will the ball shown eventually go into a corner in figure 3-17?

5. Concerning bounding pool balls, we found that if they were shot at a 45 degree angle to the side, they:
   a. might form a repeating pattern without going into a corner.
   b. might go into a corner and then come back on themselves to form a repeating pattern.
   c. might not form a repeating pattern until they eventually wound up in a corner.

Do these possiblities complete what might happen to a pool ball bounding on a table?

BIBLIOGRAPHY

Gardner, Martin. "Bouncing Balls in Polygons and Polyhedrons," *Sixth Book of Mathematical Games from Scientific American*. San Francisco: W. H. Freeman and Co., 1971, pp. 29-38.

————. "Mathematical Games," *Scientific American*, Nov. 1973. (Programmed "worms" that draw geometric figures, p. 116.)

Grant, Nicholas. "Mathematics on a Pool Table," *Mathematics Teacher*, Mar. 1971, p. 255.

Inexpensive Science Teaching Equipment Project. *Guidebook*, Vol. III, Science Teaching Center, University of Maryland, College Park, MD, 1972. (On balances, pp. 1-40.)

4

Understanding
the Laws of Probability

Mathematical concepts include: randomness, permutations, series, progressions,
sequences, ordered pairs, zero points,
binomial expansion, fractions, symmetry,
exponents, arithmetic processes, percentage

A Mathematical Tree

We can play an interesting solitaire game which simulates the
growth of a tree. We start with a line on our paper which we call a twig,
and this twig can die, grow, or double itself according to chance. If these
three possibilities each have an equal chance of taking place, what does
the line become? We must find some random way of obtaining a sequence of these possibilities. Two coins which when thrown land both
tails might be (1) The twig dies. When both land heads then (2) The twig
divides into two and each grows a unit distance. When one falls heads
and the other tails then (3) The twig grows a unit distance. Any paper
can be used to "grow the trees," but graph paper grows them more
evenly. Figure 4-1 shows the growth of a few such trees before they died.
The x's are twig deaths. Apparently this kind of tree always dies sooner
or later and we do not have to look long for the answer. We start with
one twig and with equal chances of destroying it or doubling it. After any
number of tries we must still be close to just one twig growing since we

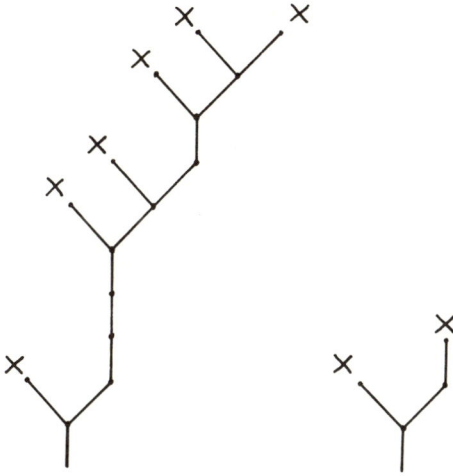

Figure 4-1. These are two examples of a kind of mathematical tree which can show some growth but dies because it lives so close to destruction. It is called a "critical tree." (See reference at end of chapter).

have as much chance of going in the (1) direction as in the (2). But if we constantly have only one twig and are continually shooting at it with one chance in four of hitting it, we will eventually hit it and end the game. In order to continue the game indefinitely we must devise some way of drifting away from this one twig position. This can be done by switching positions (2) and (3). This increases the possibility of the twig doubling so that in time the tree is apt to develop innumerable branches. At the start there is still a one out of four chance of its dying immediately. But in one hundred tries the usual twig should have fifty branches since the chance of killing twigs is half that of doubling them. The (2) position, in which growth takes place without branching, may seem like a mere delaying phase since it postpones the issue of life or death for the tree. We might consider it as adding to the "maturity" of the individual and this, of course, has its analogy in human affairs. Is our purpose in life to proliferate or to perfect the individual? A more impressive symbol than a short line for growth should be sought. Perhaps a squiggly line will do, in deference to the individual.

The Growth Game

Other games of a more complex character based on growth can be invented. We might start with the four categories, "growth," "marriage," "birth," "death," and with a given number of individuals, say 12, all immature. The order should be (1) growth, (2) marriage, (3) birth, and (4) death occuring at any time. A toss of two coins, one bright, one dull, can have four possibilities, one for each case: Two heads mean (1) for growth; a dull head and bright tail is (2) marriage; a bright head and dull tail is (3) birth; and two tails means (4) death. At the start, growth is allowed to·take place along the left of the 12 lines, and deaths (x's through the lines) takes place along the right. When growth turns up we put a circle at the top of one of the lines. When marriage turns up we join two circled lines (but only if we have at least two) with a line. A birth is recorded as a line in a row below the first and is recorded only if at least one marriage has taken place. When the first marriage occurs in any generation, all further births after it are recorded in the row below to indicate the start of a new generation. Figure 4-2 shows an example of

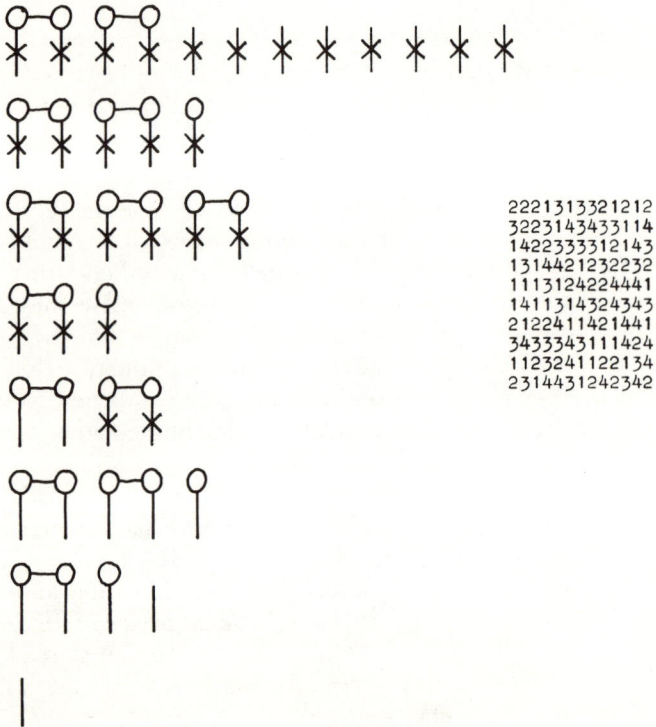

```
2221313321212
3223143433114
1422333312143
1314421232232
1113124224441
1411314324343
2122411421441
3433343111424
1123241122134
2314431242342
```

Figure 4-2. Eight generations are shown in the "Growth Game." The numbers obtained by tossing two coins are shown at the right, with (1) growth (a circle over a line), (2) marriage (a line joining 2 circles), (3) birth (a line in the next row below), and (4) death (an x through a line). The game was begun with 12 individuals in the top line.

the game record. With single births the game resembles human conditions, but it would be as easy to consider a birth as adding two or five or any number of individuals. According to the rules adopted, we can expect the game to be static since there is as much chance for a birth as for a death. In order for a birth to occur, the sequence (1), (2), (3) must take place in that order. Since this sequence has less chance than that a (4) will take place first, we can expect deaths to atrophy the original 12 individuals before the static condition occurs. The game will continue until there is a chance sequence of deaths which eliminate the original static number. While this game shows populations growing and dying, it does not explain how, obviously. The elimination of a natural enemy spurs population growth, and an epidemic curtails it. A small circle can be marked on the floor and if one or both coins fall in it, whatever number the coins turn up can be counted as effecting several individuals. The rules of the game are flexible and should be varied.

Random Motion

Another interesting way of picturing chance is to allow movement from a starting point in four directions according to the throw of two coins. With two coins and large, squared graph paper we can get a picture similar to "Brownian motion"—the bouncing about of tiny smoke particles as they are hit by molecules, observable under the microscope. A point is marked near the center of the graph paper indicating the start. If two heads appear when the coins fall then a short line upward from the start is drawn. If two tails appear the line is drawn down. If a head and tail appear, the line is drawn either left or right according to which head it is. A question to be considered is, "Do we wander far from zero point after a large number of tries?" The game might be continued until we either run off the paper or return to the zero point a given number of times. There will be some repetition of lines and this back and forth motion will not be easy to detect since one line will be right over another.

Still another method of showing random motion is to have the four directions at an angle from the original direction as shown in figure 4-3a. The four possible choices with two coins are each given one of the numbers as in the figure. Then when a new line is added it is from that new line that we determine the four directions. In this way, when the same number comes up twice in a row there is no repetition. Eight identical tosses are required for repetition to occur of this sort. An eight pointed star will form in the process. If a special sequence occurs to produce a rhombus, then repetition can occur after only four tosses. The path should look random, but we would have to use many more than four directions to get this randomness. (See figure 4-3b. and compare it

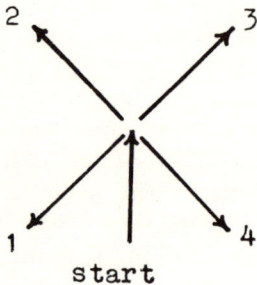

Figure 4-3a. Four possible directions are obtained from the toss of two coins.

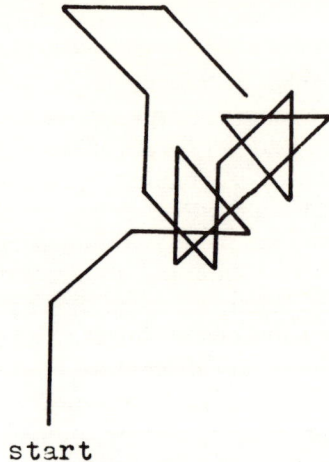

Figure 4-3b. This is an actual record of the path obtained. Graph paper is used for an easier plot.

to figure 4-4.) Also in Brownian motion, the path lengths are not all the same.

More Truly Random Motion

A strip of manila folder about 2 inches long and ½ inch wide (5 centimeter x 1 centimeter) and pointed at one end can be fastened to a starting point at the middle of any sheet of paper. It is then spun with the finger, and where the pointer tip comes to rest a pencil mark is placed. Then a line can be drawn from starting point to that point, and the little pointer centered over the next point for another spin. A next point is obtained, the line drawn, and a further spin made from the new end point. A record obtained from 34 spins is shown in figure 4-4. The line eventually goes off the paper. Will the line always go off no matter how big the paper and how small the spinner?

The Probability Board

This board originated long ago with Galton, and is built somewhat like a pinball machine. Its purpose is to illustrate quickly a series of random events. A ball or marble is rolled down the middle of an inclined board which has an array of pegs or nails in it in the triangular array shown in figure 4-5. Boards can be easily made from 3/16 inch (5 mil-

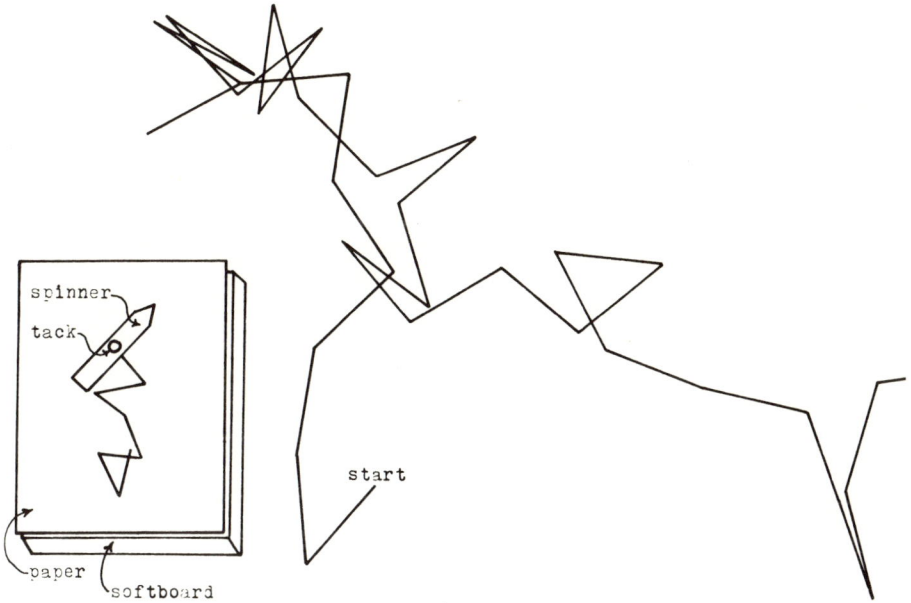

Figure 4-4. A record of a spinner direction held to each advancing point by a thumb tack and spun to give a new direction. All possible directions in a plane are available. It is quite similar to the motion of a molecule in a gas except that here each line segment is the same length.

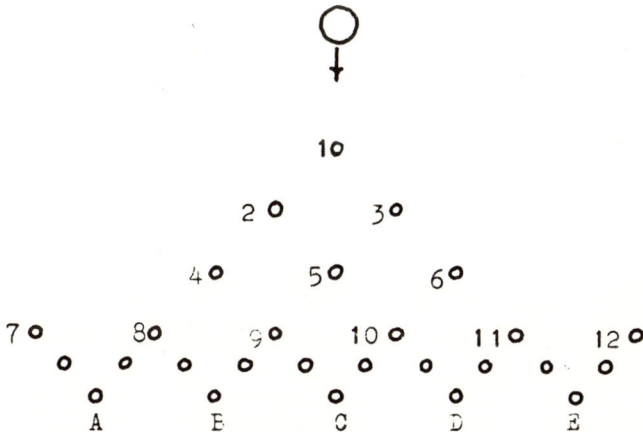

Figure 4-5. An evenly perforated ceiling tile can be made into a satisfactory probability board. The pattern above can be made with 3/16 inch dowel pegs on one such tile. Only the holes in which pegs are inserted are shown.

limeter) dowels and evenly perforated acoustic ceiling tile. The holes in the tile are ½ inch (13 millimeter) apart, and there are 22 rows of such holes in each square tile. The wood dowels are inserted in the proper holes, skipping a row of holes between each row of pins. The board is leaned against several books so that a marble will roll in the direction of the arrow in the sketch. When the marble hits pin 1 and the board is not tipped to the left or the right, the marble will have an equal chance to roll to either side of pin 1. If it should roll to the left of pin 1 and conditions are proper it should hit pin 2 at the top and roll to the left or the right with equal chance. The marble will proceed in like manner, hitting one pin in each row until it falls into one of the bins A, B, C, D, or E at the bottom. The student can keep a tally of how often the marble lands in each bin.

After practicing with the boards, the question of why the middle bins get the most marbles will come up. Class totals for each bin might be tallied on the blackboard, with each student calling out his count for each bin. It takes only five or ten minutes for each student to record 100 trials, so in a class of 25 students a total of 2500 trials can be obtained. The tilting sideways of individual boards will tend to cancel in the class total so one side of the board will not be favored over the other.

We assume that a marble has an equal chance of rolling to either side of any pin it hits. The two pathways around pin 1 are shown in figure 4-6. Then the marble hits either pin 2 or 3. The number of pathways to the left of pin 2 is one, but on the right of pin 2 there are actually two paths as shown in figure 4-7a. The marble has thus two *chances* of passing between pin 2 and pin 3, as shown in figure 4-7b.

But the boards have further rows. The outside pins represent no

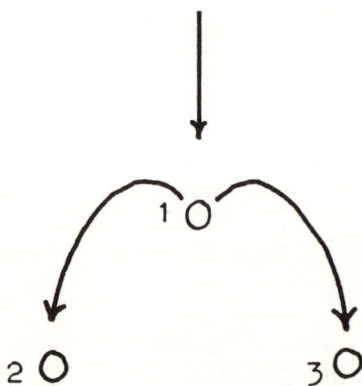

Figure 4-6. The beginning path of a marble on the probability board allows it to roll on either side of pin 1. Note that one roll of the marble seems to become two. It is actually rolling twice.

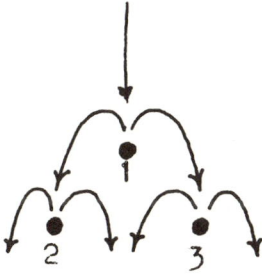

Figure 4-7a. The increased traffic between pin 2 and pin 3 is shown here.

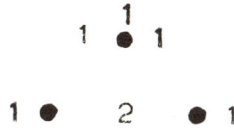

Figure 4-7b. The number of paths possible are shown.

Figure 4-8a. The increasing number of possible pathways for the marble can be obtained by tracing out each sequence of arrows to the third row.

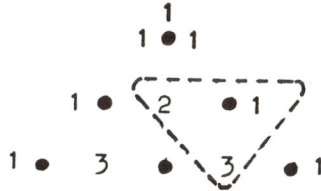

Figure 4-8b. Any number can be found by adding the two numbers closest to it above. Each number gives the paths available up to that location.

real difficulty since there is only one possible pathway on either side of such pins. Pathways between pins are complicated by the possibility of a marble rolling from either side. In the aforementioned case the two pathways between pins 2 and 3 are added to all future paths the marble takes if it first rolls between them. If, for instance, another row of pins is included, we have, in figure 4-8, a 1 3 3 1 ratio. Figure 4-8a shows how a marble may roll and figure 4-8b shows the number of different pathways possible between each pair of pins. Within the dashed area there are two pathways between the two pins in the second row and one pathway on the outside. We simply add these different pathways to find the number of different routes over which the marble may travel to roll between pins in the third row. This process continues for any number of paths directly under that pin. Figure 4-9 illustrates this for six rows.

We can see how the number of pathways increases at the middle and decreases outward. Does this mean that a bin placed under the middle pins in the sixth row will catch 20 marbles while a bin placed under the 2 pins in the second row will only catch two marbles? Obvi-

```
                              1
                         1    ●   1
                    1 ●       2       ● 1
               1 ●      3       ●     3      ● 1
          1 ●      4       ●     6      ●     4      ● 1
     1 ●     5       ●    10      ●    10      ●     5     ● 1
1 ●     6      ●    15      ●    20      ●    15      ●    6      ● 1
```

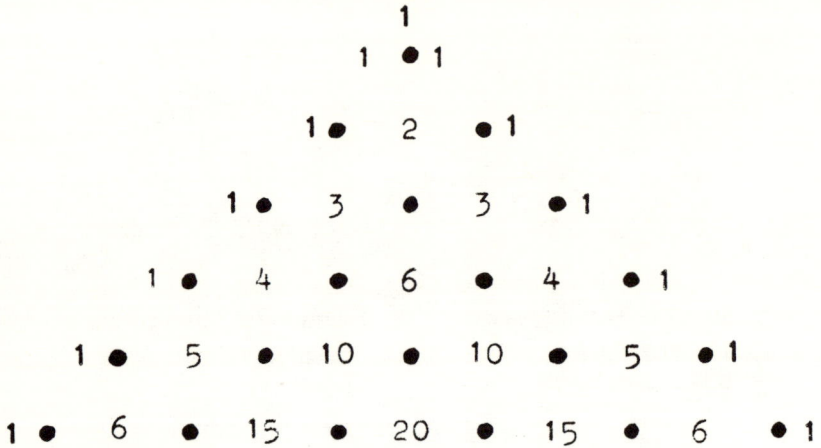

Figure 4-9. Each number in the above figure indicates the number of different pathways possible between the pins on each side of the number. What would be the numbers in the next lower row?

ously not if the marble is rolled an equal number of times in each case. The numbers indicate possible pathways. If a marble is rolled $1+2+1$ times or four times it will *probably* roll between the two pins in the second row twice. A marble would have to be rolled $1+6+15+20+15+6+1$ or 64 times for us to expect it to roll between the middle pins of the sixth row 20 times. If we can expect the marble to roll into the middle bin of the sixth row 20 times, it has 20/64 of a chance to roll in each time it is rolled down the board. Each aforementioned number, then, is actually the numerator of a fraction whose denominator is obtained by adding the number of pathways in that particular row. There is thus ½ a chance (one chance in two) for a marble to roll between the two pins in the second row.

Comparison to Tossing Coins

We can compare this reasoning with the possibility of heads or tails coming up when coins are tossed. If the marble rolls to the left we may say it is as though the coin fell heads up. If it rolls to the right it is as though tails came up. Having established that a roll to the left is the same as "heads" and a roll to the right the same as "tails," we can move on to the second row. We must imagine next that as the marble hits a pin in the second row and rolls by it, the marble becomes a second coin. Thus, if a marble rolls to the left of the pin in the first row it is "heads" for the first coin, and if it rolls to the left of the left pin in the second row it is "heads" for the second coin. Figure 4-10 shows all the possibilities for two coins, or for one coin tossed twice.

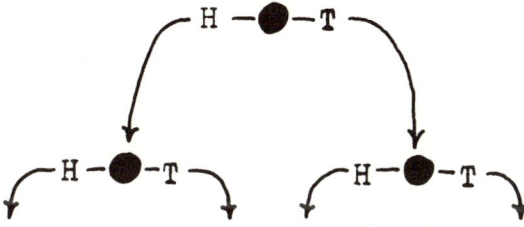

Figure 4-10. The triangular array of numbers can be obtained by tossing a coin enough times to generate the desired sequence of pathways.

Note that there are four different pathways for the marble and four different possibilities for the ways two coins can land. In each case, however, there are two results which appear the same. Do we consider head of one coin and tail of another as different from tail of one coin and head of another? If so, then there are four possibilities. If we want to consider these possibilities as the same and not distinguish between them, then we can say there are only three different ways two coins can fall and there are only three bins into which a marble may roll below the second row of pins. These considerations are important if we want to relate this study to genetics. Those marbles which roll continually to the left or continually to the right have only "leftness" or "rightness" in their ancestry. They are "homozygous." Should they alternate at any time they become heterozygous by obtaining both heads and tails in their ancestry. If dominance occurs then all head-tail and all tail-head combinations will look like pure head or pure tail depending on which characteristic dominates.

If we consider an individual as a certain combination of tosses of the coin then there are more individuals of mixed parentage (having both heads and tails in their record) than those having only heads or only tails. These regulators work within human society as well, and in the animal and plant world since nature has discovered long ago that isolation is stagnation. For whatever it is worth, the bins with the longest "pedigrees" are those on the outside of our game. The bins at the middle contain most of the "population" and are also those bins whose "parentage" is the most varied. Groups of people in the central land masses of the world where travel is easier have an ancestry composed of the many different tribes which occupied those regions. Those groups more on the periphery have interbred more frequently and this can be seen in some minor physical characteristics. Human beings have had a relatively short history and are quite mobile, so this effect has not continued for any great length of time.

Recording the Pathways

The board does not perform as well in practice as in theory. The rebound of the marble from each pin is not standard enough to insure that it will hit a pin in the next row. If the rebound off the first pin is weak, the central bins will receive a greater share of the marble rolls than calculation would bear out. If the rebound off the first pin is strong, the outer bins will receive a greater proportion of the rolls. This effect can be illustrated without difficulty and each student can analyze his board a little more fully by the following processes. An ordinary 8½ x 11 inch (22 x 28 centimeter) master sheet can be made up with the pins marked as circles. This is dittoed and a sheet given to each student. He places the sheet over the ceiling tile so that holes in the board line up with each of the holes in the paper. He then punches out each hole with a pointed pencil and inserts the pins. (If he does not punch out the holes first but inserts the pins directly the paper will wrinkle and the marble will not roll true.) The marble is then dipped in a can of lampblack, powdered graphite, or in thinned tempera paint, and rolled down the board as before. A track will be left for each such roll and it becomes plain, after ten or more rolls, if a marble misses a pin or if it consistently goes to one side of a particular pin. After some 30 rolls, the heavier paths can be easily picked out. If one side of the board has heavier paths it indicates that the board is tilted toward that side. A peculiar characteristic of marbles dipped in tempera paint is to favor the inner bin. This happens because as the paint dries it becomes sticky and severely restricts the rebound of the marble off the first pin.

The paper frequently develops areas where it is not tight on the board and these also tend to skew the results. Better results may be obtained with aluminum foil which has been blackened in a candle flame and laid on the board to replace the paper. The marble then picks up a small amount of carbon as it is rolled down the board.

In our construction we have sought to make the results truly random. We expect the marble to roll to either side of the dowel pin with equal frequency. If we were completely successful in removing all sources of error which favored one side over the other, then wouldn't the marble bounce straight up from the first pin and settle back on top of it? This does occasionally happen with these boards, and when it does we jiggle the board a little or pull at the pin in order to get a result. Something a little short of perfection is sought, where the small variations that exist are not large enough to predetermine which way the marble rolls.

Recording Pathways with Rubber Bands

Tossing coins is more truly random than the rolling of a marble down the probability board, even though it lacks much of the drama of a marble leaving a streak on the recording paper. Using a probability board, a coin, and some rubber bands, we can pictorialize the path of a marble satisfactorily and still maintain the more truly random nature of the coin toss. We let a bounce of the marble to the left of a pin (as in figure 4-10) mean a coin toss which turns up heads. A rubber band is then stretched between the two pins involved, as in figure 4-11. The coin

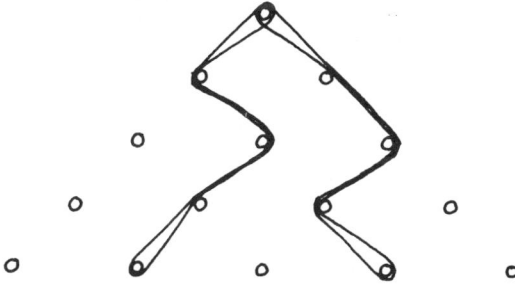

Figure 4-11. A rubber band can be stretched around the pegs to show a path on the probability board. The above paths were made by tossing a coin with heads a roll to the left of a peg and tails a roll to the right. The two paths illustrated are HTHH and TTHT. As further paths are made, a thickening of rubber bands around the middle pegs will result.

is tossed again and the rubber band is stretched farther along the path. This can be done for any number of rows and a large pegboard with many rows in it, which can be seen and used by the whole class, can be constructed. If blueprint paper is laid over the pegboard and the rubber bands are pushed down on the pegs so as to contact the paper, a permanent record can be obtained of the pathways by exposing the blueprint paper to bright light and then washing it.

Recording Pathways with Graph Paper

Recording of pathways can be obtained by using graph paper, as shown in figure 4-12. This is the simplest way since all we need is graph paper and a coin, but the pathways must be separated slightly in order to show how frequently they are traversed. This gives a slightly artificial character to the record.

The Paradox of the Three Coins

This problem concerns three coins in a box. One coin has two heads, the other two coins are normal. If we pick one coin from the box and

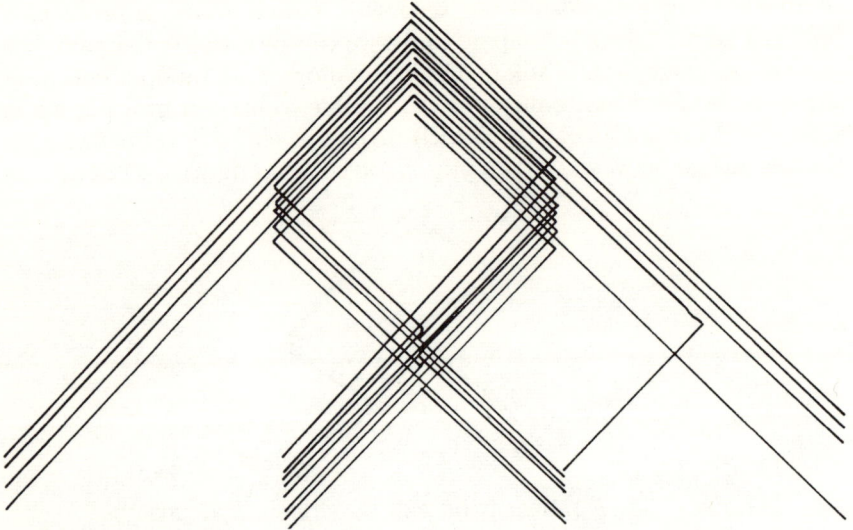

Figure 4-12. This illustrates an actual series of rolls with a coin, using graph paper to create the pattern more easily. No path was allowed to be drawn over another but was separated slightly to show where paths tended to build up.

drop it on the table, and if by chance it should land heads up, what is the chance that the other side will be heads? Since only one coin out of three has two heads, we might expect the chance to be 1 out of 3. It isn't. It is more than that; in fact it is ½. It is easy enough to try the problem. A bright penny might be considered the two-headed one, and two dull pennies the normal one. As the problem is tried, the frequency of selecting the bright penny soon indicates there is something favoring it. If the class is interested, everyone can do the problem together, and a picture of what is happening can be made more quickly. Washers instead of coins can be used, with one side colored to indicate tails. Will someone discover the reason for the frequency of the double-headed coin appearing from the practice? Whether someone discovers it or not the class will be able to better understand the solution to the problem after working it and seeing the results.

The clue to the solution of the problem is in the requirement that the coin selected from the box land heads up. If a tails appears we don't count it, and thereby reject "bad" coins. In fact, half the time a "bad" coin appears and we reject it. This inevitably increases the chance of our picking the two-headed coins. We could illustrate this more clearly by playing the game a little differently. Suppose that we didn't count either heads or tails of the "bad" coin. We would then select the "good" coin

100 percent of the time. Or suppose that we used only two coins, one normal and one double-headed. Half the time we will pick the good coin, but of course we will have more than ½. One-quarter of the time we will pick heads on the "bad" coin so at least ¼ of the time we will be "wiped out." Of the remaining ¼ chances, those in which tails were turned up, we try again, and have as much chance of picking the right coin as picking the wrong one. This means ½ x ¼, or ⅛ more chance for each. The right coin has therefore at least ½ + ⅛, or ⅝ probability of being turned up. But we are not finished. One-fourth of the reruns are tails again, and these have to also be rerun. One-half of these repeats will be the good coin, and so we must add ½ of ¼ of ¼, or 1/16 more to the good coin. This continues as we add smaller and smaller amounts. We approach ⅔ as the probability of picking the "good coin. The same reasoning applies to the three coin problem In each case we must know how many different possible ways we can choose coins. In determining the probability of any event we must know how it compares to all possible events under the given conditions. This gives us the fraction which we find easy enough to understand, and which we call "the odds."

A Marble Contest

A series of covered boxes are set up in a row. In the first are a black and a white marble. In the second there are two black marbles and a white one. In the third there are three black marbles and a white one and so on with one more black marble in each succeeding box. If marbles cannot be obtained in sufficient quantity beans can be used with the different one in each box painted. The beans must be of the same size. We start from the box with the *largest* number of marbles in it and proceed to the smallest. We reach in and pull out a marble without seeing it. If the marble is white the game is ended. If it is black we proceed to the next box. Above each box we could have a score sheet, and the student places a tally over the box from which he picks a white marble. If we have 20 boxes, what is the chance of someone going through all of them without selecting a white marble? The chance is quite small, but not so small that it won't happen now and then. It is 1 in 21 that all twenty boxes will turn up black marbles. It is quite simple to determine the chances. It is just 1 divided by the number of marbles in the first box. Since the twentieth box has 21 marbles in it, the chance of getting through all of them (picking all black marbles) is 1 in 21. We could start at either end of the row and the chances of getting through would be the same, but if we start at the end with only two marbles we are apt to be cut off sooner. We could pick from boxes at random and our chances would still be the same (as long as we didn't use any box twice).

Why is the chance of picking all black marbles 1 in 21? First, consider the first box with 21 marbles in it, 20 of which are black. The chance of picking a black marble is 20/21. The chance of picking black marbles from the first two boxes is 20/21 x 19/20 or 19/21 since the 20's cancel. We multiply these fractions because we have a 19/20 of a 20/21 chance of picking a black marble (just as we have ½ of ½ of a chance if each box had one black and one white marble). As more boxes are used the probability goes down, each time cancelling all denominators except the 21 and reducing the numerator until we obtain 1/21 as the chance of getting through all the boxes. One need not remind students that the game is like a set of actuarial tables where as our age increases so does our mortality rate.

We might present the boxes to the students without letting them look inside. After a certain number of tries a discussion can be started as to how many marbles there are in each box, and the ratio of black to white marbles. Each day, or week, the game could be changed and the students then try to determine the ratio of the marbles. One arrangement which is difficult to get through is to increase the number of black marbles up to a point, say seven or eight, and then decrease them until there is only one of each again. If we had boxes with the following numbers of marbles: 2,3,4,5,5,4,3,2 (with one white marble in each box) our chance of getting through would be 1 in 25. Other interesting arrangements can be invented. A series of boxes with a single black and a single white marble in each reduces very rapidly the chance of picking black each time. The chance of getting through twenty boxes like these, is 1 in 2^{20} (about 1 in 1,000,000), and is obtained by carrying out the multiplication of (½ x ½ x ½ x ½ . . . . .) until we have done it twenty times.

Boxes of Molecules

There are two interconnected boxes with two molecules bouncing around in them. How many ways can the two molecules be placed in the two boxes? They can both be in one, both be in the other, or one in each box. There are four ways, just as there are four ways two coins can fall. For three marbles there are eight ways they can be arranged. The chance that all three marbles are in *either* box is 2/8, or 1 in 4. As the number of molecules becomes greater the chance of them all being in one box becomes vanishingly small. But it is still a chance and, considering the number of boxes in the world, we are apt to wonder why it doesn't happen just once. The chance of all molecules of air in two connected thimbles arranging themselves in one of the thimbles is about as great as if we had a probability board which stretched from the earth to the moon and a marble rolled down it continually bounced to the left of every peg it hit.

Probability of Germination

What percentage of various seeds will germinate? Seed packets provide the highest percentage of sprouting and are a good standard with which to measure other germinating seeds. Old seed packets from previous years are good to use, as well as beans meant for cooking, grass seed, etc. A simple holder for germinating seeds which will keep them moist and yet not drown them is shown in figure 4-13. The paper towels are rolled around perhaps ten seeds, stapled flat to keep the seeds in

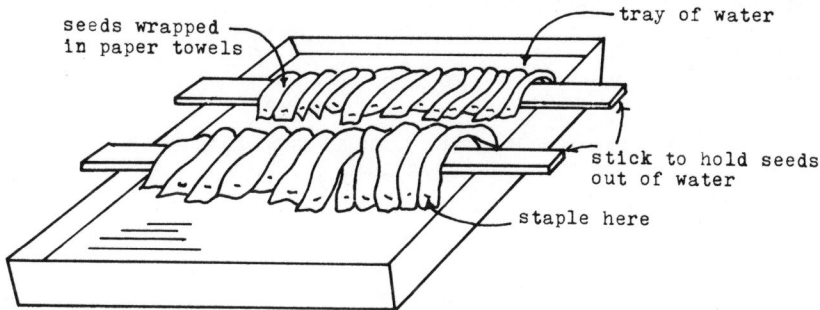

Figure 4-13. Paper towels hold seeds and keep them moist while germinating in this class-size tray. The towels can be cut, opened for inspection, and rewrapped for further growth. Names on the towels keep them identified.

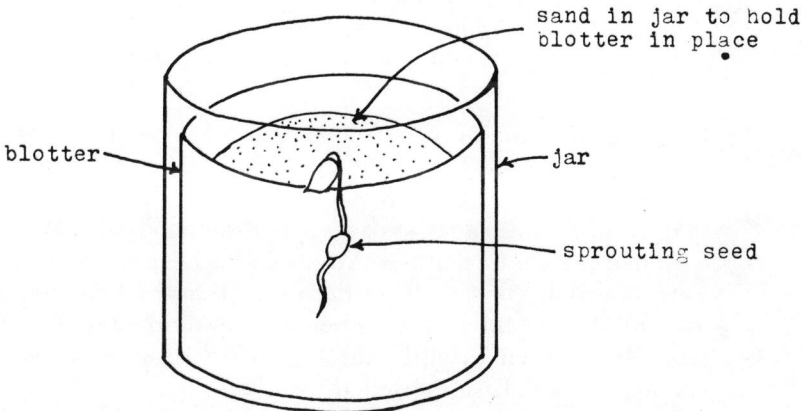

Figure 4-14. This method of sprouting seeds allows observation of growth at the root tip. Does the root grow all along its length or only at the very tip?

position, and the ends allowed to drop into the water where they act as a wick. If several students are to use the tray each can put his name on his own paper towel with a ball point pen. If water is kept in the tray and the room is warm the seeds will germinate rapidly. After germination quantitative studies can be continued on how fast the root grows by transplanting the sprouting seeds to a jar where they are held against the inside walls by a blotter as in figure 4-14. The root tip itself can be marked to determine if the tip moves as the root grows. We might reason that it cannot move since if it did it would shear off any branch roots. Is this true of plants that have roots entirely in water such as the water hyacinth, or duckweed?

Puzzles and Problems

1. Obtain the shells from the same species of snails, clams, fossils, etc., and try to find the differences between two individuals. These differences could be in the number of flutings, or marks of any kind, number of twists in the shell (if any) as well as a measurement of the overall dimensions. (This is designed to show that there are many factors at work which determine the appearance of an individual).

2. A marble is to be chosen from one of two boxes whose contents cannot be seen. If a black marble is chosen, a prize is given. If a white one is chosen, no prize is given. There are six marbles in all, four whites and two blacks. The chooser can arrange the marbles in any way he likes beforehand. However, all marbles must be used. How should he arrange them to increase his chances of getting a prize? (Once he arranges them the boxes are concealed and shuffled so that the chooser no longer knows which box is which.)

3. Let us suppose that the same chooser placed one black marble in one box and the rest of the marbles in the other. Another person put three black marbles in one box and three white ones in the other. Then the class or audience was allowed to see how each had placed the marbles. After they each chose, the results were shown to the class. It so happened that the first chooser lost and the second won. Another try was announced and the class was allowed to enter the contest in support of either chooser. They all supported the second chooser. What was wrong with their reasoning? This could actually be done as an exercise involving both choosers being "in on" the demonstration. The first one knows the boxes by some slight identifying mark and avoids winning. The second also knows which box to choose and picks the winning box. Thus, while it looks as

though the first chooser has the advantage, he never wins. What the class does as it sees him lose is the part we are testing. After about eight or ten tests, the demonstration should stop and an explanation made before the students lose faith in probability theory. What are the chances that the first chooser will lose eight times and the second win eight times consecutively? (In this game it is hard to get two boxes sufficiently identical. If the boxes are shuffled behind a screen and the chooser selects the left or the right box he has less chance of using identifying marks. To be in on the demonstration the chooser must be advised beforehand by the shuffler where the box he is to choose is put for each try.)

4. How many ways can five molecules arrange themselves between two boxes? What is the probability that all five will be in the same box?

5. The following concerns the number of ways of arranging certain items. It is not strictly concerned with probability but is the denominator only of the fraction known as the "odds." The numerator of the fraction is the number of possibilities we consider favorable among the total in the denominator. In these problems we build patterns similar to those obtained in the chapter on patterns and cycles.
   a. How many ways can you connect four hex nuts so that at least one side of each touches at least one side of another? (28 hex nuts will be sufficient for all the possibilities here.)
   b. How many ways can you arrange five hex nuts so that the above conditions apply?
   c. How many ways can you connect four square nuts as above?
   d. How many ways can you connect five square nuts?
   e. Do 5a through 5d using penciled circles to indicate where the center of the nuts are. (Only pencil and paper will be needed for this.) One arrangement is shown in figure 4-15.

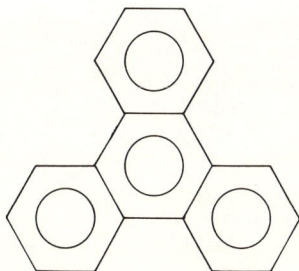

Figure 4-15. This is one of several patterns possible with four hex nuts.

BIBLIOGRAPHY

Engel, Arthur. "Teaching Probability in Intermediate Grades," *The Teaching of Probability and Statistics*. New York: John Wiley Interscience, 1970, pp. 96, 97.

Gardner, Martin. "Mathematical Games," *Scientific American,* Feb. 1968. (Tree graphs, p. 118.)

————. "Mathematical Games," *Scientific American,* July 1967. (Sprouts and brussel sprouts, p. 112.)

————. "Mathematical Games," *Scientific American,* May 1969. (The rambling random walk, p. 118.)

Association of Teachers of Mathematics. *Notes on Mathematics in Primary Schools*. London: Cambridge at the University Press, 1967. (Pascal's Triangles, pp. 204-218.)

5

The Mathematics
in Simple Machines

Mathematical concepts include: symmetry, fractions, angular measure, opposite angles, ratio, parallelograms, triangles, ellipses, perimeter, cycloids, epicycloids, rotation, axes of rotation, loci, dimension, zero point

Amplifiers

The pantograph enlarges as does a hand lens or a radio, and this
seems to be an inherent quality of much of our Machine Age gadgetry.
One quality is enlarged at the expense of another. This process of
change takes place in mathematics and is the basic theme of *number* itself.
It has become a prolific means of interpreting our world. Linkages provide enlargement in its simplest form, easily observable, manipulated,
and controlled. Reverse the enlargement device, and the process of making smaller can be observed. In either case, distortion inevitably accom-
panies the process, sometimes until the result is unrecognizable. Distortion is also worth experimenting with, and we begin with a linkage which
involves a good deal of distortion.

Linkages

Posterboard Links

Related Math: curves, radius, opposite angles, symmetry, axis of rotation

A handy way for students to explore linkage in the classroom is with strips of posterboard or stiff cardboard. These strips can be pinned to bulletin board material, to the soft type of ceiling tile, or to ordinary corrugated cardboard box material. We will refer to any material in which pins are anchored as "softboard." A sheet of paper should be placed over the softboard to make an easily renewable recording material for the designs which will be created with linked strips of posterboard. These designs portray the motion which takes place during the operation of such simple devices as eggbeaters, windshield wipers, scissors, and drawing compasses. The mathematics in them is geometry, with an undercurrent of fractions, ratio, and the raw material for many an equation.

Distortion Linkage

A simple arrangement for creating designs is to link two strips to form a T as shown in figure 5-1.

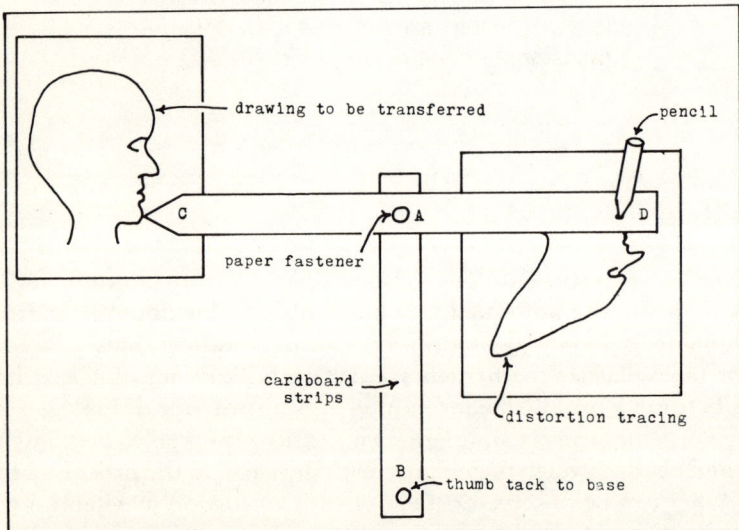

Figure 5-1. This simple experimental pantograph can be used to study distortion. Two cardboard strips are held together at A, and one strip is fastened with a thumbtack to the softboard base at B.

A design placed under C can be transferred to D. The cardboard is cut to a point at C to make the tracing of the design more accurate. A pencil must be fastened at D in order to record the movement. A hole can be punched in the cardboard for the pencil point and the pencil held by the right hand as the left directs the motion by tracing out the design. The tracing must be done slowly in order for it to be accurate. Looseness in any of the pivot points will also destroy accuracy.

The design produced by the arrangement shown in the illustration will be fairly similar to the original. However, if the length of the arms of the T is varied or if the junction of the T is near one end, or if the strips are not near the perpendicular to one another, then quite a bit of distortion will result. By moving the pencil from the end at D toward the center A, and drawing a design at each location, the type of distortion produced can be studied as it becomes more pronounced. The design for such a study should be simple, such as a circle or the profile of a face. The students might be asked what sort of design will be produced by a pencil which is placed at the junction of the two strips (point A in figure 5-1). The answer is simple—an arc of a circle, no matter what the design.

Pegboard Links

Related Math: congruency, symmetry, transformations, circles, perimeters, circular arcs, axes, loci

A more permanent arrangement of linkages can be made by using strips cut from Masonite pegboard. This material comes with holes placed ½ inch (1.25 centimeters) apart or 1 inch (2.54 centimeters) apart. Either type can be used, but in order to make sturdy strips from pegboard with holes ½ inch apart, it is necessary to cut the pegboard through alternate rows of holes. The help of the school custodian and/or the use of a table saw will be very helpful if any quantity of such strips are to be made. A handy length for the strips is 12 inches (30 centimeters).

The holes in pegboard are 3/16 inch (about 5 millimeters) in diameter. Dowels of this diameter are quite handy in linking such strips together. The fit is quite snug and some dowel lengths which are a bit off from the circular may not fit at all. A dab of soap on the dowel will make it fit into the hole in the pegboard more easily. In order to fasten the pegboard strip to the softboard a dowel peg about 4 inches (10 centimeters) long is sharpened in a pencil sharpener and, after being entered into a hole in the pegboard strip, is pushed or driven with a hammer into the softboard. If evenly perforated ceiling tile is used, the dowel can be easily pushed into one of the holes. It should not be sharpened in such a case. A device of this type is shown in figure 5-2.

The record of the designs made by tracing out a circle at D and by

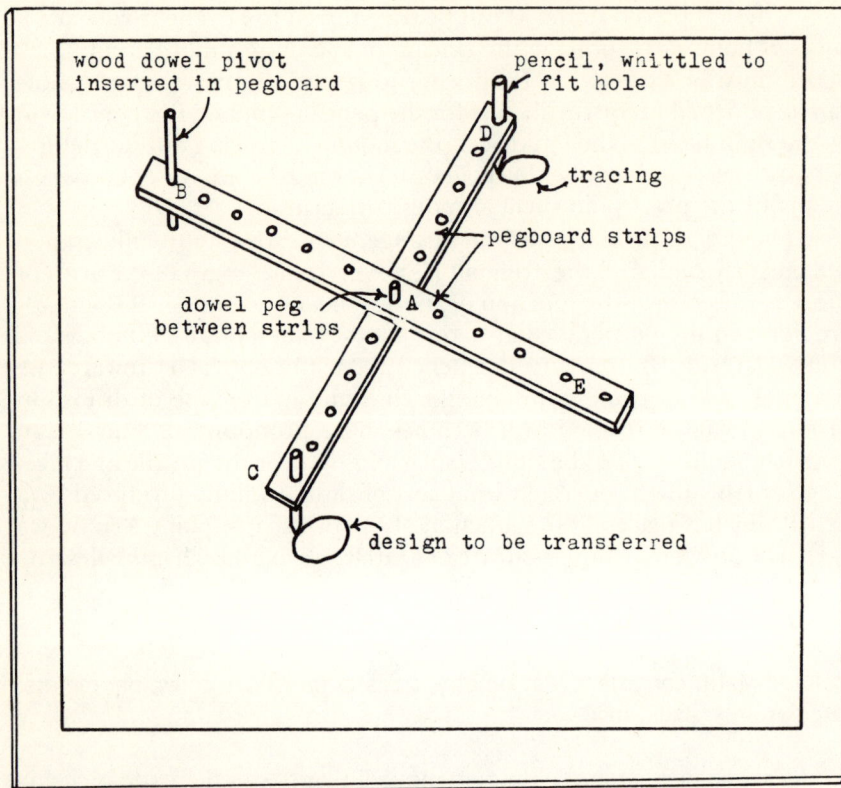

Figure 5-2. A pegboard base and strips provide a fairly sturdy arrangement of transferring pictures and studying the resulting distortion.

alternately placing the pencil in holes in the pegboard arm between C and D is shown in figure 5-3. The peg at A can also be moved along arm CD or arm BE for further experimentation. A circle is a good design to trace since the types of distortion can easily be seen.

Pantograph Linkage

Related Math: parallelograms, congruency, transformations, ratio, angles, axes, opposite sides

Additional work on linkages can be done with such devices as the pantograph, which can enlarge a design or make it smaller without distortion. It can be assembled easily from cardboard strips but is sturdier

original design
(outline of a quarter)

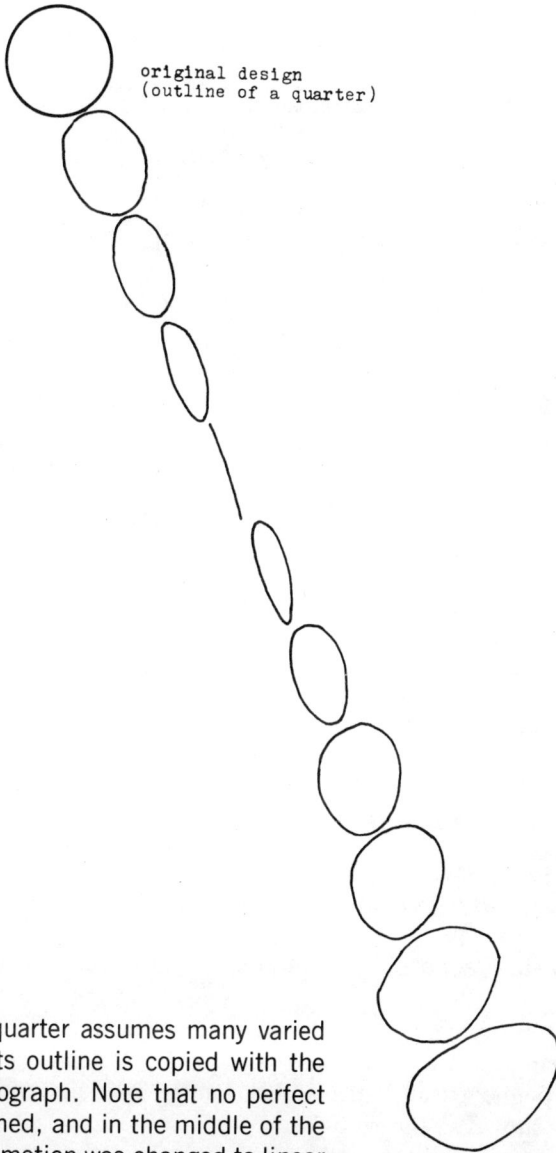

Figure 5-3. A quarter assumes many varied shapes when its outline is copied with the distorting pantograph. Note that no perfect copy was obtained, and in the middle of the figure, circular motion was changed to linear motion.

when made from Masonite pegboard (see figure 5-4). This pantograph will enlarge a drawing. If the pencil and the tracing pin are reversed, the drawing will be reduced. The drawing can be made distorted by shifting the pins so that the arms of the pantograph are no longer parallel.

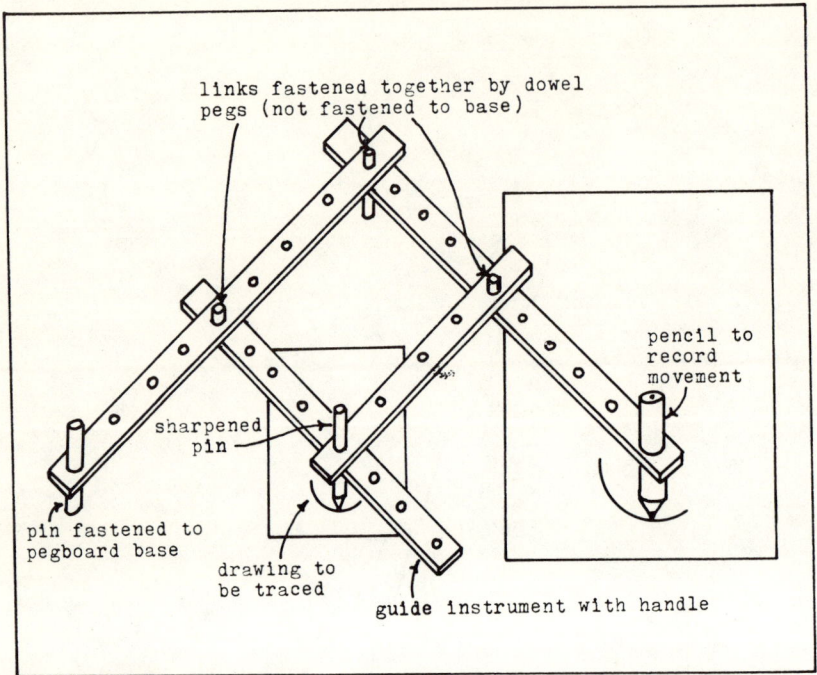

Figure 5-4. This pegboard pantograph is sturdy enough for class use. Designs can be enlarged, distorted, or made smaller. To fit the hole, the pencil must be whittled down or the hole enlarged.

Rubber Band Pantograph

Related Math: fractions, ratio, variables, radius, zero point,

A very simple pantograph can be made from a few rubber bands or a soft spring such as a shade roller spring. A dowel is fastened into a piece of pegboard and the rubber bands, marker, and pencil are attached as shown in figure 5-5.

The stretching of the rubber band is proportional to its length so the device serves well enough for small sketches. If more rubber bands are added to the end, the enlargement can be enlarged. As the sketch is copied, the pegboard tends to slide, and should therefore be held firmly to the tabletop. A sharp tipped felt pen leaves a good trace with a minimum of pressure. The rubber bands must be adjusted until the pen makes a light contact.

A good way of checking the evenness of the rubber band stretching is to place one end of a rubber band around a peg in the pegboard,

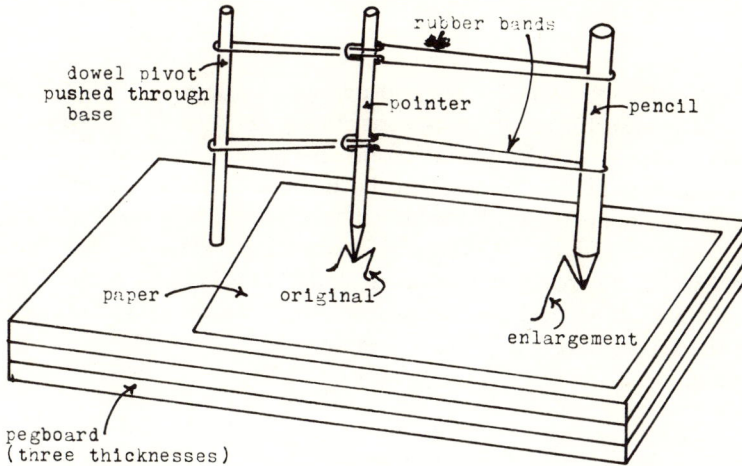

Figure 5-5. This rubber band pantograph makes enlargements with fair accuracy. It must be held to the tabletop or clamped so that it doesn't slip when the rubber bands are stretched.

stretch the rubber band over the evenly spaced holes in the board, and ink a point at the middle of the rubber band over one of these holes. Stretch the rubber band two holes farther and see if the mark is now over the next hole. (See figure 5-6.) Every unit length of the rubber band has a certain "stretchability." This experiment determines if this is uniform along the rubber band. It is therefore an experiment in fractions.

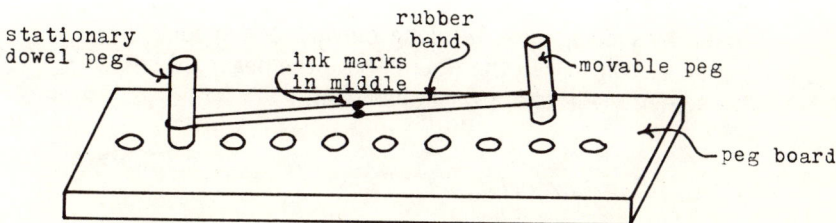

Figure 5-6. If the movable peg is moved 2 pegholes farther away from the stationary dowel peg than it was at the start then how far will the ink marks on the rubber band be stretched?

Building Curves on Curves

New possibilities will come to mind as the work with linkages continues. Whenever one curve is generated by a linkage it is worth trying to use it as the basis for another curve as shown in figure 5-7. Two links are attached, and arm LDE is slid along line AB while point C remains stationary. A pencil in the notch at D records the curve. After the complete curve is drawn, then draw the curve on the curve. Let the arm LDE slide so that the hole at L is directly over the previous curve. The new curve will be recorded at the notch at D. This second curve has two sections, one above and one below line AB. A third curve can be drawn using the second curve as a basis. The total figure is symmetrical on each side of line AB.

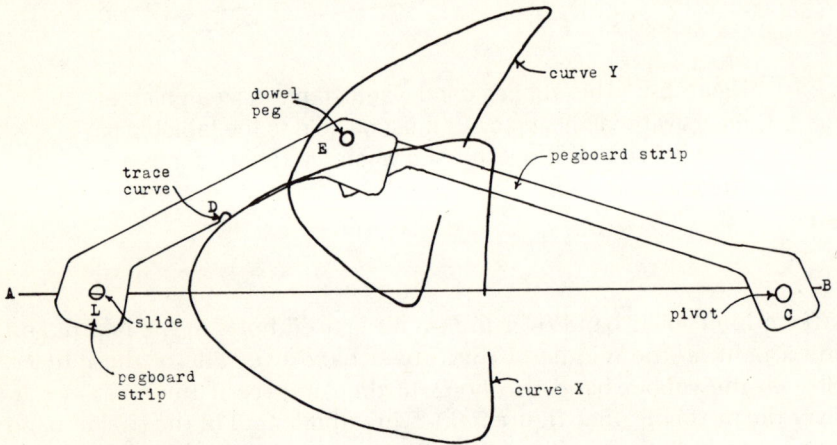

Figure 5-7. Curves are built on curves in this linkage of narrow pegboard strips. The breaks in the curve are due to a covered portion of the strip which prevented tracing in that place. Curve X was made by moving L along line AB while holding the pencil to the notch at D. Curve Y was made by moving point L along curve X and holding the pencil at point D. In the figure above the pegboard strips have been made to appear transparent.

An Everlasting Parallelogram

If the midpoints of any quadrilateral are connected, the resulting figure will be a parallelogram. Four strips of pegboard can be linked with 3/16 inch (5 millimeter) dowels, and, if they have been selected to have an odd number of holes along their length between the pegs, they will have a hole in the exact middle of each side. A dowel peg is inserted in these middle holes and a rubber band stretched across the pegs. The quadrilateral then can be flexed so that its shape changes, but no matter what its shape, the rubber band will still form a parallelogram. (See figure 5-8.) It is easy enough to add another link and try the problem with five sides. We find that we cannot get a regular pentagon, however.

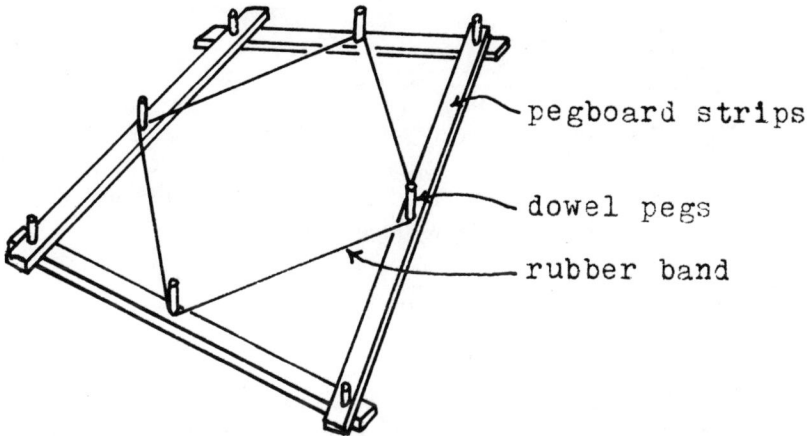

Figure 5-8. A perpetual parallelogram is formed by the rubber band no matter how the shape of the pegboard quadrilateral is changed as it is flexed on its four corner hinges.

Tin Can Linkages

Related Math: rotation, cycloids, epicycloids, circumference, ellipses, triangles, circles

A quick way to produce a curve which has some relationship to the real world is by linking two tin cans with rubber bands as shown in Figure 5-9. The rubber bands are wrapped around the cans in a figure eight to keep the cans from slipping as one can is rotated around the other. The device requires two people to operate—one to hold the middle can stationary and to press gently on the pen while the other turns the outside can. The shape of the design is somewhat like the path of the earth's moon around the sun. The center of the rolling can is the earth, the pencil is the moon, and the center of the stationary can is the sun.

A similar and more permanent apparatus can be made from plywood disks, each with a narrow (⅛ inch or 3 millimeter) velcro fabric strip fastened with glue and/or staples to the outside edge. A small hole near the edge of the disk serves to hold the pencil or pen in order to

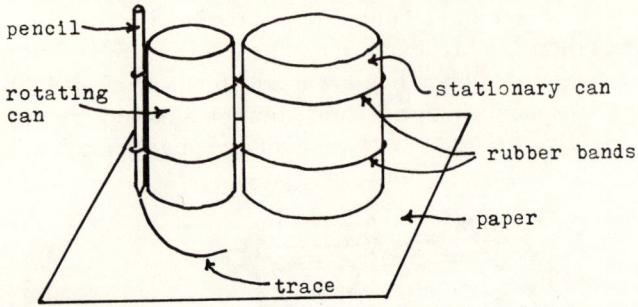

Figure 5-9. This is a quickly set-up linkage to observe the motion of a point on the circumference of a circle as it rotates about another fixed circle. Best results are achieved with two people working the device.

produce the design as shown in figure 5-10. Pegboard serves well also as material for the disks. The pegboard is too thin for stapling, but the velcro fabric can be glued with Duco cement. It must be cut from its usual ⅝ inch (1.5 centimeter) width down to about ⅛ inch (3 millimeters) to match the thickness of the pegboard. One of the holes in the pegboard can be for inserting a pencil, or a new hole close to the edge of the disk can be drilled.

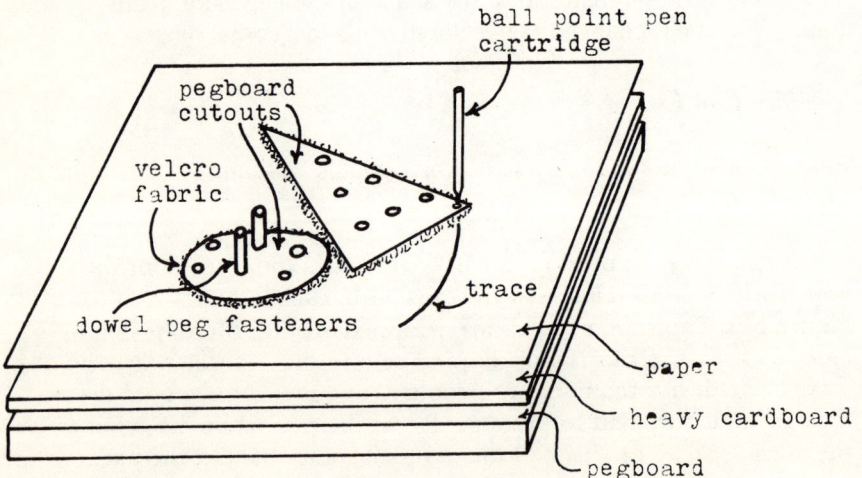

Figure 5-10. The stationary oval pegboard cut-out is held in position by dowels. Around it rotates the pegboard triangle. The velcro fabric maintains good contact between the two figures. A 1/16 inch hole (or 2 mm.) drilled at the corner allows the ball point pen cartridge to be inserted.

Disks of all sorts can be tried in order to produce a variety of designs. Oval disks, squares, and triangles all produce rather interesting curves. Unless the perimeters of both disks are the same or one is a multiple of the other, the design will not retrace itself after one revolution. Eventually it does retrace itself just as the wandering pool ball of Chapter 3 went into a corner sooner or later. Designs using an elliptical disk and a triangular disk are shown in figures 5-11 and 5-12.

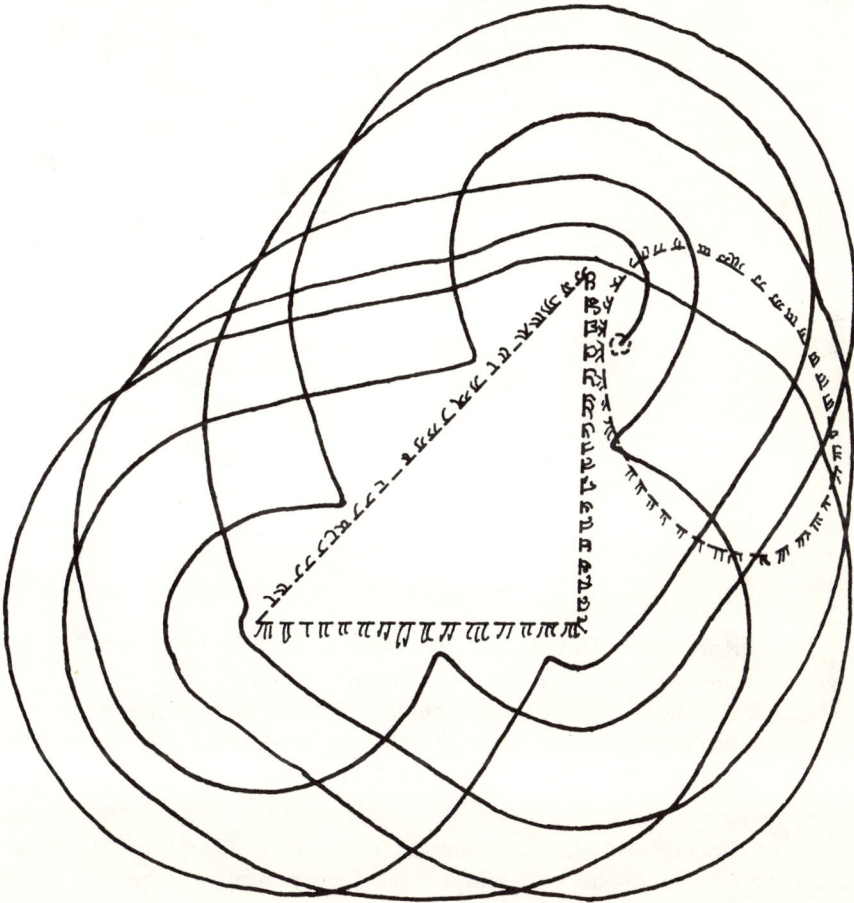

Figure 5-11. This design was made by linking a rotating ellipse to a stationary triangle. The exterior shape of the design resembles the central stationary figure. The appearance is somewhat similar to the waves coming off an obstacle protruding from the surface of a large body of water.

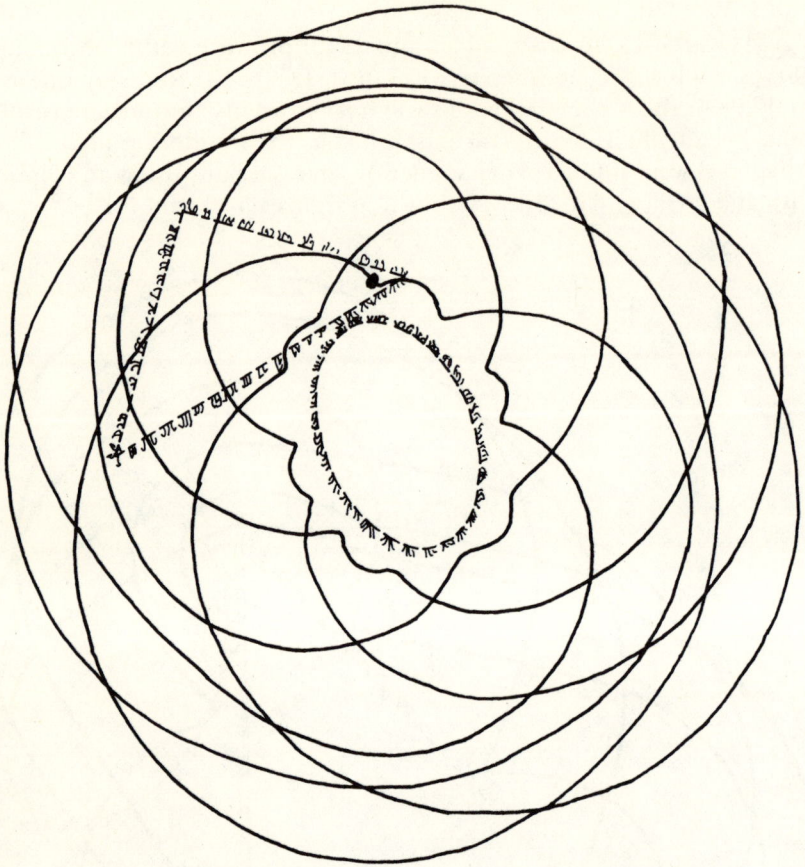

Figure 5-12. This design was made by linking the same materials used in figure 5-11 but the ellipse is stationary and the triangle rotates around it. The exterior shape is elliptical and in this case repetition of the curve occurred after several circuits of the triangle.

Interesting tracings can be obtained by rotating a disk within another larger, circular opening. Such an opening can be cut from plywood or pegboard. (See figure 5-13.) When recording the path of a point on the inner disk one hand should guide the disk around, holding it against the cut out opening while the other hand records with the pencil. The Spyrograph Game uses toothed plastic disks, and quite precise curves can be obtained from it. Unfortunately it has only circular disks and rods.

Velcro fabric can be stapled or glued to a straight edge and recordings made of disks as they are rolled along it as in figure 5-14. This

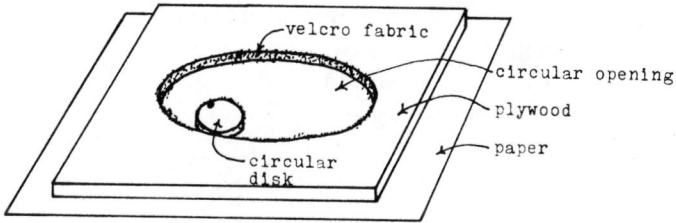

Figure 5-13. If the inside circular disk is half the diameter of the opening it revolves around, what sort of curve will be traced out by a pencil held at one point on its circumference?

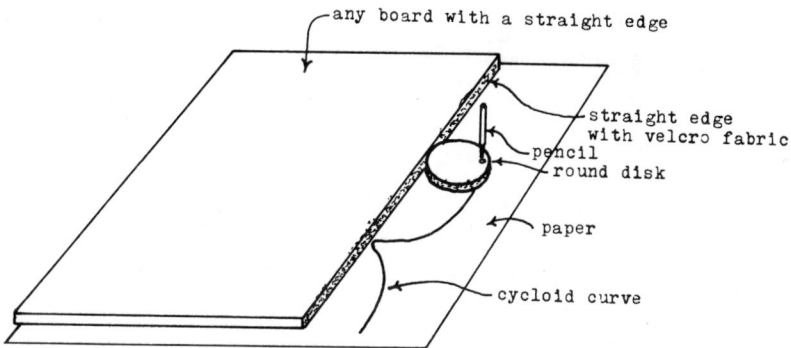

Figure 5-14. A round pegboard disk is rolled along the straight edge to produce a cycloid curve. What sort of curve would be produced by an equilateral triangle rolled the same way?

method of producing a cycloid (by rolling a round surface along a straight edge) has been known since antiquity. A wheel or disk with a piece of chalk taped to its rim can be rolled along the chalkboard to produce a cycloid.

Universal Joints

Related Math: axes, angles, radius, perpendicularity, intersecting planes, lines in planes, right angles

A universal joint or "U-joint" is a means of transferring power along a shaft at a slightly different direction from the original motion. Two shafts are connected by such a joint and the rotation of one shaft will turn the other. (The power to drive the rear wheels of an auto is obtained through a "U-joint.") We can make a U-joint with two plastic straws and a pin as shown in figure 5-15.

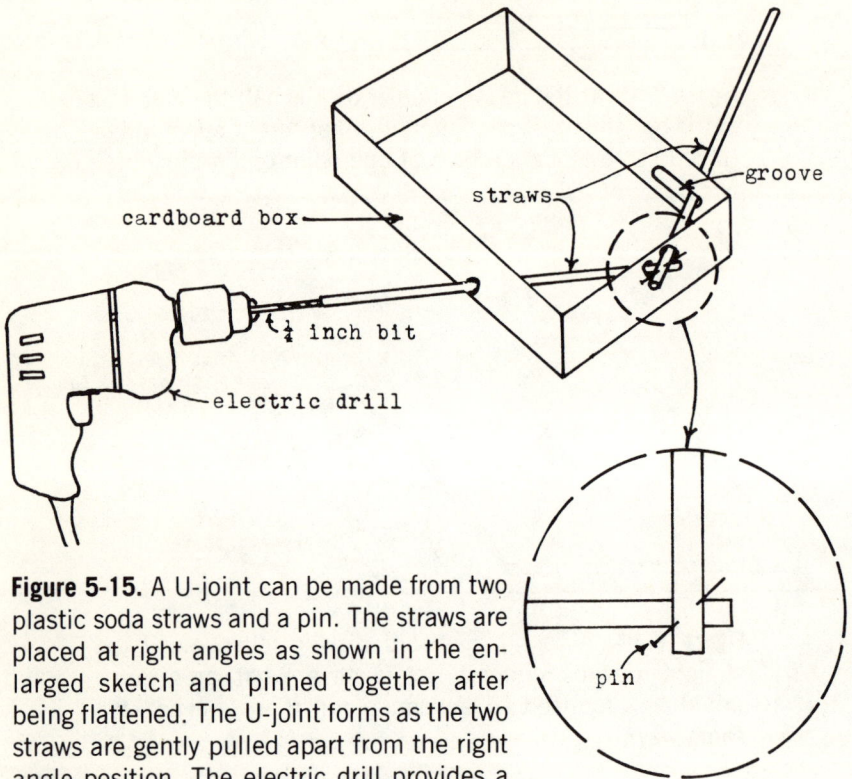

Figure 5-15. A U-joint can be made from two plastic soda straws and a pin. The straws are placed at right angles as shown in the enlarged sketch and pinned together after being flattened. The U-joint forms as the two straws are gently pulled apart from the right angle position. The electric drill provides a good source of power to turn the straws but the demonstration can be done by hand also. The groove allows further changes in the direction of the driven straw.

After the pin is stuck through the two straws, the straws are gently pulled until they are nearly in line. Two little bends will form near the pin and these are the axes which are the essential part of any U-joint. The direction of motion of one shaft can be changed nearly 90 degrees to rotate the other shaft. The pin will gyrate as the straws are twirled.

In order to study the device with more reliability, a U-joint can be constructed from two barn hinges (other hinges will do), a broomstick, a few screws, and a piece of ½ (1.27 centimeter) inch or ¾ inch (1.9 centimeter) plywood. The device is put together as shown in figure 5-16.

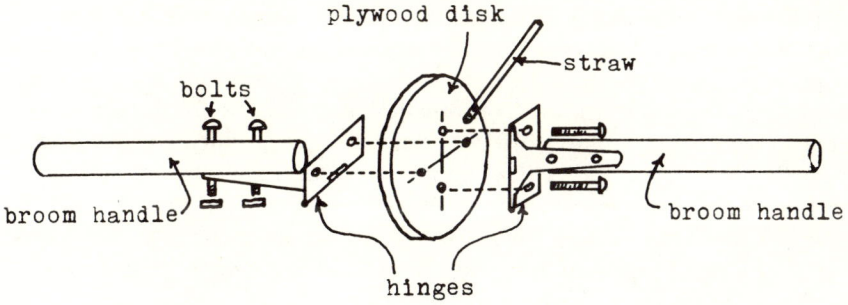

Figure 5-16. This U-joint is sturdy enough for practical use. The plywood does not need to be circular. A straw fastened along the face of the plywood will illustrate its gyrations as the shafts turn.

This is a rather sturdy U-joint, and the transmission of power can be easily observed as well as what happens to the central plywood disk. The greater the angle between the two sections of the broomstick, the more wobbling will the central plywood disk undergo. (It need not be round, but could as easily be a square of plywood). In order to see the effect best and to measure it the two shafts should rotate in sleeves attached to a base as shown in figure 5-17. The base must be firmly clamped or otherwise attached to the tabletop.

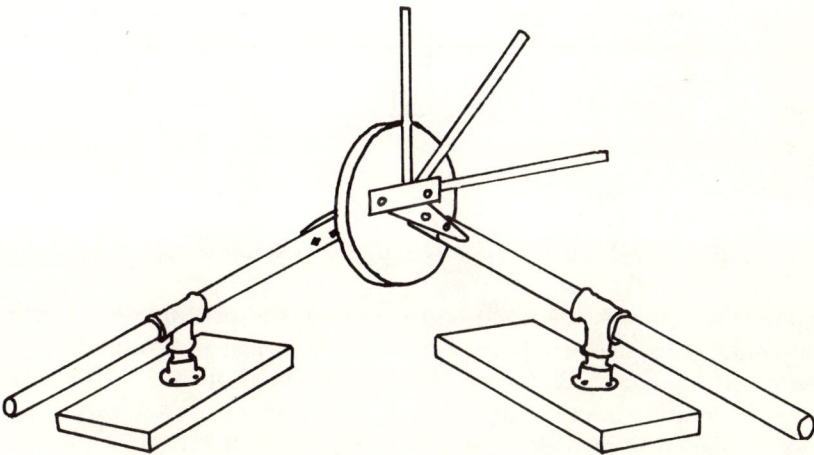

Figure 5-17. The U-joint is on stands for more accurate observation. The straws show how each part of the disk moves while the shafts rotate.

Consider this—each hinge permits flexing along one axis, but when both are combined, flexing can take place along any axis, ie., the joint is "universal." One thing to discover is that the hinge pins do not wobble although they rotate with the broomstick shaft. There are thus two axes on the wobbling, rotating disk, 90 degrees apart, which do not themselves wobble. How can a disk be held at four points around its edge without restraining it from any wobble? Yet the U-joint does wobble. A straw tacked along side a hinge pin will trace out a circle as the shafts rotate. To see the wobble more clearly tack a straw at 45 degrees to either of the hingepins and then rotate the shafts.

Balances and Weighing Devices

Related Math: parallelograms, parallels, equations, ratio, increments, horizontals, angles, verticals

Linkages are used in platform balances. The pegboard strips in figure 5-18 are fastened as are the operating members of a platform

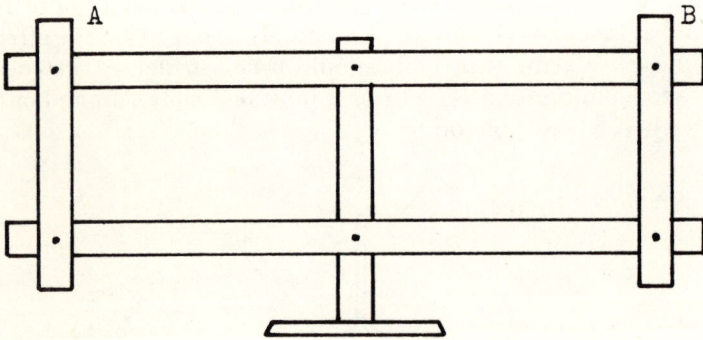

Figure 5-18. This linkage can be made from pegboard strips to simulate the operation of a platform balance.

balance. No matter how each end is tipped, the platform will remain horizontal. In a platform balance, trays are fastened at A and B. Here it is not easy to attach such trays on the ends of the pegboard, so this is not a good operating model. If it is to be used as such the dowel pegs should be well soaped to provide a minimum of friction at each joint.

The "measurements center" should have as many different types of weighing devices as possible. Defunct bathroom scales can be taken apart to observe how they operate, as well as any other inoperative scale which you might obtain. A good metal platform balance is a useful device for weighing pets, grocery items (to check on the labelled weight), and even a large balloon filled with air. See Chapter 3 for other weighing devices which can be made in the classroom.

Finding the Center

Related Math: axes, loci, symmetry, equality, rotation, zero point

If an object spins freely in air (or space) it will rotate so that one point always remains at the center of rotation. We can find this center of rotation (center of mass) by doing a few operations similar to the ones used by an auto mechanic in balancing wheels. To locate the rotation center of a baseball bat, we find the place at which we can balance it on our finger. We can start with a finger at each end and move them in toward one another. Where they meet the bat will balance and we can color a dark ring around the bat at this point. Then if we give the bat a twist and throw it up into the air it will rotate so that the ring will be the center of rotation. We can do essentially the same thing with a piece of pegboard. Any piece will do. Let the pegboard dangle from a nail held in one of the holes. Figure 5-19 shows a method of recording a line drawn vertically from such a hole. The string is chalked by rubbing ordinary chalk on it. As the pegboard and string both dangle, the string is pinched against the pegboard near the bottom with two fingers, and the string is snapped to leave a line of chalk where the string contacted the pegboard. Then another hole is chosen and the operation repeated. The point at which the two chalked lines cross will be the center of rotation. If this point is marked with bright paint and the pegboard is thrown in the air so that it also rotates like a platter, this spot will not rotate but will be the center of rotation. If flourescent paint is available and the room darkened except for a lamp rich in ultraviolet light, the spot will glow and the effect will be more pronounced. If the pegboard is blackened and a small circle of reflecting tape is stuck to the spot, we can see the spot glow in the beam of a projector when the room is darkened. The pegboard will not remain in the air long.

Balancing a Wheel

Related Math: symmetry, axes, zero point, rotation, equality, radius

We have found a significant location on a body (any body) which is known as the *center of mass*. Any material object, or *group of objects*, has a center of mass about which it could rotate if unrestrained. Naturally, we can make an object rotate about other points but when we do we sometimes have trouble because it sets up vibrations which tear the object

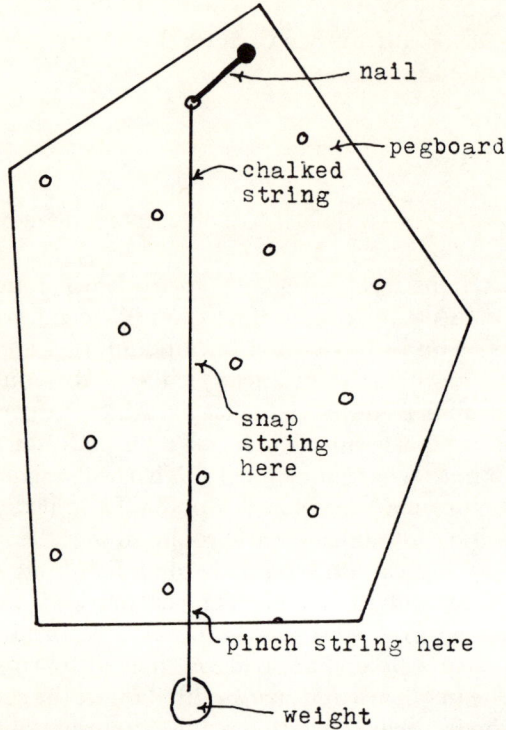

Figure 5-19. The center of mass of the odd-shaped peg-board can be found by snapping two or more chalked lines on it. Then it is thrown in the air and rotated to see if the marked point is the axis of rotation.

apart. We can show this by cutting out a pegboard disk, using a hole in the pegboard as a center for marking the circle we wish to cut. Then we attach a kite string to holes on each side of the central one and spin the disk with the string. With a little practice we can get proficient in making the disk rotate with a hum. But try to make the disk (a button will do) spin when two holes are selected which are off-center. It is very difficult and the vibration of the disk can be seen and felt, just as the wheel of a car which is out of balance can be felt at high speeds. We can try balancing the disk or button ourselves so that even though the string is in off-center holes they are closer to its center of mass (in fact should be on each side of the center of mass for proper balance). A strip of adhesive tape stuck to the right place on the disk will do the trick. Several pieces of tape may be necessary. We are balancing the disk just as a mechanic balances an automobile wheel—he uses lead weights around the rim. Figure 5-20 shows a how the device is made.

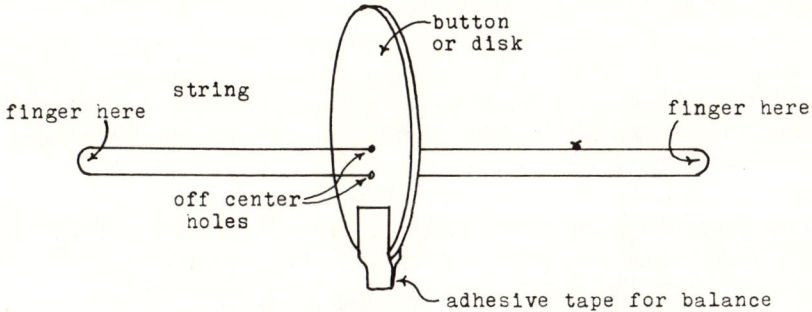

Figure 5-20. When the string is passed through off-center holes in the button or disk it will not rotate as the string is pulled. Adhesive tape can be taped to the disk however to rebalance it and allow it to rotate.

Center of the Earth-Moon System

Related Math: symmetry, ratio, rotation, axes, planes, equations, radial distance, space, points

The earth and the moon have a center about which they rotate. The earth is so much more massive than the moon that the center of rotation is actually within the earth. This center is the center of mass, and if a balance point could be put at this center, the earth-moon would balance there (assuming both were held rigidly so that they could not move apart or together). Likewise, any two *or more* bodies has a center of mass. If an object explodes in space its center of mass will remain located as though the body had not exploded. It follows that the universe (which may be exploding) has a center of mass. Any movement in the universe requires that another, opposite movement take place at the same time so that the center of mass will remain the same. If I move across the classroom something must move in the opposite direction. It is the floor against which I push and the earth itself. Since the earth is a bit more massive than I am I do not detect its movement. Since it can't be measured how can we tell it exists, ie., that Newton's third law is correct (for every action there is an equal and opposite reaction)?

Action and Reaction

Related Math: ratio, symmetry, equality, zero point

We can devise ways of showing how forces act and react and then assume that they behave the same way on a very large scale. Needed is a small wagon or toy car which will roll easily on a tabletop. A rubber band or spring can then eject a pencil or steel rod or ball which should be somewhere near the weight of the wagon. The heavier the weight of the ejected object the greater will be the movement of the wagon in the opposite direction. A compressed spring between two wagons is a good way of obtaining this action-reaction sequence. Another simple way is to suspend two differently weighted balls from strings, so that the balls just touch one another. We slip a triangular piece of styrofoam in the shape of a wedge between the balls (as in figure 5-21) and pull down rapidly on the styrofoam while holding it at its lower tip. The two balls swing out

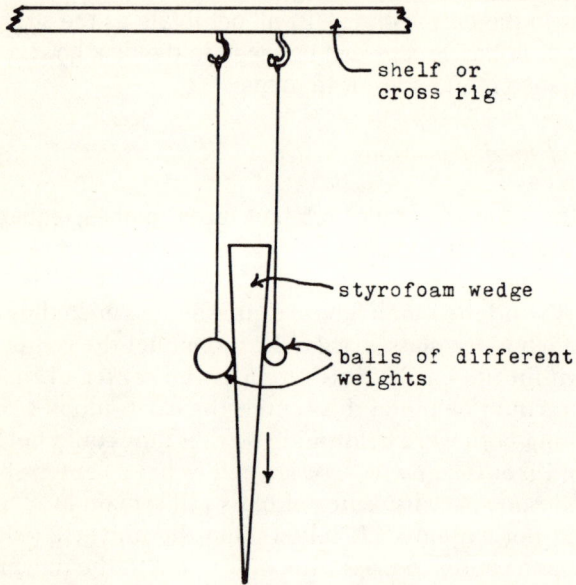

Figure 5-21. When the styrofoam wedge is pulled quickly down the two balls swing apart a distance depending on their relative masses. Which will swing farthest out?

from the styrofoam, but the lighter one swings out much farther. Any two weights will work, and the heavier one always swings out least. If you make a wedge of your hands and move your hands between the two balls quickly the balls will swing apart in the same way.

Two wagons of different weights placed on the edges of tables can be made to roll apart with a wedge between them showing that the heaviest rolls least. This wedge can be made from strap iron bent as shown in figure 5-22. The pencil is used as a means of holding the device

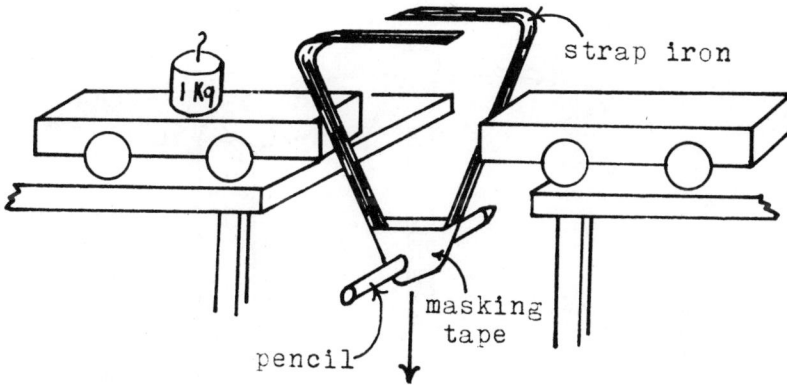

Figure 5-22. This strap iron device can be pulled downward between two wagons to show how a force affects two objects of different mass.

while pulling it down. It must be free to swing and holding by hand inhibits this a bit.

Measuring Small Distances

Related Math: fractions, ratio, zero point, decimal fractions, axis, angular measure

The micrometer offers a good deal of mathematical learning but it is expensive and can be damaged by rough handling. However, an ordinary C-clamp can detect the thickness of a single sheet of paper, and detection is the first step in measurement. The screw of the clamp should be turned by gripping the shaft, not the handle on the end since too much force will crush the paper or indent other material being measured. The jaws of the clamp should touch, not clamp, the object. The handle is useful as a means of measuring how much the screw is turned as in figure 5-23.

The actual thickness of the paper can be figured by determining how far in or out the screw moves during one complete turn of the shaft. It is easier to measure several turns so that if, for instance, there are five turns to the centimeter, then one rotation of the shaft will move the shaft 1/5 of a centimeter. If the handle moves through 1/16 of a turn for a single thickness of paper, then the paper is 1/5 of 1/16 of a centimeter thick or 1/80 of a centimeter, or .0125 centimeter. While any bolt and nut can be rigged to make a crude micrometer, the clamp has the advan-

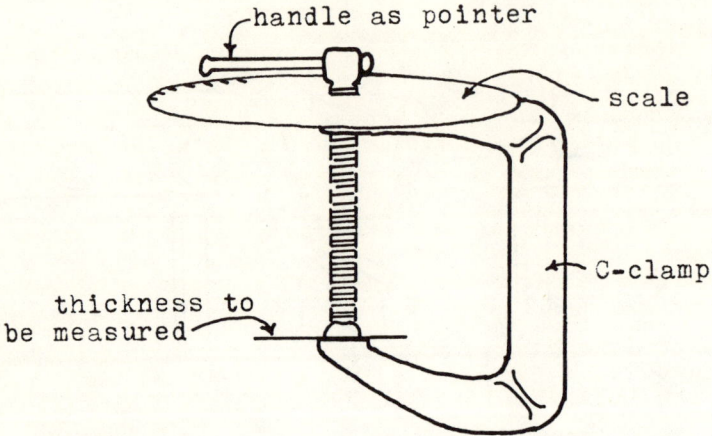

Figure 5-23. The thickness of an object can be obtained by setting it in a C-clamp and adjusting the clamp till it touches the object. Calibration of the C-clamp micrometer can be made with a feeler gauge.

tage of needing no fabrication and the jaws are quite rigid, which is an important consideration.

A feeler gauge should be included in the tools area and this device helps calibrate the C-clamp micrometer. This gauge consists of strips of metal of carefully determined thickness which are printed on each strip. If a gauge can be obtained with a .006 inch (.015 centimeter) strip as the thinnest strip on it, reasonably good calibration of the C-clamp micrometer can be made. The clamp I used, with 3 inch (15.24 centimeter) jaws, could go down to about .003 of an inch (.0076 centimeter). With the thickness gauge as a comparator, the thickness of other unknown material can be obtained reasonably well. A scale in the form of a cardboard disk placed under the handle will allow more precise readings. The jaws of the clamp when closed should be the zero point on the scale.

Puzzles and Problems

1. We have two quarters, and one of them rolls around the other which remains stationary. How many times does the rolling quarter rotate before returning to its original position? (Any coin with knurled edges will do. The knurling prevents slipping of one coin against the other and provides a means of picturing the location of the rolling quarter. For instance, after it has rolled halfway around the stationary quarter, in what position will the rotating quarter be?)

2. The wheel of Aristotle—A circle within a circle rolls along a track as in figure 5-24. If the large circle rolls along track B, the smaller one will then follow track A. How can these tracks, AA' and BB', be the same length? If BB' is one revolution of the larger, then AA', the same length, must be one revolution of the smaller circle—but this is impossible. Why?

Figure 5-24. If the large circle rolls on track BB' does the attached small circle roll on track AA'?

3. In problem 2, if the larger circle rolled on a track around the outside of still another circle, as in figure 5-25, the smaller circle would then actually rotate on a track larger than the larger circle—which is even more impossible, if this can be. Why?

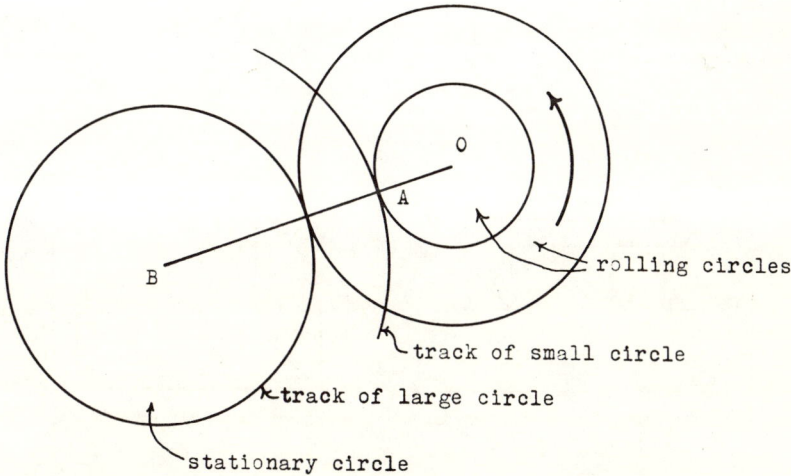

Figure 5-25. The smaller circle has a longer track than the larger one.

The following problems (4-9) and others similar can be worked out
with or without the actual linkages. The linkages in problems 8 and 9
might be interesting enough to construct. An X is a point where the link
is fastened to the table. The links are fastened to one another at the dots.
The object is to draw an arrow to show the direction of motion at B in
each case, resulting from the movement at A indicated by the arrow.

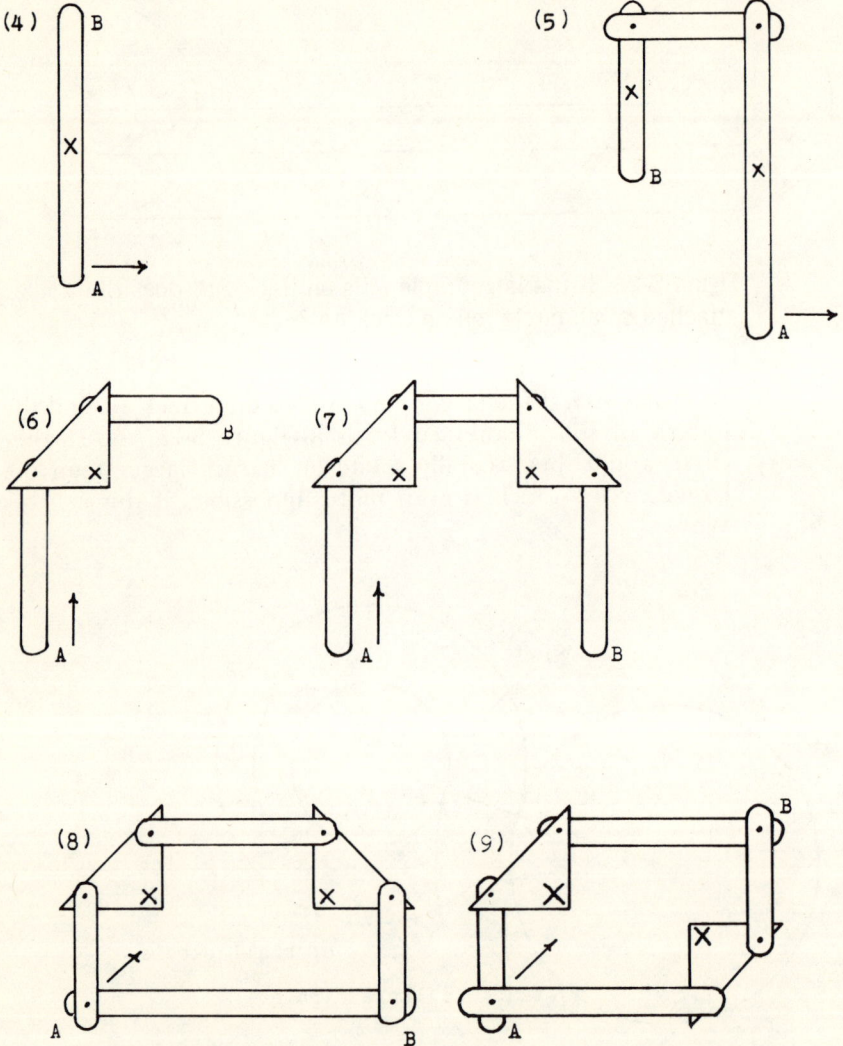

Figure 5-26. The above are some linkage problems which
students might find interesting.

10. In figures 8 and 9, if the letter "F" is traced out at A, what will it look like as it emerges from the machine at B?

11. A family lived in a house supported on a single pillar just one meter on a side as in figure 5-27. The house was 10 meters on a side and the pillar protected it against the frequent floods that occurred in their area. But the family grew, so they doubled the dimensions of their house, and, in order to be sure that the pillar was strong enough to support it, they doubled each side of the pillar. Yet the new pillar bent and the house lay over on its side the first night they spent in it. What did they do wrong?

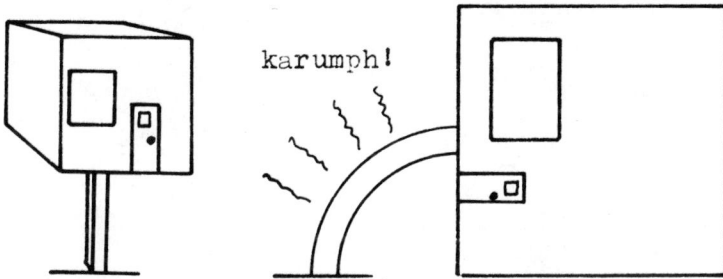

Figure 5-27. The pillar that failed.

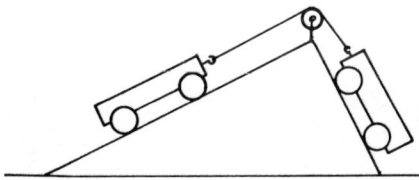

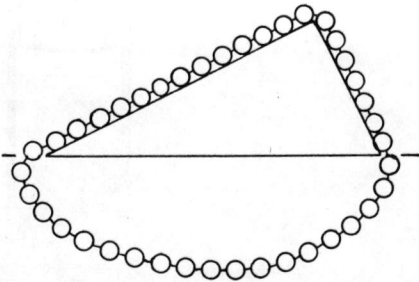

Figure 5-28. If the cars are not in equilibrium, why is the chain?

12. Consider figure 5-28. The car on the steep incline, if it is the same weight as the other one, will pull the other car down. Yet the chain is in equilibrium even though it is draped over the same hill as the cars. We assume that there is a hollow under the hill for the chain to hang down into, and that the chain is frictionless. What could you do to the chain so that it would move as do the cars?

13. In figure 5-29a we have a square pulley with a rope under it and being pulled upward at X. The pulley will turn as shown by the arrow. How far up will the square pulley go in one-quarter turn? How far up will the rope be pulled during one quarter turn of the pulley?

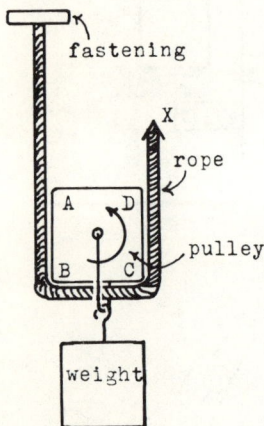

Figure 5-29a. The rope is fastened.

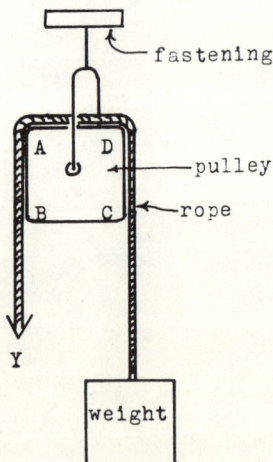

Figure 5-29b. The pulley is fastened.

14. In figure 5-29b we have the square pulley hung from the ceiling with a weight suspended from it to keep the rope taut. When the rope is pulled down at Y the pulley turns. For one-quarter turn of the pulley how far does the rope go down at Y? How far up does the weight go? Which pulley in figure 5-29 might be easier to use to lift a heavy weight?

15. How can you make a rubber band pantograph that distorts?

BIBLIOGRAPHY

Cundy, H. M. and A. P. Rollett. *Mathematical Models.* Oxford: Clarendon Press, 1961. (Good for linkages.)

Inexpensive Science Teaching Equipment Project. *Guidebook*, Vol. III. Science Teaching Center, University of Maryland, College Park, MD, 1972. (Action and reaction carts are described.)

Lockwood, E. H. *A Book of Curves.* New York: Cambridge University Press, 1963.

6

Mental Exercises
in Math

Mathematical concepts include: determinant, function, logic, binary system, tables, graph theory, fractions, probability, topology, arithmetic processes, numbers and number theory, estimating, exponents, decimals, ratio, game strategy

Neuron Games

Related Math: truth tables, Boolean algebra, equations, sequences, binary system

Nerves carry the messages which control body functions and they also interact to produce thought. These "neurons" have their own method of operation, and we can abstract some of these so that they can be dealt with mathematically. One neuron can be activated by something touched, another by something seen, still others are parts of thought processes, or regulation of the heartbeat. Each has a cell body and an extension, or axon, at the end of which there are a number of branches. Impulses travel from the cell body through the axon and out into the branches. From there the impulses trigger other adjacent neurons, or, in some cases, muscles or glands. Many intricate connections between neurons are possible—to the point where thought occurs. Perhaps equally important with activation of one neuron by another is the role of a neuron in inhibiting another from being activated.

142

Rarely does one neuron activate only one other, although this does take place in the eye where the picture received by the eye must be transmitted unblurred to the brain. Let us assume that a neuron requires activation by two "bulbs" as shown in figure 6-1. We oversimplify the neuron in order to see more easily the process of transmission of a nerve impulse. In figure 6-1 the nerve impulse travels from the cell body along the axon and to the bulbs. Since the bulbs are both connected to the same axon, an impulse along the axon activates both bulbs, and neuron 2 is fired. If neuron 1 fires at time t we can say that neuron 2 fires at time t + 1 where the 1 indicates the amount of time necessary for the impulse to travel along one neuron and cross the junction between that neuron and the next one.

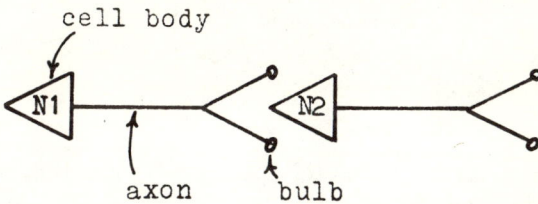

Figure 6-1. If neuron N1 is activated its bulbs will in turn activate neuron N2. There is a time delay so that if neuron N1 is activated at time t, we say neuron N2 is activated at t+1.

A Shorthand Description of Neuron Activity

It is helpful to describe neuron activity mathematically. There are two ways: by a shorthand and by tables. We can abbreviate the statement, "N1 firing at time t" to "N1 (t)." The operation of N1 firing N2 can be abbreviated: If N1 (t), then N2(t+1). This can be further abbreviated to the standard expression: N1 (t) = N2 (t+1).

Suppose the action of the neurons shown in figure 6-2 is to be

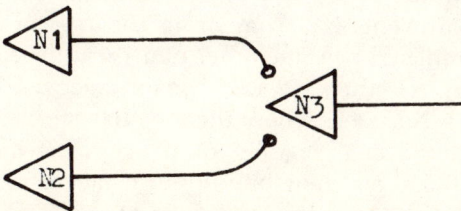

Figure 6-2. Neuron N3 will fire only if both neuron N1 and neuron N2 fire together.

described. We can say in this case: N1 (t) $\wedge$ N2 (t) = N3 (t+1). The inverted V sign means "and." (Already the notation is becoming difficult but it is concise and we will continue just a bit further.) The expression means: "If N1 fires at time t or N2 fires at time t, then N3 will fire at time t+1."

In figure 6-3 if either N1 or N2 fires N3 is activated. We can abbreviate this operation: N1 (t) $\vee$ N2 (t) = N3 (t+1). The V sign means "or" and we read the expression as: "If N1 fires at time t or N2 fires at time t then N3 will fire at time t+1."

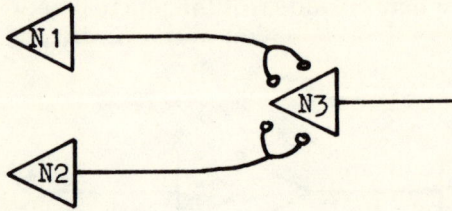

Figure 6-3. Either neuron N1 or neuron N2 is sufficient to activate neuron N3.

Just as complicated actions and thoughts can be inhibited, so one neuron can inhibit the firing of another. In figure 6-4 as long as N1 fires, N2 cannot.

Figure 6-4. The loop at the end of the axon of neuron N1 prevents N2 from firing. If neuron N1 fires at time t, neuron N2 does not fire at t+1 even if other neurons are trying to activate it.

The loop around the cell body is arbitrarily chosen to indicate that the firing of N1 prevents N2 from firing for as long as N1 is active. Thus, if N2 is stimulated by some other neuron at the same time as it is being inhibited by N1, then N2 will remain inactive. This can be abbreviated: N1 (t) = $\overline{\text{N2 (t+1)}}$, where the long bar means "does not fire."

For practice let us analyze a few simple circuits which students can use also. Figure 6-5 shows how one impulse can result in a continual series of impulses—in fact we have provided no way to stop the impulses. If representative, figure 6-5 illustrates the need in the body for continual stimulation such as the heartbeat.

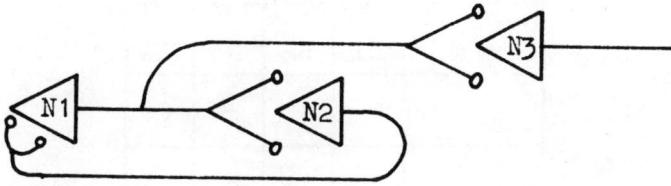

Figure 6-5. A single impulse to N1 will keep this circuit going. N3 fires at t+1, t+3, t+5, etc.

The frequency of the impulses is determined by how long it takes for the nerve impulse to jump the gap or "synapse" between the neurons. If an inhibitory circuit is added we can stop the impulses when we wish, as shown in figure 6-6, where we get three impulses to N3 before N4 inhibits passage. The impulses must be timed so that they arrive together since the inhibitory impulse must act while the exciting impulse acts in order to be effective. In the case of figure 6-6, if N4 fires at a certain time, then N1 will not fire one time unit later, no matter how much it is stimulated.

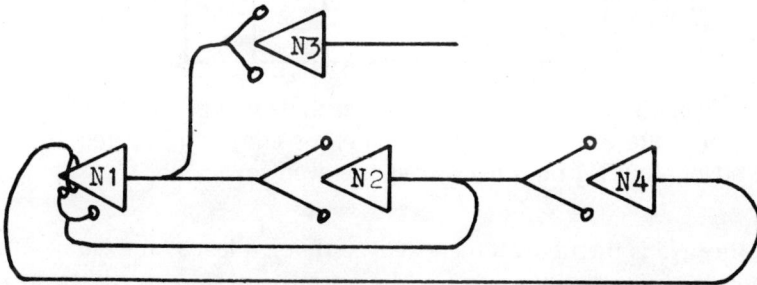

Figure 6-6. This sequence of neurons is already capable of some versatility. A single excitation of neuron N1 will keep the circuit going indefinitely but two excitations of N1 in a row will stop the circuit in 5 time units (t+5).

Neuron Tables

With these admonitions let us make a table, figure 6-7, of the activity in the circuit described in figure 6-6. We imagine a constant series of impulses "rapping at the door" of neuron N1. These impulses are at time t, t+1, t+2, t+3, etc. When a neuron fires we mark an F under its symbol and when it does not fire we mark an O. We start with N1 firing at time t.

	N1	N2	N3	N4
t	F	O	O	O
t + 1	F	F	F	O
t + 2	F	F	F	F
t + 3	O	F	F	F
t + 4	O	O	O	F
t + 5	O	O	O	O
t + 6	F	O	O	O
t + 7	F	F	F	O
t + 8	F	F	F	F

Figure 6-7. This table shows how each neuron in the circuit of figure 6-6 behaves if neuron N1 is constantly excited. Note that N1 does not always fire even so.

Since N3 is the neuron to be activated, ie., it leads on to some other undescribed circuit, we can read the pattern of N3 directly from the table as a cycle of FFFOOOFFF, or "yes yes yes no no no yes yes yes." Note also that the circuit is broken down into elements in the table. If N1 fires, then one time unit later N2 will fire. If N4 fires, then one time unit later N1 will not fire. The heavy line under the t+5 times indicates a complete cycle (the sequence FOOO for t+6 is the same as the first row).

Hot-Cold Sensations

Figure 6-8 shows neurons which give a hot (H2) sensation and those which give cold (C2). N is part of both circuits.

We can see that activating H1 directly activates H2. Activating C1 is more complex and we shall use a table to determine what happens. We shall first consider what happens when C1 is activated only once and then when it is activated repeatedly.

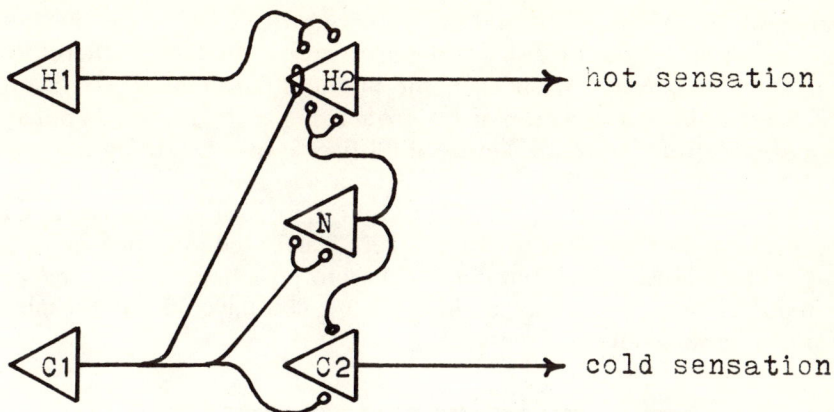

Figure 6-8. This simplified neuron circuit will explain how a momentary cold sensation can appear as a hot sensation. C1 is activated by cold objects and H1 is activated by hot objects.

Since like a crossword puzzle it is easier to fill in first what we know, we can fill in as much as is shown in figure 6-9 without considering much of the circuit. Since C1 is activated just once at time t, we put an F in that

	H1	C1	N	H2	C2
t	O	F	O	O	O
t + 1	O	O			
t + 2	O	O			
t + 3	O	O			

Figure 6-9. This is the start of the neuron table for figure 6-8. C1 is activated just once. H1 is not to be fired in this exercise so its column can be filled in right away. C1 will not be fired again hence the zeroes below the initial firing. Other neurons fire later than C1 hence the zeroes in the first row.

box and zeros under it to indicate only one firing. Also, we can put zeroes for N, H2, and C2 since they are activated by C1 and therefore can fire only *after* time t. Checking the circuit of figure 6-8 we see that if C1 fires at time t nothing can stop N from firing at t+1, so we can put an F in the box for N at t+1. Likewise, if C1 fires at time t, nothing can stop H2 from *not* firing at t+1. So we can put a zero under H2 at time t+1. Looking at the diagram again, this time at C2, we see that both N and C1 must fire at the same time in order to get C2 activated. At time t, according to the table, C1 fires, but not N. Therefore C2 does not fire and we can put a zero in the t+1 square below it. We now have filled in the table for t+1 as shown in figure 6-10.

	H1	C1	N	H2	C2
t	0	F	0	0	0
t + 1	0	0	F	0	0
t + 2	0	0			
t + 3	0	0			

Figure 6-10. The table for the neuron circuit of figure 6-8 is shown complete to time t + 1.

For time t+2, N does not fire because its activator, C1, did not fire at t+1. Therefore, we can put a zero under N for time t+2. H2 can fire, and indeed will since N, its activator, has just fired at t+1, and C1, which *can* stop it, has not fired at t+1. (The explanation is so much longer than the operation. With practice the tables can be filled out quickly—even for complex circuits.) We mark F under H2 at time t+2. C2 cannot fire since both C1 and N have not fired together, hence we give it another zero. We have shown here that a cold sensation can produce the feeling of heat if it is momentary. (At time t+3, all neurons are back to the zero condition.) The complete table is shown in figure 6-11.

In order to see what happens when a series of cold impulses are sent along C1, we start with an F in each column of C1 and work out the details as before. We wind up with the diagram shown in figure 6-12. A cold sensation is felt, indicated by the F's in the C2 column, and they are not preceded by a hot feeling. Does this all seem to be in accord with the facts? Try it with a piece of ice. They say it works.

	H1	C1	N	H2	C2
t	O	F	O	O	O
t + 1	O	O	F	O	O
t + 2	O	O	O	F	O
t + 3	O	O	O	O	O

Figure 6-11. This is the completed neuron table for the circuit of figure 6-8 when the cold sensing neuron C1 is activated once.

	H1	C1	N	H2	C2
t	O	F	O	O	O
t + 1	O	F	F	O	O
t + 2	O	F	F	O	F
t + 3	O	F	F	O	F
t + 4	O	F	F	O	F

Figure 6-12. This is the completed neuron table for the circuit of figure 6-8 when C1 is activated continuously (a continous sensation of cold).

It is fun to make up circuits and then make tables of them. For clarity of results, one neuron should trigger the circuit, as the "entrance neuron." If there is more than one neuron entrance then operation of the circuit becomes involved and actually behaves like two circuits or more, depending on the number of entrance neurons. No matter how complex the circuit, however, they all seem to yield to the table form of representation. We are dealing with elementary thought and it is interesting to speculate what the circuits "mean." No matter what circuit we devise, it probably is used somewhere in the brain. And any circuit can become the "gate" for another. When we consider that any neuron in any circuit can trigger other neurons which lead to other circuits we begin to see how complex a system we have. The neurons described here have only a few connections to others and require only two bulbs to be fired. Real neurons frequently have hundreds of bulbs and can fire up to one hundred other neurons. Besides actually firing other neurons, a neuron can excite others so that they might be fired more easily. In our diagram it is like the firing of one neuron which has only one bulb near the body of another neuron. Since two bulbs are necessary for firing, the second neuron is not fired, but it is closer to being fired.

Not So Secret Codes

Related Math: binary numbers, addition, zeroes

With adding machine tape and a paper punch we can make a series of punches on the tape which will spell a word according to a simple system of addition. Figure 6-13 shows how this is done. We must have

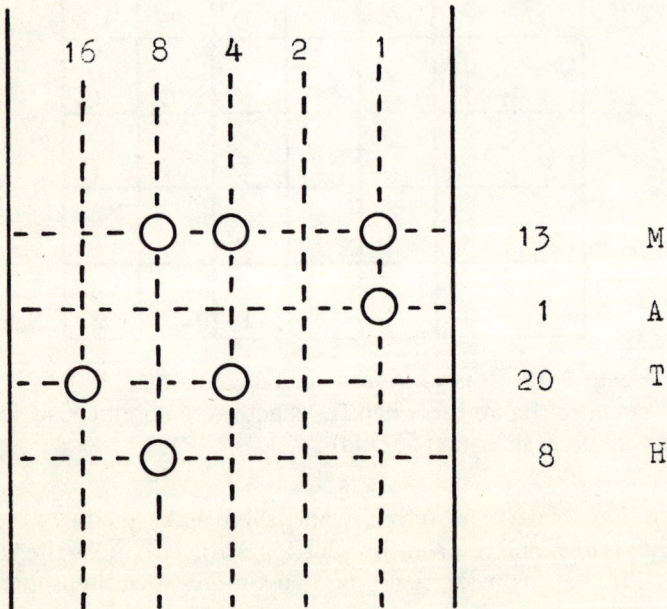

Figure 6-13. Adding machine tape can be punched to form numbers representing the letters of the alphabet.

five tracks along the paper and across these tracks at regular intervals are letters punched across the paper according to our code.

In this coding system, in which a line across the tape intersects a track, we can punch a hole or leave the intersection unpunched. Therefore, there are only two possibilities for each intersection. We simply add the value of each track that has a punch in it. In the figure 6-13 we have shown the sums in the decimal system (13, 1, 20, 8) and if we number each letter in the alphabet in order, we obtain the word "math" for this sequence. The tape record we have produced is very similar to telemeter tape in which the punched circles are read electronically and automatically operate typewriter keys to print out the message on the tape. If such tape is available—already used—its message can be deciphered.

Making the Code Binary

If we examine the placement of the punched circles in figure 6-13 and replace them with "1's" (placing zeroes where 1's are absent) we will obtain binary numbers. For the word "math" we obtain: 1101 - 1 - 10100 - 1000. Using this method, we can write words on ordinary paper. Writing the words in a column is less confusing than in a row. Thus the word "mathematics" would look like this:

(See abacus section, this chapter for more on the binary system).

1101

1

10100

1000

101

1101

1

10100

1001

11

10011

Networks

Related Math: graph theory, fractions, inverting

An interesting game can be played with paper and pencil which has applicability to traffic patterns, irrigation, and electric circuits. We first

start with a pipe, represented by a pencil line, which then divides. If it
divides in two, we assume half of whatever the pipe carries goes into each
branch. If it divides in three, then each branch gets 1/3 of what was in the
original. Figure 6-14 shows a fairly simple circuit.

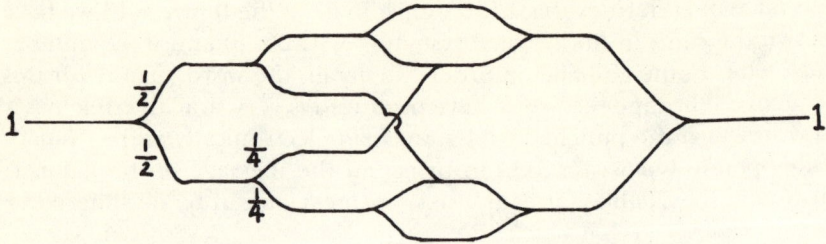

Figure 6-14. This network shows how the "pipe" divides.
Since we assume there are no leaks, the amount leaving
the network is the same amount entering. Can you determine the other fractional parts in each branch?

Note that one pipe goes in and one pipe comes out. The unit divides
into fractions and then its parts rejoin to reappear as one unit again. The
challenge is to find some network which requires a little thought to solve.
One which is a bit puzzling is to arrange the pipe in the form of a cube as
shown in figure 6-15.

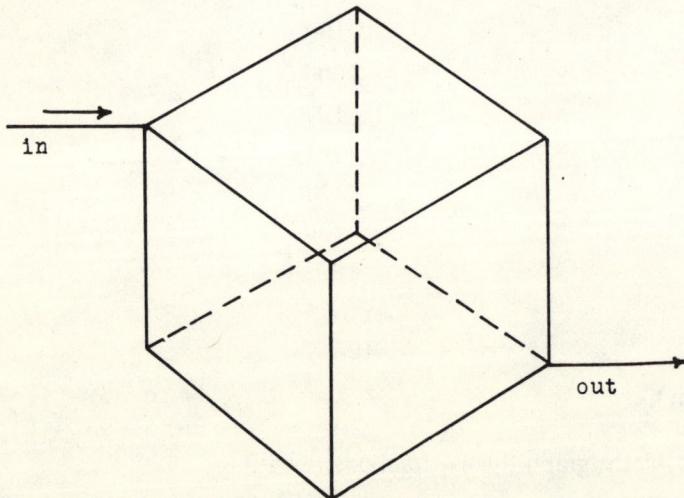

Figure 6-15. This cubic arrangement of pipes disguises the
direction of flow in many of the segments.

The pipe divides into three on the way in and three branches rejoin on the way out. These can easily be connected in the line of flow as in figure 6-16. Connecting the remaining branches properly so that they all lie in the direction of flow is an interesting exercise which we will not complete here. There is a complication in this work in which branching results in a pipe lying across the route as in figure 6-17.

Figure 6-16. The three entrance and the three exit pipes of the cubic arrangment of figure 6-15 are shown. Can you connect the rest of the pipes properly?

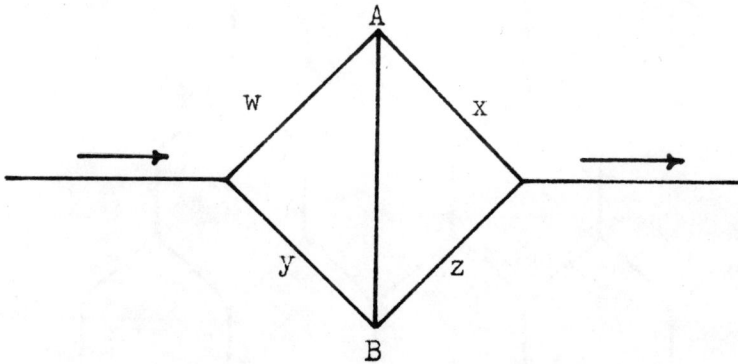

Figure 6-17. Pipe AB lies across the direction of flow. What determines if there is any flow through it?

Ideally, we can expect no flow through pipe AB. But if one of the pipes lettered w, x, y, or z is longer or in any way restricted, then a flow will take place across AB. In our discussion on the branching of pipes we did not consider length in any branch. We can find sufficiently complex arrangements even so. If we did consider length and constructed pipes in the outline of a rectangular box we would have a more complicated problem. Less flow will take place through the longer pipes (assuming all the segments have a uniform diameter).

Probability Board Branching

Another branching illustrates the probability board discussed in
Chapter 4. This is shown in figure 6-18.

Note that the outermost branches each carry half as much as their
preceding branch but that inner ones have rejoinings which result in the
fractions listed across the base of the figure. Since there are six termini in
figure 6-18, what would the network fractions be like if these termini
became the entrance to the network rather than the exit? If each of the
six new entrances carried 1/6 of the total of whatever is in the pipe as

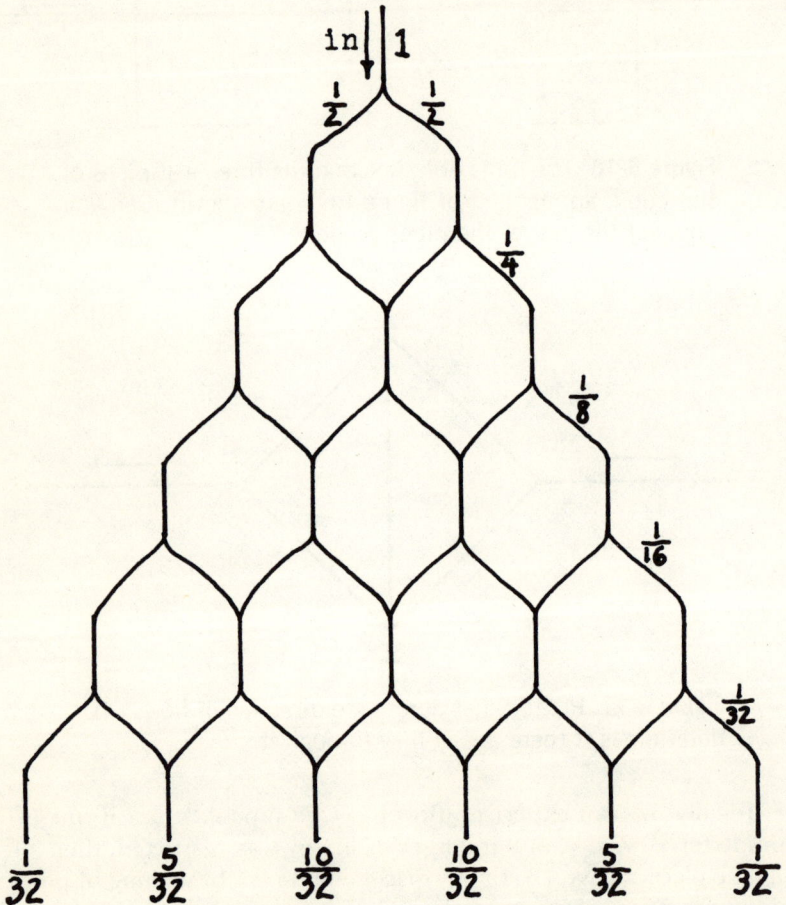

Figure 6-18. This branching of pipes closely resembles the
"probability board" (Pascal's triangle) of Chapter 4.

shown in figure 6-19 (a backward Pascal triangle) we would have most of the material carried on the margins, unlike before where less was carried there. Would the fractions be the same if we started with the proportions shown at the bottom of figure 6-18 and worked backward up to the top? We might dub this situation a "reverse Pascal."

It is worthwhile exploring the byways of any new idea. In this case a network of the units of figure 6-19 might be folded onto itself to form a tube similar in appearance to a net stocking. Figure 6-20a is a sketch of one section of a simple three dimensional network. Figures 6-20b, c, and d show various ways of diagramming the network.

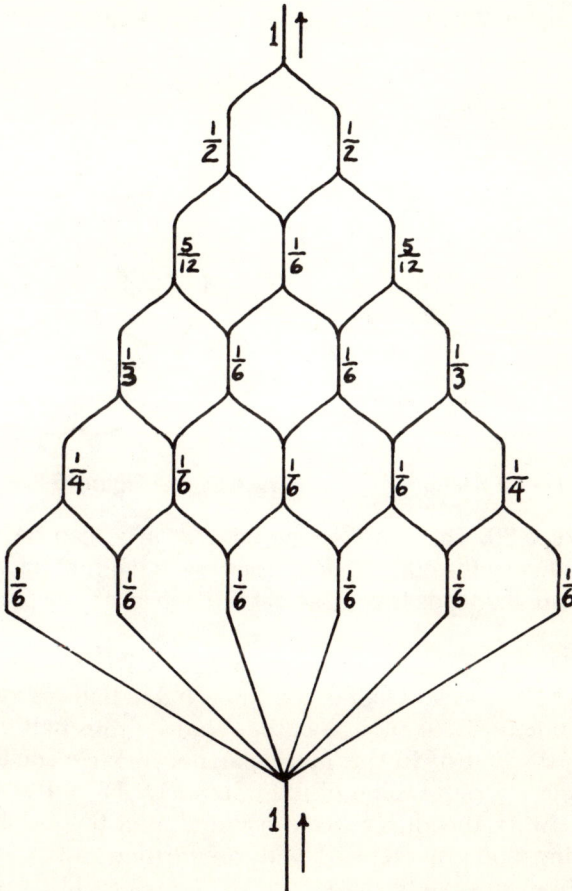

Figure 6-19. The flow in this system is opposite from the usual Pascal triangle. The amount in the outer pipes increases uniformly while the amount in the inner ones remains constant.

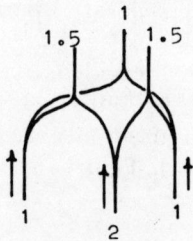

Figure 6-20a.

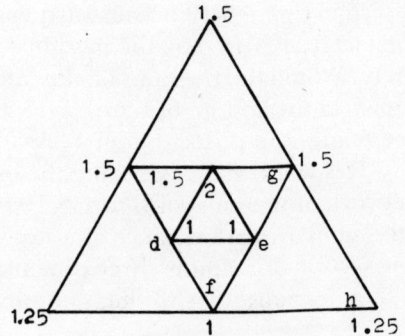

Figure 6-20b.

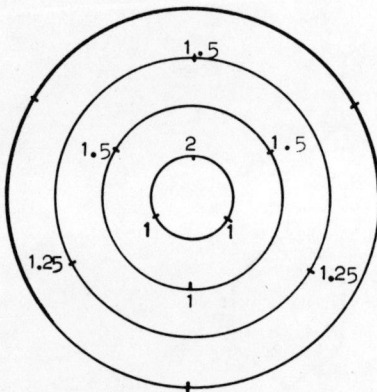

Figure 6-20c.

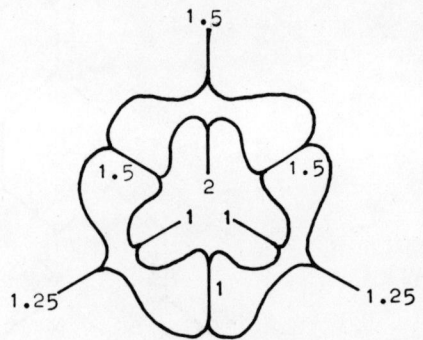

Figure 6-20d.

Figure 6-20. The original pipe network in a. can be represented by the other figures. The flow in the first figure is
upward and tends to average out differences in the pipes.

The rules for filling the triangles or circles are the same as before.
As shown in 6-20b, we add half of the value at d to half the value at e and
obtain the value for f. Likewise, half the value at f plus half the value at g
gives us the value at h. In this particular network we started with one
branch having twice the value of the others (1,2,1), but as we progress
along the network this difference in value diminishes. At figure 6-20d
we are looking along the network with the farther end stretched out so
that all the branches can be drawn without crossing. This last design is a
rather intriguing one. Similar ones resembling stained glass windows can
be developed, starting with four or five branches, or any number, as long
as we have enough patience to tie them together and branch them again
properly.

The Abacus

Related Math: arithmetic processes, number systems, decimals, factors, multiples, modulus principle

The abacus is a versatile and beautifully simple instrument for illustrating the structure of various number systems. It also provides a rather intriguing method of practicing addition and subtraction. Here we will discuss the use of the Chinese and Japanese abacus. These instruments will continue to be useful to the student long after he has left the classroom.

A 15 rod Japanese abacus is available from Edmund Scientific Co., Barrington, New Jersey. A 9 rod type is satisfactory for classroom use. It will allow numbers with 9 digits to be set. The abacus work may be done with the whole class if sufficient abaci are on hand. The clicking of beads as a whole class works on a problem can give a teacher reassurance that all is going well, at least at that point of time. An abacus and study sheets can be kept at the measurements center for individual work. Most students enjoy working with the abacus. Minimum help from the teacher is needed if a series of study sheets of increasing difficulty are developed (see end of chapter).

The basic idea of the abacus is to record by movable beads the value of a number. Once a number is "set" on the abacus another number may be added to it with about as much ease (to the practiced operator) as if the first number was not there. Thus sums can be recorded on the abacus about as rapidly as numbers can be set on it. Figure 6-21 shows a Chinese and a Japanese abacus each with the number 637 set on it. Beads have been moved to the bar from above and below the bar. These are the beads which we count. The beads above the bar on the rod farthest to the right count 5 and those below count 1. The beads on the next rod to the left each count 10 times more, thus they count 10 below the rod and 50 above. This increase in value continues so that the third rod is the hundreds place, the fourth rod is the thousands place, etc.

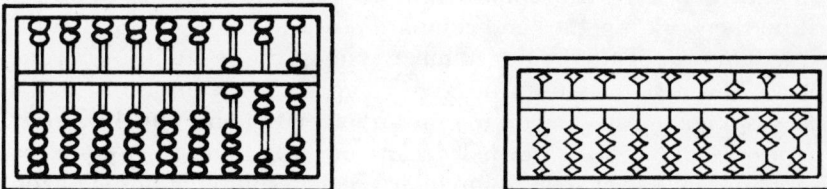

Figure 6-21. A Chinese abacus is at the left and Japanese at the right. Each has the number 637 set on it.

The advantage of the Chinese abacus is that less must be carried in the head of the operator. It is easier for the beginner and will be the one used in this chapter for computations in the decimal system. To streamline it, the topmost and bottommost beads can be taped, and it becomes a Japanese abacus. Suppose 20 is added to the number 637. On the Chinese abacus the two remaining ten beads in the second row from the right can be pushed up to the bar. Since there are now five beads in this second row they may be exchanged for one bead above the bar. When 20 is added to 637 on the Japanese abacus a different approach must be used since there is only one bead left unmoved on the second rod from the right. We can add 20 by bringing down the 5 bead on the rod (actually this bead has a value of 50) while returning the three beads to their position away from the bar. In effect we add 50 and subtract 30. If we add 4 to 637 on the Chinese abacus the same problem arises of not having enough counters. This operation of subtracting in one's head means that the operator is an active participant in finding sums and perhaps accounts for the interest students often develop in the device.

Getting Used to the Abacus

The following are a few hints in getting started with the abacus.

1. The abacus must be used with the rods horizontal. If they are inclined the beads tend to fall out of position. This is one source of error. Sometimes a too violent push will result in beads moving out of place, also.

2. An exercise which helps get used to addition on the abacus is to add 6's up to about 60. On the Chinese abacus this can be done with a minimum of mental addition. Adding 2's up to 30 is more difficult, as is 3's or 4's or 8's. Adding 7's is tricky and good practice. The operator of the abacus will become aware of patterns as he adds a number continuously since the various placements of the beads will recur.

3. Adding columns of figures is a standard and rather deadly method of drill in arithmetic classes. Use of the abacus gives such addition a flavor and serves to fix in students minds the facts of addition just as well. If there are sufficient abaci for each student it is good to have a class do the work together and compare results.

4. The use of the binary number system can be studied with the abacus. This system is used in large computers and its use with the abacus is a good introduction to other number systems. For the binary system only one bead is needed on any one rod. The rest should be covered or taped over so as not to interfere with computations. The top section of a Japanese abacus has only one bead on it and can be used as is. The one bead when moved to the rod counts 1 and when moved away from the rod counts 0. Counting in the binary system goes this way: 1,

10, 11, 100, 101, 110, 111, 1000, 1001, 1010, 1011, etc. Only 1 and 0 appear in the system. Some of these numbers are illustrated in figure 6-22. In actuality, of course, 10 in the binary system has all the characteristics we give to 2 in our common decimal system. Other number systems can be studied by using the proper number of beads on each rod. A two bead system, for instance, would be counted as 1, 2, 10, 11, 12, 20, 21, 22, 100, 101, etc. Addition and subtraction operations in such systems could be performed on the abacus as long as the proper number of beads was placed on the rods.

Figure 6-22. The top row of a Japanese abacus can be used as is for the binary system. 10 and 1110 are set in the above figures showing part of the top row.

A Trial and Error Slide Rule

Related Math: estimating, bisectors, exponents, logarithms, decimals, averages, arithmetic processes

This can be a reasonably accurate instrument if made carefully, but it is better to make an inaccurate instrument than to tediously mark lines to within an accuracy of a half millimeter. It is the process of manufacture as much as its use afterwards which is instructive. Two strips of paper with straight edges or thin cardboard are required for drawing the lines and serving as multipliers. Figure 6-23 is a step-by-step explanation of how to begin.

As the instrument is constructed, the pattern which emerges is that the distance between each number remains the same since we added the same distance each time. But the numbers marking off these distances increase more rapidly—in fact they double. Also, examining the distance between the end of the rule and 4, we find it is the same as the distance between 4 and 16. We might expect then that if we could locate "3" that doubling the distance between the end of the rule and 3 would give us 9. Other numbers can be put on the slide rule. Figure 6-24 is a step-by-step explanation of this.

The numbers 5 and 7 are also obtained by estimating. 24 can be found by the labelling of the product of 8 and 3. Folding the rule in two on the 24 mark will give the square root of 24, or 4.9. This is close to 5

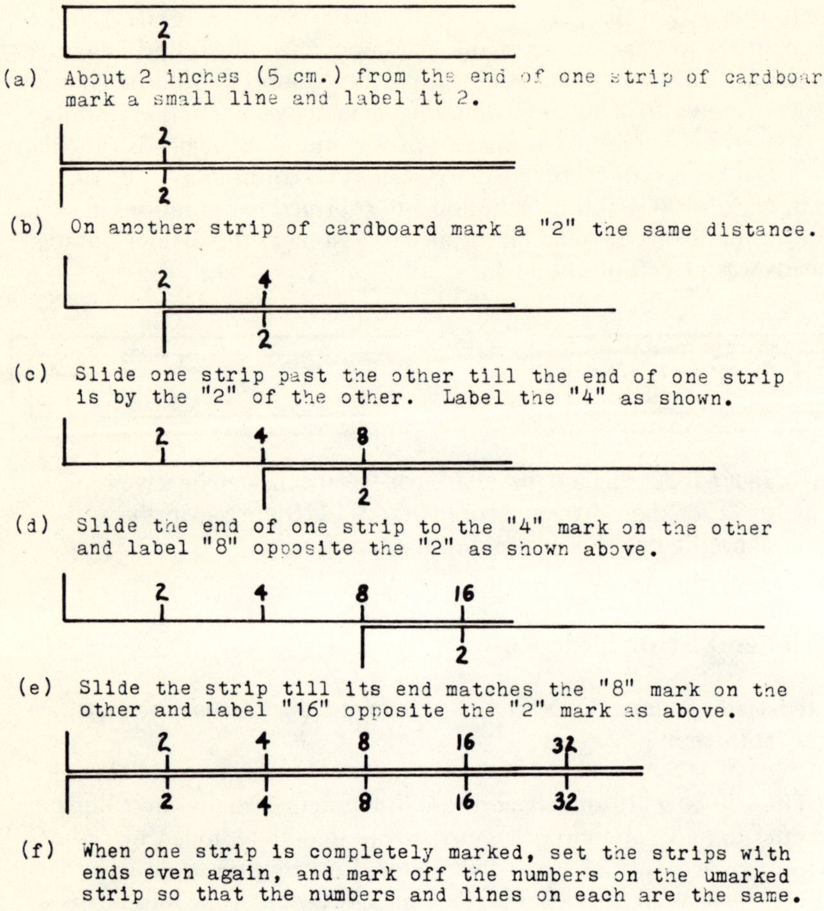
2
(a) About 2 inches (5 cm.) from the end of one strip of cardboard, mark a small line and label it 2.
2
2
(b) On another strip of cardboard mark a "2" the same distance.
2 4
2
(c) Slide one strip past the other till the end of one strip is by the "2" of the other. Label the "4" as shown.
2 4 8
2
(d) Slide the end of one strip to the "4" mark on the other and label "8" opposite the "2" as shown above.
2 4 8 16
2
(e) Slide the strip till its end matches the "8" mark on the other and label "16" opposite the "2" mark as above.
2 4 8 16 32
2 4 8 16 32
(f) When one strip is completely marked, set the strips with ends even again, and mark off the numbers on the umarked strip so that the numbers and lines on each are the same.

Figure 6-23. Beginning steps of the Do-it-yourself slide rule.

and we can find the square root of 27, which is 5.2, in order to give us another mark a little more than 5. Then 5 can be estimated between the two marks.

The number seven can be found by a study of 12. The number which when multiplied by itself equals 12 is 3.464. When this is multiplied by two we get 6.928, a good number for a lower limit. For an upper limit we can multiply 1.414 by 5 and obtain 7.07. Between these two numbers we estimate 7.

We can now find half of 5, half of 7, half of 9, and a third, or a fifth, or a seventh of various numbers. One error in marking a number will lead to errors in all numbers based on it. The slide rule can be checked

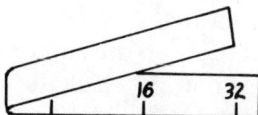

(a) Mark off on the strip half the distance to the "32" mark. This distance can be found by folding the strip in two.

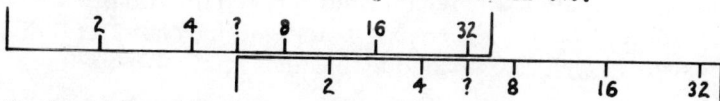

(b) Fit the two strips together as above. The position of the question mark should be half way between 4 and 8 as well. The value of this point is 5.66 or the square root of 32 (see appendix for square root table).

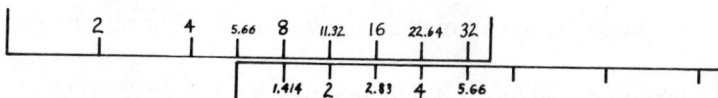

(c) Once 5.66 is found, the other numbers shown above can be found. 5.66 x 2 = 11.32 etc.

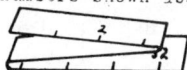

(d) By folding the strip in thirds we can obtain a mark for the cube root of 32 which is 3.18.

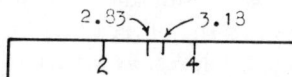

(e) The mark for "3" can be placed midway between 2.83 and 3.18. This is close enough for our purpose. Once "3" has been obtained, then 6, 9, 12, etc. can be found.

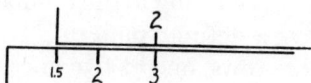

(f) The "1.5" mark can be determined as shown above. Many other numbers can be marked by a similar method.

Figure 6-24. Filling in the slide rule.

by multiplying several of the numbers already marked to see if the result falls in the right place. It is not so much the accuracy of the instrument which is critical here, but the process of laying out and studying numbers and how these numbers must change when we add two lengths to obtain a product. If the student is stimulated to make a more accurate second slide rule perhaps he learns as much or more than if his first instrument is sufficient. Log graph paper can be cut in strips and used to make up a serviceable slide rule. It should be pasted, without stretching, onto heavy paper, wood, or pressed wood.

The lower end of a slide rule is labelled "1." This is not too difficult to determine since the product of a number and "1" is that number, so if we place the "2" mark of one strip over the "2" mark of the other, the ends will coincide. But the 1 on the end of the slide rule could also be .1 or 100 or 10,000. If it is not 1, then all the other numbers we marked on the rule are changed by a factor of 10, also.

Division can be done with the slide rule, and, after some practice with multiplication, the relationship between the two processes can show how to do division. Set 3 x 2 = 6 and you have also set 6 divided by 3 equals 2, as well as 6 divided by 2 equals 3.

Paper and Pencil Games

Related Math: inductive method, tables, number theory, the paradox

Games are so much fun in a math class that the teacher may become guilty about playing them, or allowing students to. They provide a hearty break from the usual routine and should be pursued as long as interest holds. One such game is the 20 line game. A row of 20 lines is placed on the blackboard or paper, and each of the two players takes turns in erasing or crossing out one, two, or three lines starting from one end and working toward the other end of the row. The one who crosses out the last line wins (or loses, as a variation). There is a very definite strategy necessary to win the game, but it is better to develop the strategy by playing. As with many such games, a good method of attack is to simplify. Who wins and how would he win if only one line is used, two lines, three, etc.? A table of winner and loser, according to the number of lines with which the game started, will have a definite pattern.

Nim is a closely related game with three rows, one of five lines, one of four, and one of three. Players take turns removing any number of lines from any one row during each turn. The last one to remove a line wins or loses as desired. Again, a strategy can be developed by first considering just one line in each row, and then adding lines, each time determining who is the winner.

Mathematical riddles are also an important addition to the math class. In this category also are the optical and sensory illusions whose understanding forces us to rely on logic rather than the senses. Martin Gardner of the *Scientific American* magazine has done much to popularize such riddles, particularly the type whose answer requires breaking a usual pattern of thought. For instance, why should a barber in Geneva prefer to cut the hair of two Frenchman, rather than one German? Some readers will find this completely obvious: the barber gets more money. Others will be completely mystified. There are many riddles and problems we cannot solve, not because they are difficult, but because our thought patterns lead away from the solution. How many times higher is the sixth floor than the third floor? Twice as high? Not if you draw a diagram and number the flights of stairs.

Puzzles and Problems and Riddles

1. Make up a table of the following circuits (figure 6-25), according to the time of each neuron firing (F) or not firing (0). Two bulbs from another neuron, or neurons, are needed to fire a neuron and both bulbs must be firing at the same time. A loop around the body of a neuron means that neuron is inhibited by the neuron attached to the loop. One neuron firing at time "t" will cause a neuron properly excited by two of its bulbs to fire at time "t+1." The first table is shown partly completed. Assume that N1 fires at every time interval.

2. Place a familiar mathematical expression between 1 and 2 to obtain a number greater than 1 and less than 2.

3. A father and a son are sitting on a porch. "I am a father," said one. "I am a son," said the other. Who is which if at least one of them is lying?

4. Why is a manhole cover circular rather than square?

5. A goose weighs 10 pounds and ½ of its weight. How much does it weigh?

6. From the cardboard back of a standard size paper (8½ x 11 inches) cut the shape shown in figure 6-26.

Split a ½ inch (1.25 centimeter) dowel at the end with a knife so that the cardboard can be squeezed into the split as shown. Hold the dowel with the cardboard above it at arms length in a dimly lit room and turn the dowel slowly in one direction for several complete turns with one eye closed. As you turn the dowel the cardboard above it seems to move one way for half a turn, then it seems to turn in the opposite direction. A window sash with four panes of glass can be drawn on the cardboard to strengthen the illusion. If someone else turns the cardboard, then the conflict between what you are doing (turning in one direction) and what you see (a back and forth motion) will not be so strong, but you may see the illusion more easily by changing your position until the back and forth motion appears. Use a black background and light the cardboard from different directions until the illusion is so strong you can see it with both eyes open. Then punch a sharpened pencil through the middle of the cardboard so that it is stuck there and observe what affect this has. You will find two visual impressions in sharp conflict. (The pencil will seem to move through the cardboard noiselessly and without rupturing it.)

7. Cross the second and third fingers and press down with them on a marble. Two marbles will be felt. Why? Is there any habit pattern here which is being altered?

(a)

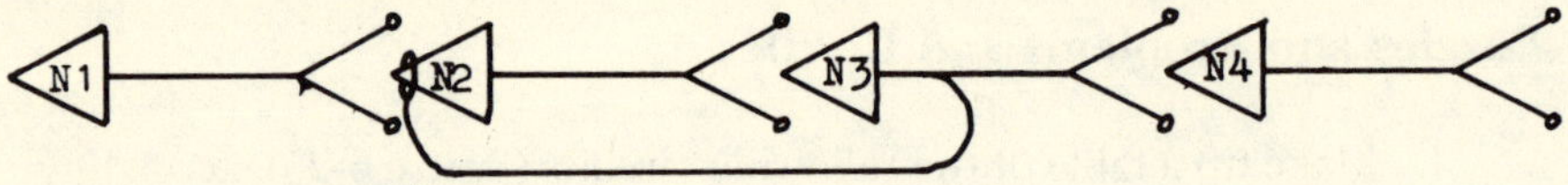

		N1	N2	N3	N4
t		F			
t + 1		F			
t + 2		F			
t + 3		F			
t + 4		F			
t + 5		F			

Figure 6-25. Each neuron circuit can be described in the form of a table such as the one for (a) begun on the left.

(b)

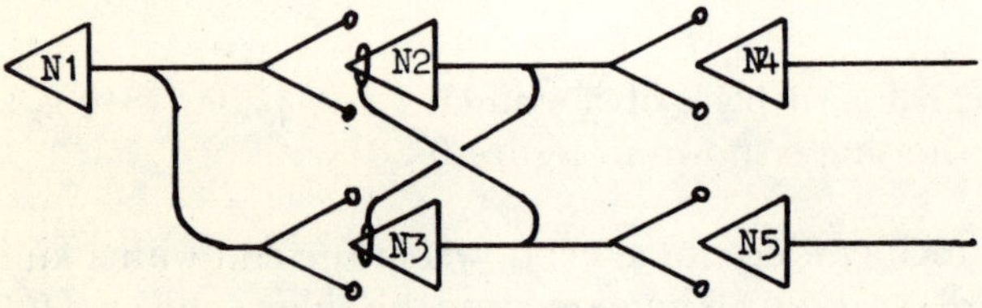

(c)

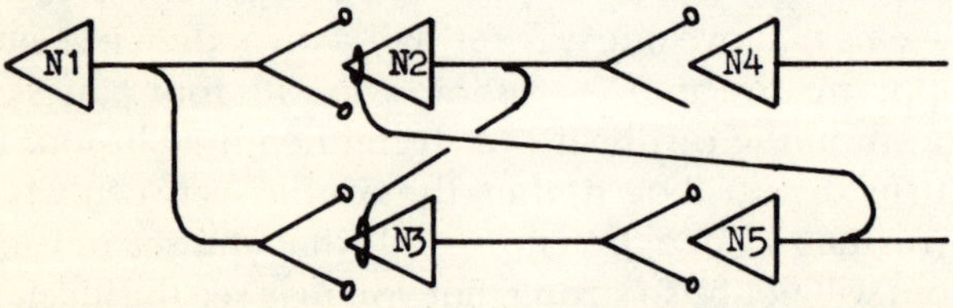

(d)

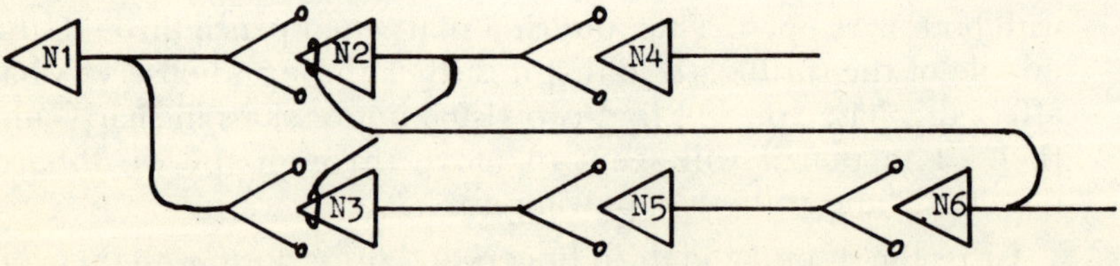

heavy cardboard

$8\frac{1}{2}''$
(22 cm)

—11''—
(28 cm)

$4\frac{1}{4}''$ (11 cm)

$\frac{1}{2}''$ dowel about 1 foot or more long, or 2 cm by 30 cm.

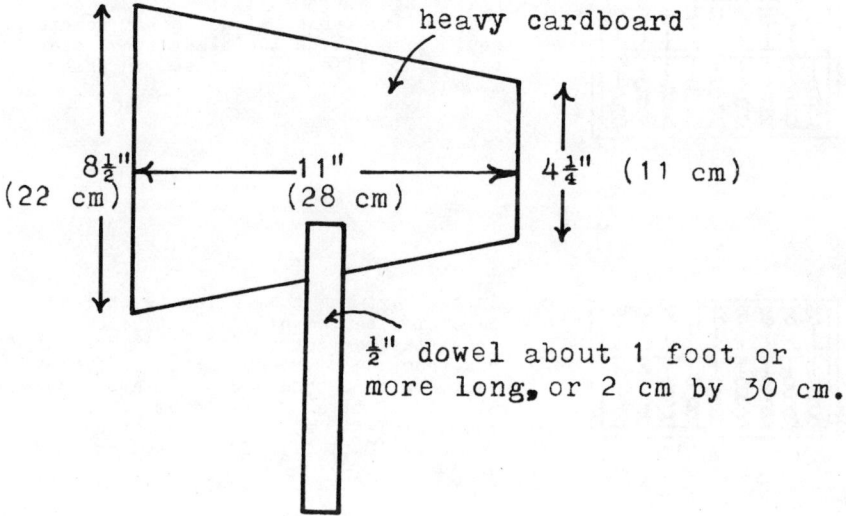

Figure 6-26. If the cardboard is rotated slowly by the dowel it seems to go backward and forward. The illusion is stronger with a dark background.

8. If one marble can be made to feel like two, can we get two to feel like one? Cross your second and third fingers and hold two marbles on the now outside edges of your fingers. A stronger illusion is possible by holding two pencils (or having someone else hold them) against those parts of your crossed fingers which usually are in contact with a pencil.

9. Why does a slide rule begin with the number 1 rather than 0 as on an ordinary ruler?

10. Twin sisters, yet only one has a nephew. How come? Can they have a brother with sons?

The following exercises are designated for the student to use without much additional instruction by the teacher. Those who do not read well will need help and the teacher should be ready to give assistance when needed. A Chinese abacus is shown but a Japanese abacus will do nicely.

Abacus I

It is easy to add using an abacus. You will notice that the beads move freely on the rods. If we wish to set a number on the abacus we move beads to the center according to certain rules as shown in figure 6-27.

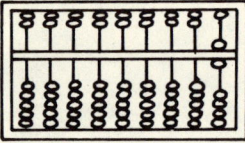

a. In the row farthest to the right, each
    of the five beads below the bar counts
    one. Each of the two beads above the
    bar counts five. Six is set on this
    abacus.

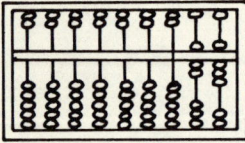

b. In the next row to the left each bead
    below the bar counts "10" and each bead
    above the bar counts "50". In the third
    row from the right each bead below the
    bar counts 100 and each bead above counts
    500. In fact as you go from one rod to
    the next left, each bead increases in
    value by 10 times. "78" is set on this
    abacus.

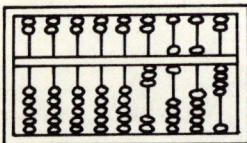

c. What is the value set on each abacus? In
    the last figures the unimportant parts
    have been left out.

_____?

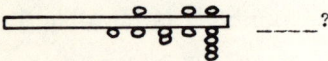

____?

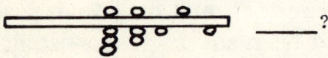

_____?

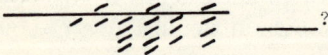

_____?

Figure 6-27.

Adding numbers on the abacus is not much more difficult than setting numbers. How do we add? Just set one number, and then add another number right on top of it. This is explained in figure 6-28.

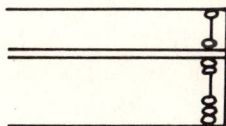
a. This is 7. If we wish to add 7 to it we bring down the other "5" bead to the bar and two of the "1" beads up to the bar.

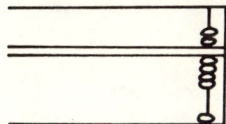
b. This is 14. In order to make any further adding easy we can "exchange" the two "5" beads from the first rod for a "10" bead on the second rod.

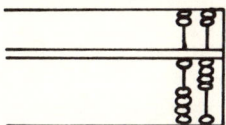
c. This is 14 in its finished form ready for further addition.

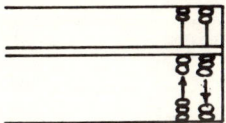
d. When we add 9 to 14 we move the beads as shown by the arrows (add 10, subtract 1).

Figure 6-28.

Abacus II

1. Add the following sums on the abacus and write the answer you get for each problem:
   a. 3 + 3 + 4 =_____
   b. 5 + 6 + 6 =_____
   c. 636 + 723 =_____(On the abacus we add from the *left*, that is we start with the beads on the rods farthest left and work to the right, just the opposite from usual addition and subtraction).
   d. Add 3 + 3 + 3 . . . . . . 17 times.
   e. Add 7 + 7 + 7 . . . . . . 21 times. This is a good exercise both on the Chinese and the Japanese abacus.
   f. Add 8 + 8 + 8 . . . . . . 16 times.
   g. Add 9 + 9 + 9 . . . . . . until you reach a four digit number, that is, until you begin to use the fourth rod on the abacus.

2. From a monthly bank statement add with the abacus all the deposits made and the amount in the account at the beginning of the month. From this total subtract, using the abacus, all the charges to the account. You should obtain the amount in the account at the end of the month.

3. From a cash register receipt from a supermarket add all the items with the abacus to see if you get the total on the receipt.

BIBLIOGRAPHY

Association of Teachers of Mathematics. *Notes on Mathematics in the Primary Schools*. London: Cambridge at the University Press, 1967. (Networks, pp. 218-223.)

Gardner, Martin. "Mathematical Games," *Scientific American*, Jan. 1970. (The abacus, p. 124.)

McConnell, John. "An Application of Boolean Algebra to Biology," *School Science and Mathematics*, April 1971, p. 318.

Rogers, Margaret Anne. "The Rationale of Slide Rule Manipulation," *Mathematics Teacher*, May 1970. (A description of a technique used in the eleventh grade, p. 398.)

7

Some Ideas from Topology, the Rubber Sheet Geometry

Mathematical concepts include: area,
size, shape, space, polygons, spheres,
planes, cuts, limits, boundaries, curves,
points, length, area, thickness, edges,
vertices, graph theory

The Four Color Map Problem

Several ideas from topology can be incorporated in an introductory mathematics program, yet these ideas lead directly to conclusions which puzzle mathematicians. In fact, we might say that there is nearly ideal material in this area on which to work. The four color map problem is easily understood, interesting to play with, and a challenge as well since no one has yet solved it.

No map has yet been devised, and it is hard to see how there can be on a plane surface, which requires more than four different colors to color the various countries, no matter how complex their shape. We assume that a country is not more than one continuous area. Students who come up with maps which seem to require five or more colors can always be shown a simpler way to color the map so that only four colors are required.

After students have had plenty of chance to devise a map that requires more than four colors and are familiar with borders and complicated arrangements of them, it is good to discuss the question of proof.

Proof depends on certain rules laid down beforehand. Since we are dealing with divisions of space, of lines which we choose to end or not to end, our conclusions have much to do with the predetermined rules. If these rules are logical and don't conflict, we may go far into the subject. In this case, size and shape are not important, but "holes" are important, and "what touches what." This is not so different from some aspects of the real world which change shape, like a rubber sheet. Definitions are important. Does a surface have thickness? We assume it doesn't, for we cannot increase the thickness although we are allowed to change the shape of any figure at will. In the four color problem it is useful to distinguish between border and boundary. A border lies between two countries while a boundary is the margin of a country which may lie on the exterior of the map. The following points are just a few that can come up in a discussion of what is relevant to the four color problem. (See also figure 7-1.)

1. Every country has at least one boundary and it is continuous.
2. Every country is in only one piece.
3. A country cannot border itself.
4. No more than two countries can have a border in common.
5. The interior border of a country may enclose one or more countries.
6. There can be no border between an interior and an exterior boundary.
7. All land on the interior of a map is owned by some country, ie., there are no "holes" in a map. We can say that this is due either to innate greed or that even holes require color.
8. There is no way to join four countries each to each other, without enclosing one of them.
9. No more than four countries can be joined together so that each touches the other three.
10. There can be no more than three colors necessary on the exterior of any map or the four color problem cannot be proved. (If we imagine one country surrounding all the others on the map it will require a color different from any on the exterior of the map it surrounds.)

These propositions may or may not help prove that four colors are sufficient to color a map. But they and many others similar help sharpen the understanding of the problem and of topology. Students should be encouraged to think up such truisms for they have questionable value to the student *unless* he thinks them up.

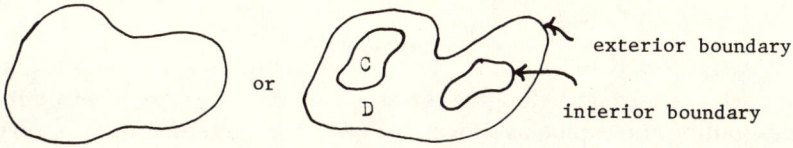

a. Every country has at least one boundary and every country is
    in only one piece. A country may enclose one or more others.
    There can be no border between an interior and an exterior boundary.

b. A country cannot border on itself.

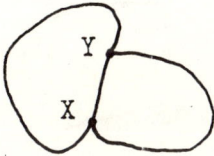

c. A border can separate no more than two countries. A border has
    either two ends (X and Y) or no ends as in figure 7-1a (between
    country C and country D). A map consisting of two countries has
    only one border. The border between two countries can never be
    longer than the boundary of either.

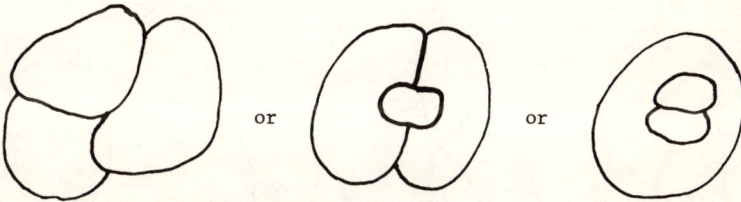

d. Two countries, each bordering a third, can meet. A border end
    which lies in the interior of a map must join at least three
    countries.

Figure 7-1. The above concepts help students understand
the four color map problem.

Shrinking Countries

Another way to look at the problem is to put in a point as a "capital" for each country and elongate the shape of each country until we have lines joining the capital as shown in figure 7-2. Note that one country is enclosed and that we need only three colors on the exterior of the map. If we start with figure 7-2c we can easily reconstruct the map by first marking each line in the middle with a short cross mark as shown in figure 7-2d. These marks are then connected around each capital.

If we surround the countries in figure 7-2 with a country (as in figure 7-3a) then lines to A, B, D, and E from F do not show that all these countries are surrounded. In order to show this, a line has to be drawn about the countries encircled and the line connected to the capital of the

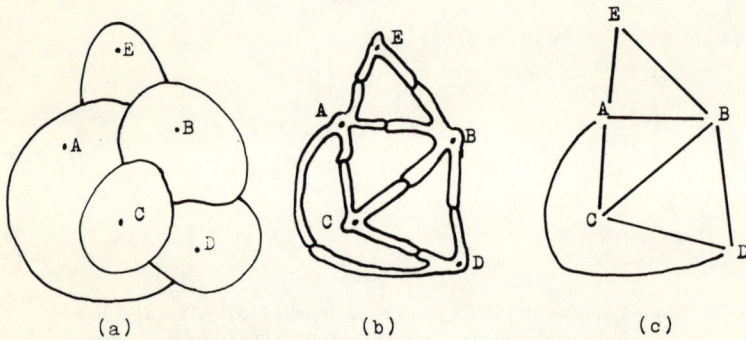

(a)   (b)   (c)

The capitols, A, B, C, D, and E of the mapped
countries are joined according to their borders.
Border intersections become holes as in (b).

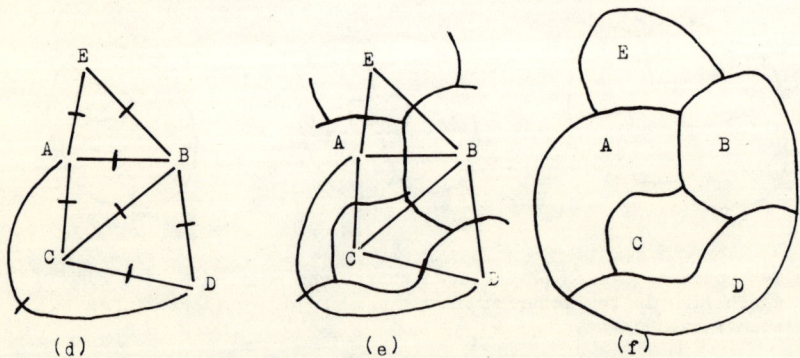

(d)   (e)   (f)

Figure 7-2. A method of reconstructing the map is shown.
The finished map at (f) may not have the same shapes in
the countries but it is identical to (a) as far as connections
between countries are concerned.

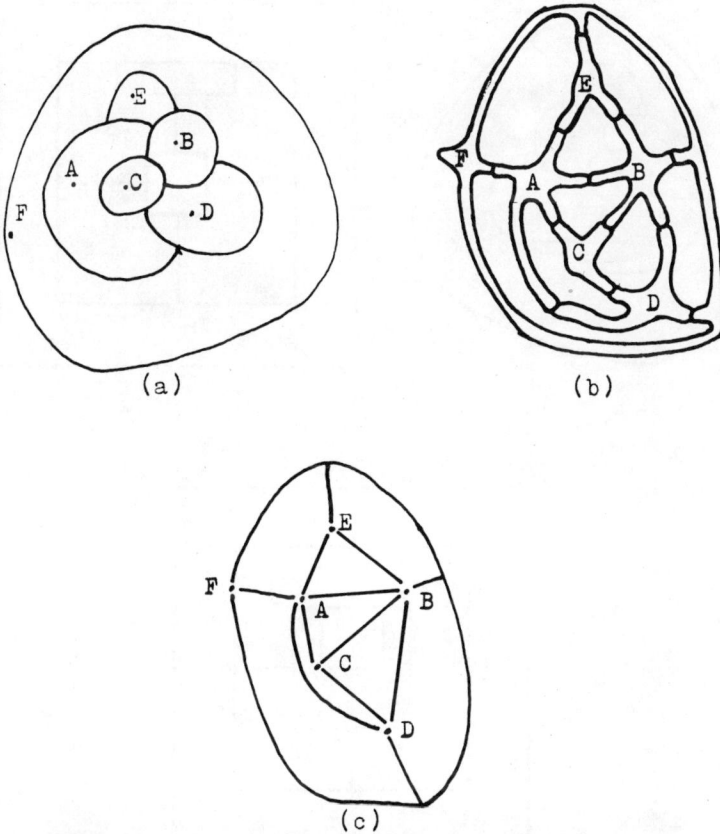

(a)

(b)

(c)

Figure 7-3. This is how an encircling country F can be added to the scheme of joining capitals. Note that it is the only country capable of bordering any further added countries.

encircling country as in figure 7-3c. Figure 7-3a and b show how such a line surrounding the countries is derived from the original map.

Examining figure 7-3a, it is easy to imagine that the rest of the world (or universe) is outside country F. By continually expanding the exterior boundary of F, F would become as large as we wished, in fact it could include the universe, curving around if necessary. Likewise, since size doesn't mean anything in this subject we could begin with the map of figure 7-3a and make country C the universe. Country F which surrounded the other countries, would now lie within the map. (See figure 7-4.)

Proof of the four color problem is tantalizing in its closeness—one might set the problem aside with the assertion that it is obvious. After all,

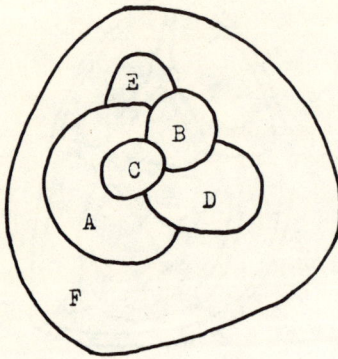

(a)

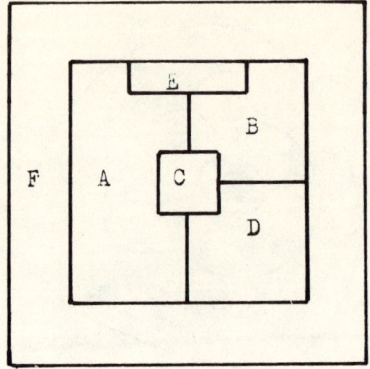

(b)

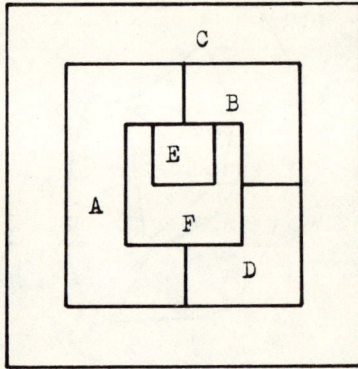

(c)

Figure 7-4. The maps at (a) and at (b) are the same. The map at (c) is obtained by imagining a hole punched in country C and the hole then expanded until it becomes the outside border of the map. At the same time, imagine the previous map exterior to shrink to a point.

when more than three countries are joined, must we not enclose one of them completely as in figure 7-3a (allowing the enclosed color to be used again) or separate two of the countries (allowing both to be colored the same)? Unfortunately, while this is true, we must show that any map with any configuration of countries requires only four colors. We cannot seem to find proof for maps unmade.

The four color map problem illustrates the fundamental idea of topology. Each country must be allowed to have an area, that is, it must consist of more than a point. With this area goes a border which is a line surrounding the country and this line has length. But beyond these assumptions we need no further conditions. The country can be pulled into any shape and its border altered in any way as long as it still surrounds the country. If we are working on the surface of a sphere, then the surface which consists of one country is equivalent to the sphere with a tiny hole.

The Moebius Strip and Its Construction

If we split a ring we ought to get two rings. If the ring is twisted, then splitting it does not cut it in two, but into a longer ring. This is the moebius strip and it is a facinating puzzle. It can be made from various materials. Several ways are shown in figure 7-5.

The ends of the paper strip in figure 7-5a are twisted one half turn before the ends are joined with staples or glue. The velcro moebius strip consists of two strips of the fabric stuck together. The ends of the double

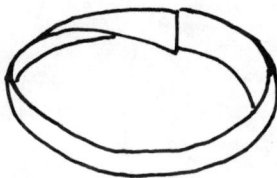

(a) paper moebius

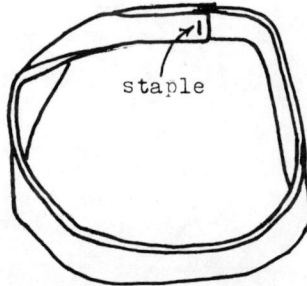

(b) Velcro Moebius

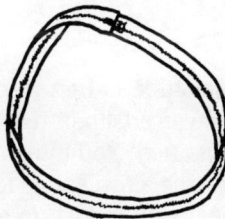

(c) zipper moebius

Figure 7-5. Velcro fabric provides a back-to-back arrangement of the strips and can be put back together for another try.

strip are fastened with staples after the usual 180 degree rotation of an end. The velcro material allows for pulling the strip apart and putting it back together.

Can a moebius strip be made out of a doughnut? We might succeed if we could flatten the doughnut, or use a deflated inner tube. Then a crosscut and a half twist and we would have it. Then we could mark where we wish to split and inflate the inner tube. Figure 7-6 shows what we would have. We could take a solid rubber ring and cut it with a razor and (as shown in figure 7-6) produce a ring twice as large instead of the two we might expect. The solid rubber will tend to return to its original shape so that the device can be opened and closed easily.

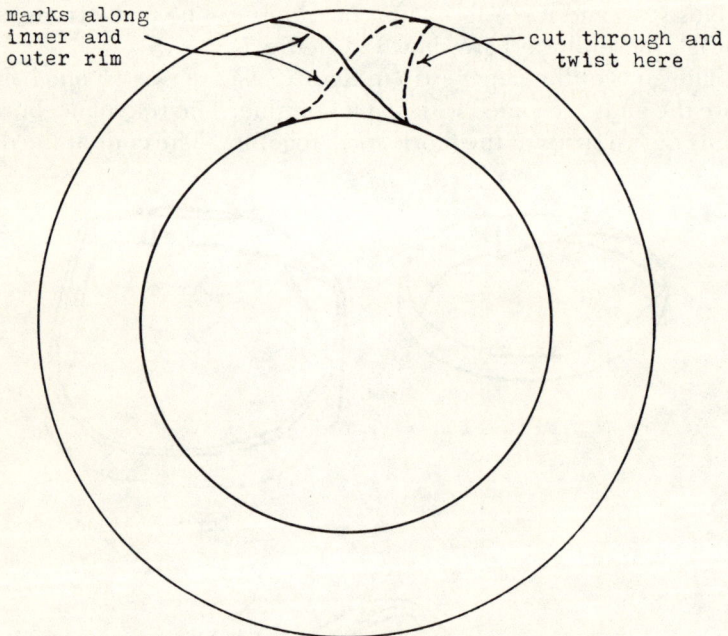

marks along inner and outer rim

cut through and twist here

Figure 7-6. If an inner tube is flattened, cut through and the ends of the cut reversed, then reinflated, a "moebius doughnut" will be obtained. You must mark the inner and outer margins where the cuts are made or the moebius character of the object will be lost on reinflation.

Pencil Cross

Hex is a simple, intriguing board game which was quite popular a few years ago—until someone spoiled all the fun by showing how to make a sure win for the person who moves first. The players sat at adjoining sides of a four-sided figure and with hexagonal tiles tried to make a continuous path from their side to the one opposite. Since the paths being formed during the play were at right angles, only one person could win and there was always a winner. The board was a network of hexagons, and the tiles (colored differently for each player) were placed over these hexagons. The game is still worth playing since a skilled person can easily win over a less skilled, even if he goes second. The game illustrates that two bands cannot cross in the plane unless they are allowed to share a common area somewhere in each band. The problem is as common as any road intersection.

We can play a similar game without the board by using ordinary graph paper—the larger the squares, the easier to play. In Pencil Cross each player uses a different color for his pencil. A move consists of drawing a line along the edge of a square or a diagonal. Neither player is allowed to touch any of his opponent's lines. A line can be started anywhere and discontinued at any time. Pencil Cross has a greater selection of moves (eight) than does Hex (six). A standard game of Hex should be available for comparison. A game of Pencil Cross is shown in figure 7-7. To distinguish the players, one is a dashed line, the other is continuous.

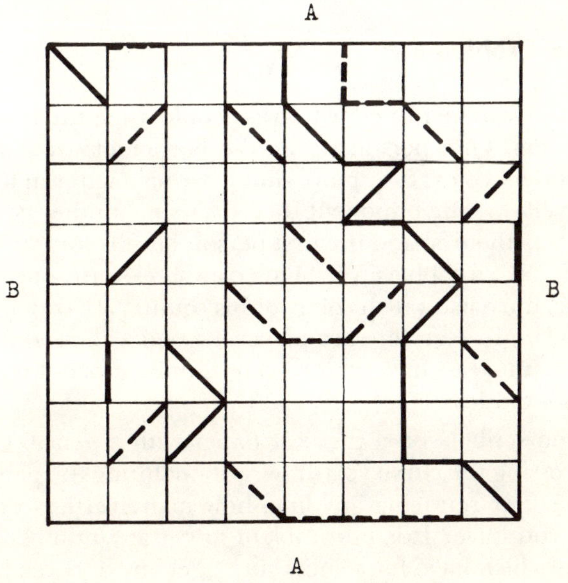

Figure 7-7. This game of two players is won when one player marks a continuous line between the sides. One player works from A to A, the other from B to B. Opponents lines must not touch or cross. The A player has won the game shown.

Who Wins in Pencil Cross?

Since there are eight directions of play in Pencil Cross, is there still an assured win for the first player? The game illustrated was played with eight squares on a side, but when we play with up to five squares on a side, it is an "easy win" for the first player. In fact, a five by four board in which the second player only has to move four units to his opponents five is still a sure win for the first player. Since we can alter the number of squares on a side at will, are there any dimensions which will give the players an even chance, or is it inherent in the game that no matter what the dimensions of the board, there is a sure win for one of the players? This last possibility is likely because if we assume that even with his best move the first player can have no sure win, then it follows that the second player must not have a best move in response which will give him a win, or the game would be determined. This reasoning can go on until all the possible moves on the board are exhausted without either player winning. But we know that there is always a winner (since the only way to prevent the opponent from winning is to win yourself). Therefore there is no board of any dimensions which will not give either the first or the second player an advantage. This is true of course for any game in which there must be a winner, unless perhaps winning is by pure chance.

Puzzles and Problems

1. A game can be played with two people using the four color map problem. One person draws the border of a country and his opponent colors it or more simply writes a letter in it such as "Y" for yellow. The opponent then draws in another country which borders the first and the first person must color it in or write the letter "B" for blue in it. This continues until one person (the loser) must use a fifth color for his country. In order to make the game more even for each player, no one is allowed to encircle all the countries. Once the problem is understood it is not difficult to avoid a loss.

2. If you scribble on a piece of paper with a pencil, crossing and recrossing the curve you draw, but not lifting the pencil from the paper nor retracing any line, how many vertices of three lines can you have? It is no problem to get any number of intersections which have four lines, but to get any of three lines coming together without lifting the pencil off the paper you have to be a little more careful. Can you trace out the edges of a cube with a pencil without taking it off the edge? (There are eight corners to the cube each of which has a three-edged vertex.) How many complete corners of the cube can you trace? Can you trace out the edges of a four-sided pyramid? (The base of the pyramid has

four three-edged vertices.) Can you trace out a double four-sided pyramid? (This figure consists of two pyramids with bases stuck together.)

3. If you have a spool of wire and bend it into the outline of a cube, what is the least number of pieces of wire you can use?

4. How many soldering joints will you need in the cube in problem 3 to seal all the corners?

5. A fundamental idea in topology can be studied by means of a puzzle. It is this: We have found after much deliberation that any closed curve that does not recross itself has an outside and an inside. We call such a curve a "Jordan curve" after its inventor, (or discoverer, if you prefer). If you are inside such a curve and cross the curve once, you are obviously on the outside. If you cross it twice you must be back on the inside, if three times you are back outside again, etc. Present your opponent a complex curve such as the one shown in figure 7-8, and challenge him quickly to tell if a point such as A is on the inside or outside of it. (You draw a line, straight or curved—so long as it is continuous, from A to the outside of the curve to find the answer.)

Figure 7-8. This curve is closed (no ends can be seen) and it obviously does not cross. Therefore it has a definite inside and outside. Is point A inside or outside?

6. Mathematicians, physicists, and engineers love to invent games in their spare time, probably to relieve their minds of demanding routines. This game was described in the July 1967 *Scientific American* in Martin Gardner's column on Mathematical Games (p. 112). It is called "Sprouts" and is the brainchild of John Horton Conway and Michael Stewart Paterson. On a piece of paper, you start with any number of spots, but less than three is uninteresting. You can start by connecting one spot to another, and somewhere along the line of connection you place another

spot. You may also draw a circle around a spot in which case you place a spot on the edge of the circle somewhere. You may also start from one spot and encircle one or more others, in which case you also place another spot on the margin of the circle somewhere. Finally and importantly no more than three lines are allowed to be connected to each spot. While it is fun to play the game alone, you can also do so with an opponent, in which case each takes a turn at drawing the proper lines. The one who finally has no place left to draw a line loses (or wins if you like).

This game has, incidentally, a similarity to the growth of a map, as a comparison of the diagram in figure 7-9 will show.

7. The device of figure 7-10 is made of batons and strong string. The object is to separate the batons without cutting the string or taking it off. It can be done. Two people tied by the wrists this way can separate themselves with a minimum of difficulty once the secret is learned. The loops around the shafts of the batons must be loose enough that a string can be slipped under them, but not so loose as to come off the end.

8. Once this procedure has been mastered you can try the more complex arrangements shown in figure 7-11. The object is still the same—to separate the batons. People can be substituted for batons and are helpful in keeping the ropes from tangling. Bracelets are good to use for the wrist loops.

9. Even a couple of twists can be undone and the loop freed as in figure 7-12a. A ruler with holes, string, and buttons provides another variation as shown in figure 7-12b.

10. Make any complicated map of various countries. Can you draw a continuous line through them which will go through each country only once and not cross itself? Can you prove that this is true for any map?

11. Country C in figure 7-13 is surrounded in the following maps. Reverse the map so that the border of country C is the exterior boundary of the map and all that is now outside of C's border is inside. You can change the shape of countries but they must each border the same countries as they did before. The first example of figure 7-13 is completed.

12. Transpose the arrangements of "capitals" and "roads" to a straight line, with all connections as before and no lines crossing. This first one is done (in figure 7-14).

13. Can you change the letters and still arrange to connect the capitals properly? For instance, can you solve 7-14c above with this line of capitals?

A. I. G. F. B. D. C. E. H.

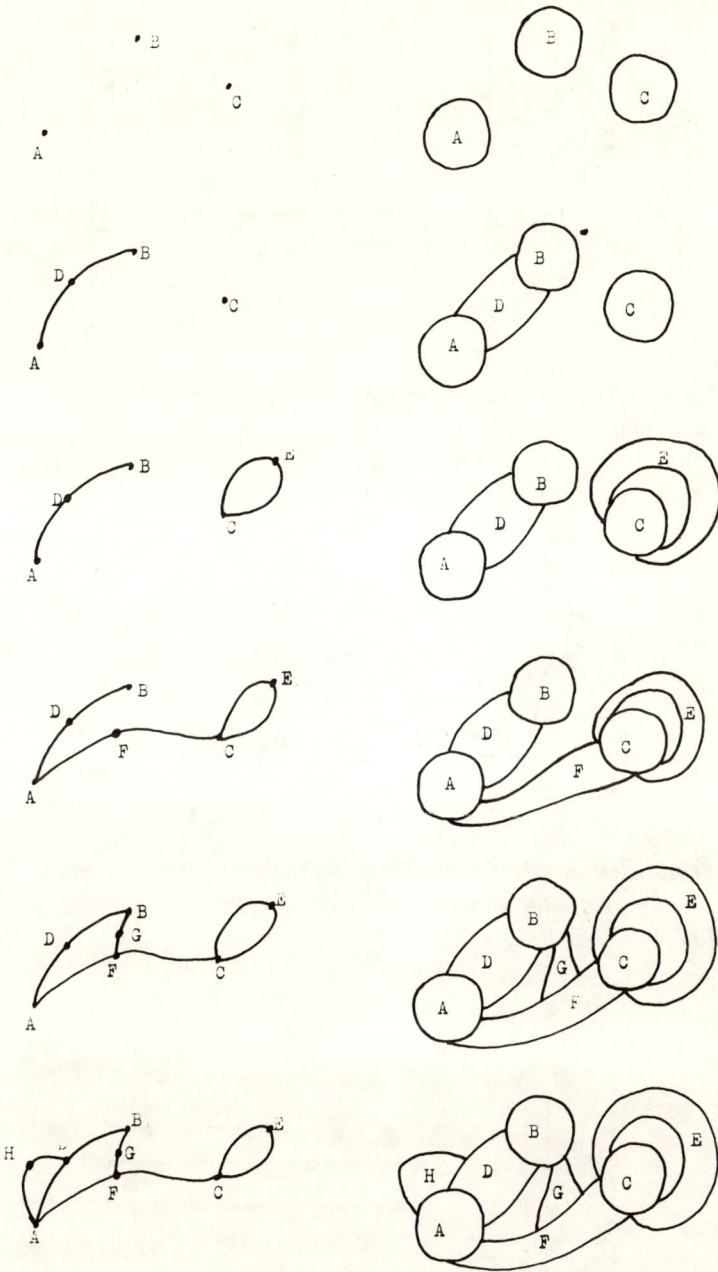

Figure 7-9. There is a similarity between the game of "Sprouts" and the growth of a map. The map however provides for unlimited addition of countries.

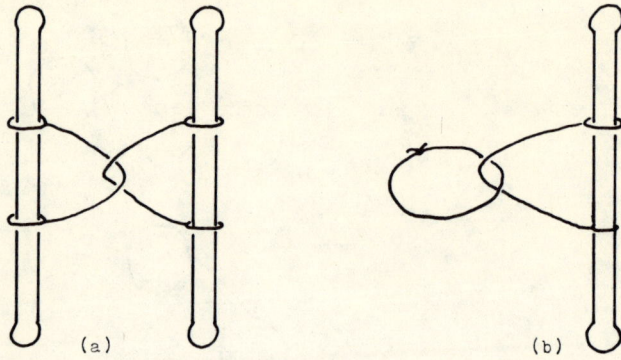

Figure 7-10. The two batons can be easily separated. The variation at (b) is no more difficult.

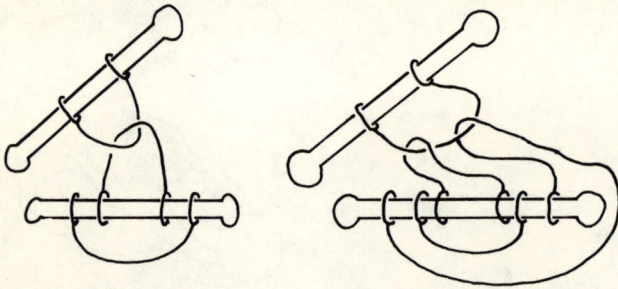

Figure 7-11. A few more complicated arrangements are shown. The batons can be separated without removing any of the strings from them.

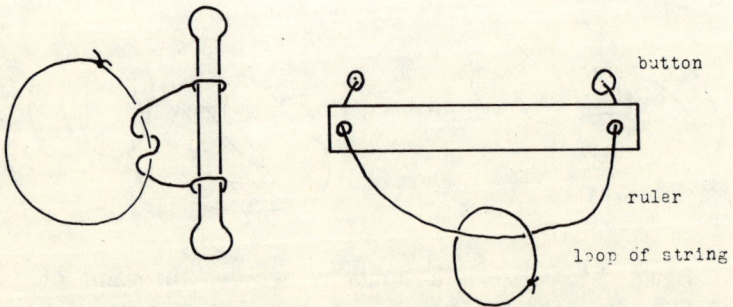

Figure 7-12. Variations of the baton separation trick are shown.

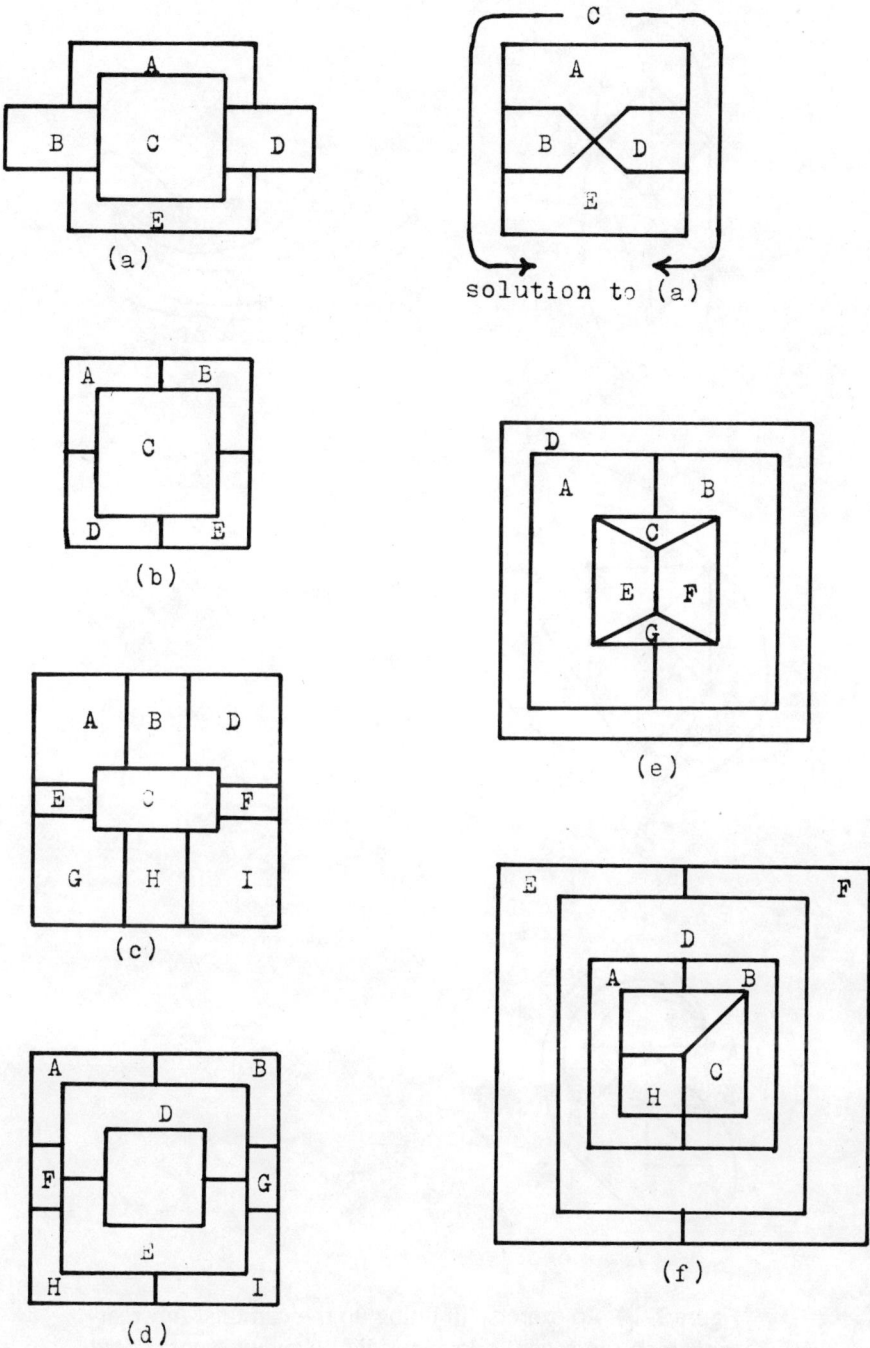

Figure 7-13. Some problems in inverting maps. (a) has been done.

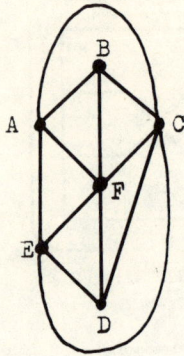

(a)

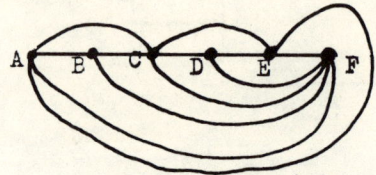

solution of (a)

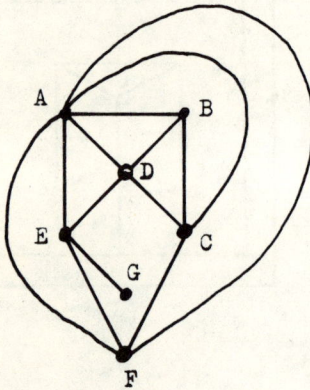

(b)

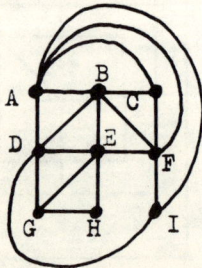

(c)

Figure 7-14. An exercise in lining up the capitals. Any rearrangement on a continuous surface, even with occasional holes, ought to be possible.

BIBLIOGRAPHY

Association of Teachers of Mathematics, *Notes on Mathematics in Primary School*. London: Cambridge at the University Press, 1967. (Hex is described on pp. 234-235.)

Dienes, Zoltan P. *Mathematics in the Primary School*. Toronto, Canada: Macmillan and Co. Ltd., 1966, pp. 148-153.

Gardner, Martin. "Mathematical Games," *Scientific American*, Dec. 1972. (The two hole torus, p. 102.)

Laible, Jon M. "Try Graph Theory for a Change," *Mathematics Teacher*, Nov. 1970. (Some work for high school students, p. 557.)

8

Establishing
the Classroom Math Laboratory

Room Layout

So much depends on materials and equipment in a mathematics lab program that the room must be carefully laid out in order for work to proceed efficiently. Any classroom will do however, and one needs only a minimum of equipment to get started. Storage areas are very handy. A room that has "area centers" already has some plan on which both students and teacher can focus. Storage of equipment should be near the area in which it is to be used, in its "area center." If the room is used for other subjects besides mathematics, then one area—the "math center"—could include much of the equipment found useful. A "weighing and measuring center" would have much mathematics involved in it, as would an "electricity center," particularly if an ammeter and voltmeter were included. A worktable is an essential part of the area center with space for at least two students to work. The following list of area centers is not intended as definitive, nor even appropriate for every classroom. It may suggest some productive types you might use in your own classroom. Many times several areas can be included in one.

Tools	Abacus, slide rule, adding machine
Photography	Energy
Plants	Puzzles and games
Pets	Rocks and minerals
Strength of materials	Electricity
Mechanics	Weighing devices
Optical	Shapes and patterns
Probability	Human measurements

The following are some standard items to include in the preceding categories:

Area centers

Tools—The following tools should be held by nails to a board frame with the outline of the tool painted onto the frame for easy replacement: hammer, hacksaw, pliers (standard, long-nosed, cutting, silversmith's), screwdrivers, adjustable wrench, handsaw, square, carpenters level, hand drill with bits, metal cutting shears, and chisel. Also needed, but not necessarily on the frame: eyelet punch and eyelets, paper punch, hand pressure and vacuum pump, cork borer set, feeler gauge, manufactured micrometer, C-clamps from small to large sizes, lubricating oil, string, wood glue, glass cutter, reaming tool, file and wood rasp, steel measuring tape, and assorted nuts, bolts, screws, and nails. A workbench with a vice and anvil on it is important.

Photography—pans for chemicals (can be cut from the bottom of plastic gallon jugs), photographic developer, photographic fixer, plastic bottles for storing chemicals, printing box (can also be used as a tracing device), plastic tongs (or even band-iron tongs), photographic paper (overage paper is all right), blueprint paper, diazo paper. This area should be in a dark part of the room.

Plants—assorted plastic or metal trays (can be made from the bottoms of plastic jugs), several pounds of beans, peas, lentils (from the grocery), peat moss, sand, soil, plant minerals, tongue depressors (for marking planted seeds), glass frames and blotters (for studying the growth of seeds), paper towels, microscope, hand lenses, shelves for storing sprouting seeds.

Pets—Spring scale or balance for weighing pets and their food, mazes for studying learning behaviour, measuring cups, dustpan, broom, scraper, pads and clipboards.

Strength of materials—a shelf with enough free space underneath to suspend things from hooks fastened to the bottom of the shelf (or cross rigs), rubber bands of various sizes, wire of various sizes, a kit of various other materials to be tested, clothespins (for gripping light items to be suspended).

Mechanical devices and machines—Anything small and intricate such as clocks can be placed in this area (and a good supply of shelf space is helpful), assorted pegboard strips for linkage work, straws, pins, posterboard, evenly perforated ceiling tile, a manufactured pantograph, empty thread spools, small wagons, gyroscope, rotation counters (available from science supply and surplus stores), auto speedometer (from junkyard), ball bearings.

Optical—lenses, prisms, mirrors (flat and curved), glass towel bars, old eyeglass lenses (available from optometrists free), colored filters,

Polaroid filters, moiré pattern materials, magnifiers, plastic fresnel lens, demonstration pinhole camera, kaleidoscope.

Probability—perforated ceiling tile, pegboard in squares about one foot on a side (see Chapter 4), dowel pegs, marbles, graph paper.

Calculating devices—abacus, slide rule, adding machine, punched file cards.

Energy—solar furnace, bunsen burners, propane burner, hot plate, cloudchamber (can be made from dry ice, alcohol, and a bottle), radiometer, thermometers (many and varied types).

Puzzles and games—Tower of Hanoi (can be made from Masonite disks), the soma cube puzzle (both six and seven piece versions—see references), the games of Hex, Spyrograph, Etch-a-sketch.

Rocks, minerals, crystals—set of wood crystal models, specimens of crystalline minerals, alum, acetamide, naphthaline (for making crystals).

Electricity—dry cells, storage battery, connecting wire, electromagnets, solenoids, permanent magnets, voltmeters, ammeters, switches, small electric bulbs and sockets for them, magnetic compasses, soldering gun and solder, binding posts and clips.

Weighing and measuring devices—platform balances, spring scales, rubber band scales (student made), many small washers or nuts of the same size for weights, sets of standard weights, rulers, plastic triangles, measuring tapes, T-squares, (both for student use and for the blackboard), compasses, micrometer, hour glasses, clock with large face and sweep second hand.

Shapes, patterns, cycles, waves—bike fork (for vibration studies), neon bulb (for observing alternating current), stroboscope, "slinky" springs, shade roller springs, maps, stereo photos, adding machine tape, stamp pad, protractor stamp, polar coordinate stamp, standard grid stamp.

Human measurements—stethoscope, Ames window (trapezoidal window for optical illusion, see problem 6, Chapter 6), mirrors, finger mazes, colorblind test diagrams.

The Cross Rig

In order to suspend something, a shelf is needed under which hooks have been placed to hold the string or wire used. Sometimes the shelf has little or no space underneath. In any case such space is usually limited and the design of the cross rig apparatus is to make such suspension possible and convenient. It is more stable than a ringstand and more versatile. Two lengths of ⅜ inch (about 1 centimeter) pipe are fastened to a table-top (see figure 8-1) by screwing them into pipe flanges on top of the table or set into it from underneath. A good deal more work is involved in this operation than any busy teacher might want to tackle. It is included here as one way to solve this problem of suspension, whoever involved with the classroom does the installation.

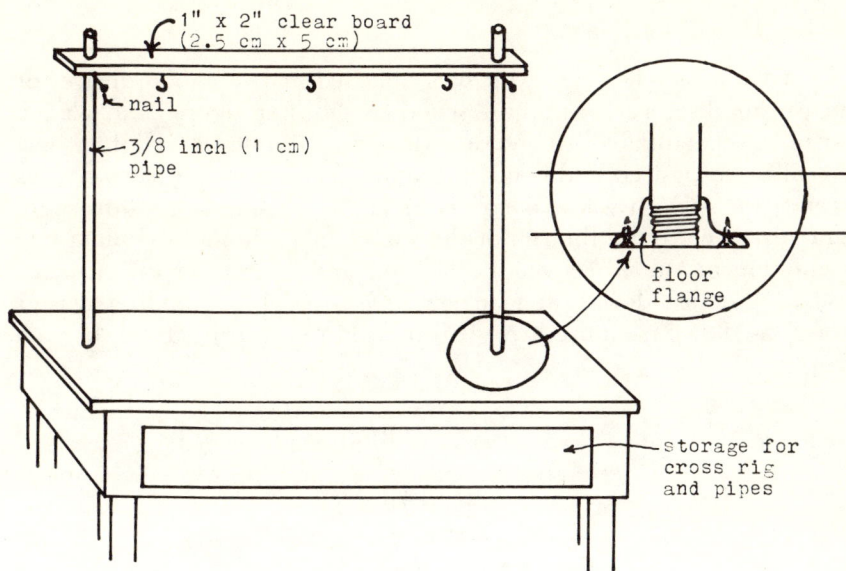

Figure 8-1. The cross rig can be installed on a tabletop and disassembled for storing when not in use. It solves the problem of providing adequate space under suspended objects.

Map Enlargement

A small section of a map can be enlarged. Topographic maps which include the school are particularly useful if pertinent portions of them can be blown up several times larger. The map portion to be enlarged is oiled with vegetable oil so that it is translucent and this part (preferably cut out) is placed in a slide holder of a slide projector. Since these projectors project only areas somewhat less than 35 millimeters in width, only a small portion of the original map can be projected at any one time. This is usually sufficient if a detailed map of the area around the school is desired. The 7½ minute topographic maps from the U. S. Geological Survey work well for this.

A Tracing Box

A frame with a frosted glass top and lit from underneath by a lightbulb is a useful device for tracing maps, designs, and drawings. These devices can be purchased ready-made, but can also be fabricated in the classroom. A large window over a box with an electric lamp in it will do. The frame should be at least a foot square.

A Measuring Wheel

A front bicycle wheel with fork attached makes a good device for measuring distances around the school as shown in figure 8-2a. Wedge (or tie) a small inflated balloon near the rim of the wheel. Roll the wheel the distance desired and count the number of times the balloon rubs against the fork. It will make a loud sound each time it goes through. The distance around the rim of the wheel can be found by rolling one revolution of the wheel on the ground and measuring the distance rolled. A similar device on a smaller scale is simply a round typewriter eraser as shown in figure 8-2b. It is useful in measuring distances on a map.

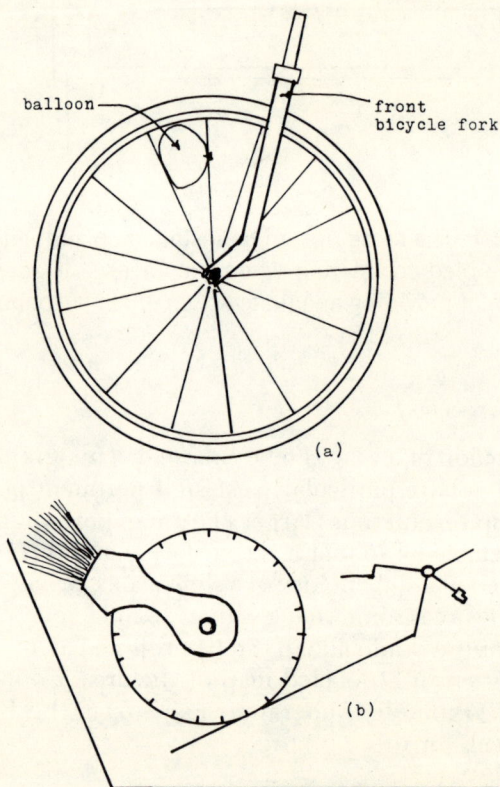

Figure 8-2. The bicycle wheel can be rolled along the ground for quick measurement of large distances. The balloon makes a loud sound whenever it goes through the bicycle fork. Distances on a map can be measured with a new ink eraser which can be marked along its margin to calibrate it.

Reversing a Tire Pump for Vacuum

A vacuum supply is handy to have, and while there are hand vacuum pumps available from science supply houses which work well, if budget problems prevent their acquisition then a regular tire pump can be modified to create a drop in pressure. The leather disk inside the pump is first reversed so that the lip protrudes upward instead of down. Then, at the base of the pump where the hose enters the body, the fitting must be removed and another fitting without a valve used as a replacement. The hose is then put back on the new fitting. The pump will then be ready for such vacuum work as checking how much tar and byproducts of cigarette smoke can be drawn through a filter (see Chapter 2, "Testing Cigarette Smoke"). The old fitting can also be fitted on the hose in a reversed position (as in figure 8-3) so that a higher vacuum can be built up.

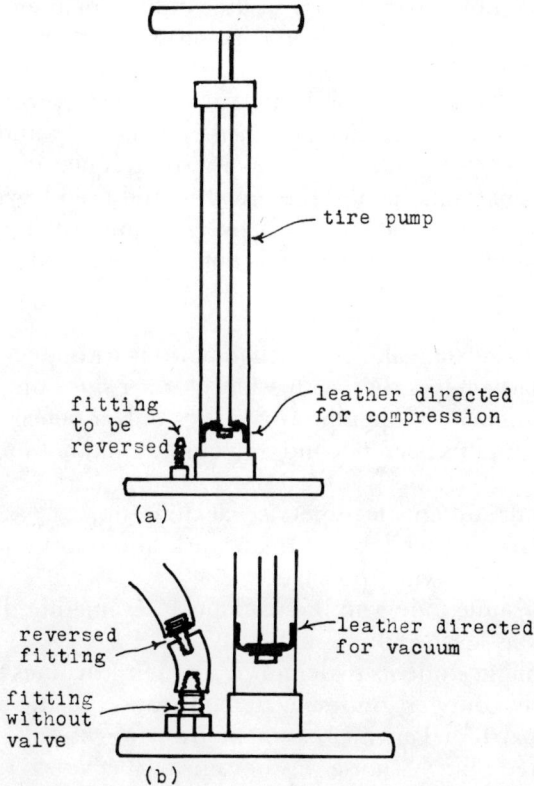

Figure 8-3. The tire pump can be made to produce a vacuum by reversing the lip of the leather piston inside the pump chamber and by changing the fitting on the pump base as shown.

Classroom Order

It is sad that neatness still has a higher priority than student interest and accomplishment. Neatness, however, is conspicuous, as is a messy classroom. Where work is being done, no matter where, we find things disarranged. When there is much material in the classroom it is considerably more difficult to keep it in order or even to provide a place for the materials. Add to this a large class with no previous experience in a classroom lab program and we will be guaranteed a messy room during and most likely after their visit. As students become familiar with the program this messiness diminishes. It will never decrease to the point of being really clean, however; nor can we expect the room to look as neat as a classroom in which students are purposely kept away from any materials which are likely to disarrange the order of the room.

Noise is another criterion used to judge the efficiency of a classroom. Absolute quiet, particularly in the study of mathematics, is often held to be the ultimate in efficient learning. Visitors are brought down quiet halls with pride. If loud voices come from one of the rooms, this is often taken as a "loss of control" by that teacher. Yet a program based on a classroom laboratory, particularly in the elementary and junior high school, cannot be very quiet. Students will be frequently moving about the room, getting material and returning it, and even leaving the room with it now and then. The conflict between a quiet room and the noise generating aspects of a lab program is not easily resolved. The following steps alleviate the problem:

a. Try to alternate alternate active periods with quiet ones. This is easier with mathematics than with science or art since the performance of strictly mathematical operations requires only a pencil and paper, if that. Such operations need not and no doubt should not start with pencil and paper.

b. Appoint students to supervise cleaning up.

c. Don't try to pack too much lab work into one session.

d. Go outdoors when possible.

e. Spend some time with the students in evaluating the lab experience. (What was learned?)

f. Ask willing students to demonstrate their learnings to other classes, particularly younger grades. A demonstration of the abacus or the probability board, or Pencil Cross or moiré patterns—all serve to show those interested that the noise was not unproductive.

g. Avoid competitive situations between students, particularly in classes already competitive.

BIBLIOGRAPHY

Dienes, Zoltan P. *Mathematics in the Primary School*, Toronto, Canada: Macmillan and Co. Ltd., 1966. (Classroom organization, Ch.'9.)

Gardner, Martin. *Second Scientific American Book of Mathematical Puzzles and Diversion.* New York: Simon and Schuster, 1961. (Cube puzzles, pp. 65-67.)

Steinhaus, H. *Mathematical Snapshots,* New York: Oxford University Press, 1969. (Cube Puzzles.)

Vrana, Ralph. *Junior High School Science Activities.* West Nyack, New York: Parker Publishing Company, Inc., 1969. (Cross rigs, pp. 179, 180; the laboratory approach, Chapter 1.)

Appendices

Appendix A

Melting Point Temperature, in Degrees Centigrade

Butter	31 - 31.5
Camphor	177.7
Copper	1083
Glass	1100
Glycerine	17
Lead	327.4
Paraffin	55
Sugar	160
Sulfur	113 (rhombic)
	119 (monoclinic)
Tin	232
Water	0
Zinc	420

Appendix B

The following table of Squares, Cubes, and Roots is from the HANDBOOK OF CHEMISTRY AND PHYSICS with permission from the Chemical Rubber Co., 18901 Cranwood Parkway, Cleveland, Ohio 44128, publishers. A more complete table may be obtained from their latest handbook.

NUMERICAL TABLE

RECIPROCALS, POWERS AND ROOTS OF NUMBERS, CIRCUMFERENCES AND AREAS FOR NUMBERS (DIAMETERS) FROM 1 TO 1000

n	$1000\frac{1}{n}$	n^2	n^3	$\sqrt{n}$	$\sqrt[3]{n}$	Circum. of circle πn	Area of circle $\frac{1}{4}\pi n^2$
1	1000.00	1	1	1.	1.60000	3.14159	.79
2	500.00	4	8	1.414	1.25992	6.28319	3.14
3	333.33	9	27	1.732	1.44225	9.42478	7.07
4	250.00	16	64	2.000	1.58740	12.5664	12.57
5	200.00	25	125	2.236	1.70998	15.7080	19.64
6	166.67	36	216	2.449	1.81712	18.8496	28.27
7	142.86	49	343	2.646	1.91293	21.9911	38.49
8	125.00	64	512	2.828	2.00000	25.1327	50.27
9	111.11	81	729	3.000	2.08008	28.2743	63.62
10	100.00	100	1000	3.162	2.15443	31.4159	78.5
11	90.9091	121	1331	3.3166	2.22398	34.5575	95.0
12	83.3333	144	1728	3.4641	2.28943	37.6991	113.1
13	76.9231	169	2197	3.6056	2.35133	40.8407	132.7
14	71.4286	196	2744	3.7417	2.41014	43.9823	153.9
15	66.6667	225	3375	3.8730	2.46621	47.1239	176.7
16	62.5000	256	4096	4.0000	2.51984	50.2655	201.1
17	58.8235	289	4913	4.1231	2.57128	53.4071	227.0
18	55.5556	324	5832	4.2426	2.62074	56.5487	254.5
19	52.6316	361	6859	4.3589	2.66840	59.6903	283.5
20	50.0000	400	8000	4.4721	2.71442	62.8319	314.2
21	47.6190	441	9261	4.5826	2.75892	65.9734	346.4
22	45.4545	484	10648	4.6904	2.80204	69.1150	380.1
23	43.4783	529	12167	4.7958	2.84387	72.2566	415.5
24	41.6667	576	13824	4.8990	2.88450	75.3982	452.4
25	40.0000	625	15625	5.0000	2.92402	78.5398	490.9
26	38.4615	676	17576	5.0990	2.96250	81.6814	530.9
27	37.0370	729	19683	5.1962	3.00000	84.8230	572.6
28	35.7143	784	21952	5.2915	3.03659	87.9646	615.8
29	34.4828	841	24389	5.3852	3.07232	91.1062	660.5
30	33.3333	900	27000	5.4772	3.10723	94.2478	706.9
31	32.2581	961	29791	5.5678	3.14138	97.3894	754.8
32	31.2500	1024	32768	5.6569	3.17480	100.531	804.3
33	30.3030	1089	35937	5.7446	3.20753	103.673	855.3
34	29.4118	1156	39304	5.8310	3.23961	106.814	907.9
35	28.5714	1225	42875	5.9161	3.27107	109.956	962.1
36	27.7778	1296	46656	6.0000	3.30193	113.097	1017.9
37	27.0270	1369	50653	6.0828	3.33222	116.239	1075.2
38	26.3158	1444	54872	6.1644	3.36198	119.381	1134.1
39	25.6410	1521	59319	6.2450	3.39121	122.522	1194.6
40	25.0000	1600	64000	6.3246	3.41995	125.664	1256.6
41	24.3902	1681	68921	6.4031	3.44822	128.805	1320.3
42	23.8095	1764	74088	6.4807	3.47603	131.947	1385.4
43	23.2558	1849	79507	6.5574	3.50340	135.088	1452.2
44	22.7273	1936	85184	6.6332	3.53035	138.230	1520.5
45	22.2222	2025	91125	6.7082	3.55689	141.372	1590.4
46	21.7391	2116	97336	6.7823	3.58305	144.513	1661.9
47	21.2766	2209	103823	6.8557	3.60883	147.655	1734.9
48	20.8333	2304	110592	6.9282	3.63424	150.796	1809.6
49	20.4082	2401	117649	7.0000	3.65931	153.938	1885.7
50	20.0000	2500	125000	7.0711	3.68403	157.080	1963.5

NUMERICAL TABLE (Continued)

n	$1000\dfrac{1}{n}$	n^2	n^3	$\sqrt{n}$	$\sqrt[3]{n}$	Circum. of circle πn	Area of circle $\frac{1}{4}\pi n^2$
51	19.6078	2601	132651	7.1414	3.70843	160.221	2042.8
52	19.2308	2704	140608	7.2111	3.73251	163.363	2123.7
53	18.8679	2809	148877	7.2801	3.75629	166.504	2206.2
54	18.5185	2916	157464	7.3485	3.77976	169.646	2290.2
55	18.1818	3025	166375	7.4162	3.80295	172.788	2375.8
56	17.8571	3136	175616	7.4833	3.82586	175.929	2463.0
57	17.5439	3249	185193	7.5498	3.84850	179.071	2551.8
58	17.2414	3364	195112	7.6158	3.87088	182.212	2642.1
59	16.9492	3481	205379	7.6811	3.89300	185.354	2734.0
60	16.6667	3600	216000	7.7460	3.91487	188.496	2827.4
61	16.3934	3721	226981	7.8102	3.93650	191.637	2922.5
62	16.1290	3844	238328	7.8740	3.95789	194.779	3019.1
63	15.8730	3969	250047	7.9373	3.97906	197.920	3117.3
64	15.6250	4096	262144	8.0000	4.00000	201.062	3217.0
65	15.3846	4225	274625	8.0623	4.02073	204.204	3318.3
66	15.1515	4356	287496	8.1240	4.04124	207.345	3421.2
67	14.9254	4489	300763	8.1854	4.06155	210.487	3525.7
68	14.7059	4624	314432	8.2462	4.08166	213.628	3631.7
69	14.4928	4761	328509	8.3066	4.10157	216.770	3739.3
70	14.2857	4900	343000	8.3666	4.12129	219.911	3848.5
71	14.0845	5041	357911	8.4261	4.14082	223.053	3959.2
72	13.8889	5184	373248	8.4853	4.16017	226.195	4071.5
73	13.6986	5329	389017	8.5440	4.17934	229.336	4185.4
74	13.5135	5476	405224	8.6023	4.19834	232.478	4300.8
75	13.3333	5625	421875	8.6603	4.21716	235.619	4417.9
76	13.1579	5776	438976	8.7178	4.23582	238.761	4536.5
77	12.9870	5929	456533	8.7750	4.25432	241.903	4656.6
78	12.8205	6084	474552	8.8318	4.27266	245.044	4778.4
79	12.6582	6241	493039	8.8882	4.29084	·248.186	4901.7
80	12.5000	6400	512000	8.9443	4.30887	251.327	5026.6
81	12.3457	6561	531441	9.0000	4.32675	254.469	5153.0
82	12.1951	6724	551368	9.0554	4.34448	257.611	5281.0
83	12.0482	6889	571787	9.1104	4.36207	260.752	5410.6
84	11.9048	7056	592704	9.1652	4.37952	263.894	5541.8
85	11.7647	7225	614125	9.2195	4.39683	267.035	5674.5
86	11.6279	7396	636056	9.2736	4.41400	270.177	5808.8
87	11.4943	7569	658503	9.3274	4.43105	273.319	5944.7
88	11.3636	7744	681472	9.3808	4.44796	276.460	6082.1
89	11.2360	7921	704969	9.4340	4.46475	279.602	6221.1
90	11.1111	8100	729000	9.4868	4.48140	282.743	6361.7
91	10.9890	8281	753571	9.5394	4.49794	285.885	6503.9
92	10.8696	8464	778688	9.5917	4.51436	289.027	6647.6
93	10.7527	8649	804357	9.6437	4.53065	292.168	6792.9
94	10.6383	8836	830584	9.6951	4.54684	295.310	6939.8
95	10.5263	9025	857375	9.7468	4.56290	298.451	7088.2
96	10.4167	9216	884736	9.7980	4.57886	301.593	7238.2
97	10.3093	9409	912673	9.8489	4.59470	304.734	7389.8
98	10.2041	9604	941192	9.8995	4.61044	307.876	7543.0
99	10.1010	9801	970299	9.9499	4.62607	311.018	7697.7
100	10.0000	10000	1000000	10.0000	4.64159	314.159	7854.0

Index

A

abacus, 157-159, 165-168
acceleration, 84
    of gravity, 85
action-reaction 133-135
aerial photographs, 20, 21
air pollution, 67
air thermometer, 86, 87
alum, 40
amplitude, 33
angle, 27, 31, 37, 39, 44, 46, 52
area
    of rectangle 60
    of triangle 59
area centers, 187
atoms, 22, 24
average, 34
axis, 37, 39, 130
axon, 142

B

balances, 130
balancing, 132
bicycle fork vibrations, 33, 34
binary code, 151
binomial numbers, 104
bisectors, 71
boundary, 170
Brownian motion, 99
burning glasses, 88
byproducts of cigarette smoke, 58

C

calculating devices area center, 188
calibration
    of C-clamp micrometer, 136
    of measuring wheel, 190
    of rangefinder, 43, 44
    of wind speed, 80
camera lucida, 22
camera, pinhole, 46-48
cardboard models, 25
center of mass, 131-133
Centigrade, 86
chords, 71

chromatography, 66
cigarette smoke, 58
circle, 65, 71
circular motion, 37
circumference, 25
click wheel, 44, 190
closed tube, 34
codes, 150
colors, 66
compass (drawing), 25, 37
concave mirror 55, 70
concentric circles, 25, 28
contour lines, 52, 54
coordinates, 37
corduroy, 28
critical tree, 97
cross rig, 188
cross-section, 50
crystal models, 23, 24
cube, 22, 25, 27
cubic system, minerals, 23
cycles, 33, 34
cycloid, 127

D

denominator, 104
design, 22, 28, 29, 31, 116-119
diagonal, 52
diameter, 25, 46
dimensions, of onion cell, 72
distance measurement, 43, 44
distortion, 115-119
dominance, 105
dot pattern, 29, 31
double vision, 48
drumhead, 36

E

earth, 48, 123, 133
edge, 28
electric circuit patterns, 151-153
electric current, 37
electric fields, 31
electricity, 24
elevation, 49, 51
ellipse, 66, 71, 125, 126